ALL HANDS ALOFT!

By the same author

THE CAPE HORN BREED

ALL HANDS ALOFT!

W. H. S. JONES

Master Mariner

JARROLDS

JARROLDS PUBLISHERS (LONDON) LTD
178–202 Great Portland Street, London W1

AN IMPRINT OF THE HUTCHINSON GROUP

London Melbourne Sydney
Auckland Bombay Toronto
Johannesburg New York

First published 1969

*This book has been set in Baskerville, printed in Great Britain
on Antique Wove paper by Anchor Press, and
bound by Wm. Brendon, both of Tiptree, Essex*

09 098100 6

ACKNOWLEDGMENTS

Grateful acknowledgment is made to the undermentioned for assistance in obtaining documents, photographs, and other material information to enable this narrative to be presented in historically accurate detail.

The Colonial Secretary's Office, Nassau, N.P. Bahamas

Ministry of Transport, Llantrisant Road, Llandaff, Cardiff

D. Carmichael, Assistant General Secretary, Merchant Navy and Airline Officers' Association, London

J. H. Burlinson of Florida, U.S.A.

L. B. Finberg, Harbour Master, Wilmington, North Carolina, U.S.A.

James E. Townsend, Assistant Collector of Customs, Wilmington, North Carolina, U.S.A.

Charles P. Bethel, Development Board, Nassau, N.P. Bahamas

Captain A. B. Gerrard, Nowra, New South Wales, Australia

Nautical Photo Agency Collection, National Maritime Museum, Greenwich

M. J. Muldoon, Melbourne, Australia

The author and Frederick Muller Ltd. for the extract from *Silent Sentinels* by Commander R. Langton-Jones, R.N., D.S.O.

The true romance of the deep lies in the obscure story of the sailorman, as he is to be found on the merchantman's quarter deck or forecastle, and not at all in those shiver-my-timbers-like absurdities which have so long and so impudently usurped Jack's place in the appreciation of the public of this sea-girt country.

'On the Fo'c'sle Head'
by
W. CLARK RUSSELL, 1884

CONTENTS

ILLUSTRATIONS

SAILS OF A THREE-MASTED BARQUE

1	Flying jib	11	Mainsail
2	Outer jib	12	Main lower topsail
3	Inner jib	13	Main upper topsail
4	Fore topmast staysail	14	Main lower topgallant sail
5	Foresail	15	Main upper topgallant sail
6	Fore lower topsail	16	Mizzen topmast staysail
7	Fore upper topsail	17	Mizzen topgallant staysail
8	Fore lower topgallant sail	18	Spanker
9	Fore upper topgallant sail	19	Gaff topsail
10	Main topmast staysail		

NOTE
Tops'l   Topsail
T'gans'l   Topgallant sail
Stays'l   Staysail

PREFACE

For eighteen months, from September 1909 to March 1911, I served as Second Mate in the barque *Caithness-Shire* on a voyage from Port Talbot in Wales, around Cape Horn to ports in Chile and Peru, on the West Coast of the Americas, and thence around Cape Horn to Wilmington, in North Carolina.

This story is based on notes I made soon after returning to England from this voyage, and a vivid recollection of events in which I participated, which the advancing years have not erased from memory.

A true narrative of actual experience, as an officer in one of the last square-rigged vessels to sail the world's trade routes, may convey to readers the difficulties under which both the shipowner and shipmaster laboured in an endeavour to compete with the ever-growing fleet of steam-driven vessels, which were abrogating to themselves both the prime seamen and the cargoes they carried in wind-driven ships throughout a glorious era in maritime history, as they sought to distribute the life-giving products of the earth among the peoples of the world.

There cannot be many men alive today who either owned these vessels or sailed them regularly to and fro around Cape Horn, which was the last trade route on which the sunset glow of a dying era was destined to set.

It is therefore well that those who still survive and are able to record the last struggle for survival should do so, that future generations may know the trials and dangers which beset those dwindling few, who persisted to the end against the overwhelming odds set against them.

In *The Cape Horn Breed* I have described in detail a disastrous voyage around Cape Horn in the last days of sail, an experience which was frequently encountered by those who battled their way against the ferocious winter gales of the dreaded Cape. My aim now, in writing this story, is to contribute authentic data which recalls what, in contrast, could be described as a normal voyage in the last days of sail, except for its ending, which however, in some respects, was only too frequent throughout the sail era.

All names of personnel who sailed from Port Talbot in *Caithness-Shire*, also dates of arrival and departure from various ports, changes of crew, and wages paid to personnel during the voyage, scale of provisions, and substitutes for same, issued by the British Board of Trade, and the Master's judicial authority over the crew, are taken from official documents of the voyage, as also the report of the inquiry into the subsequent total loss of the vessel.

Happily the way of life recorded in these pages has now receded into the mists of tradition, but it may still serve to remind those who today traverse the great oceans in comfort and safety of the courage and tenacity of both the ship-masters and crews who, in the sail era, had garnered from the scattered earth a volume of trade which had built an Empire.

Even today brave men try, and even succeed in, conquering the Cape of Storms as they sail over the many rotting skeletons of tall ships which were sent, by storm and tempest, to a last resting place beneath these raging waters, erasing for ever a very gallant breed of men who unflinchingly faced the hazards of these perilous seas as they sought to conquer them.

W. H. S. JONES

Melbourne

I

LOOKING FOR A SHIP

On the first day of September, in the year 1909, I stood on a sandy beach, to the westward of the entrance to Port Talbot dock, in South Wales, and watched the Scottish barque *Caithness-Shire* being slowly towed towards the dock entrance nearby. I had just turned twenty years of age, but I looked older. My muscles had been hardened and my features tanned by exposure to the frosts and sleet of Cape Horn and the burning heat of the tropic sun during four years of voyaging as an apprentice to the profession of an officer in the mercantile marine in the full-rigged ship *British Isles*, one of the crack sailing-vessels of her day.

In my youth I had become, in fact, an experienced Cape Horn sailor, as throughout the fourth year of my apprenticeship I had served as uncertificated Second Mate in the *British Isles*, and so had rounded the Horn in her as an officer of the watch, under the renowned Captain Barker, on both the eastward and westward passages, a tough responsibility for a youth in his nineteenth year.

After being paid off from the *British Isles* I had spent some three months ashore in England, and now I was 'looking for a ship' in which to go to sea again, before my meagre funds became exhausted. It was with this in mind that I eyed the *Caithness-Shire* as she was towed into the dock at Port Talbot, apparently to load coal for a Cape Horn voyage, as she was high out of the water in ballast trim, but I eyed her with misgivings, for she was by no means a smart-looking vessel, in my opinion. She was what was known as a 'bald-headed barque'—with square sails on the fore and main masts, and a spanker and gaff topsail on the mizzen mast, but no royals above the topgallants—and she was smaller than the *British Isles*, but with few pretensions to beauty.

One obvious advantage of a bald-headed barque, I realised with a feeling of hopeful anticipation, was that her reduced sail area and comparatively stumpy topmasts would mean less of the hazardous work aloft, less hounding of seamen to risk their lives at perilous heights to furl, or make sail, in changes of weather; but there would remain more than enough of that, in a Cape Horn Snorter, in the handling of her No. 1 storm topsails and courses on the fore and main.

I decided to go on board as soon as she was berthed, to see if I could be signed on in her as an uncertificated Second Mate.

That was a further reason for my misgivings—the fact that I had not yet obtained a Second Mate's Certificate.

It was foolish, I knew, in my inmost thoughts, that I had not stayed ashore until I passed that examination: but at twenty years of age a man thinks that he has plenty of time in hand, and in my case I had nearly spent the sixty pounds with which I had been paid off from the *British Isles*, and I was too proud, or too foolish, to ask my parents for a loan.

I was determined to make my own way in the world, and another voyage in sail seemed to be the only way in which I could pursue my calling, and at the same time retain the status of an officer which I had reached in my previous ship by four years of trials and tribulations.

As a member of the afterguard I would have every opportunity for learning, by daily contact with the Master and Mate, many of the problems besetting those who had the responsibility of sailing a large vessel across the seas, and, in port, effectively conducting the business of the ship with agents, port authorities, and other interested parties, which would be denied me if I had to ship as a bosun or A.B.

It had not occurred to me to look for a job in a tramp steamer. I knew nothing of them except that they were ugly smoke-belching warehouses which were increasingly stealing the ocean trade from the wind-driven ships.

Besides, being as yet uncertificated, I would have had no chance of employment in a steamer, except as an able seaman.

I hoped that my good discharge from the *British Isles*, and rather flattering testimonial from Captain Barker, would persuade some Master of a sailing-vessel to sign me on as an uncertificated Second Mate, a practice that was frequently adopted in sailing-ships in those days when so many qualified young officers were giving up sail as soon as they passed for Second Mate, and going into steamers.

I well knew that I should have obtained my certificate before going to sea again, but at twenty impulses are often stronger than good judgment in the matter of a career, and I was looking for a ship at Port Talbot as the result of a sudden and stubborn, rather than of a well-considered, decision.

It was an impulse which, in the sequel, would cause me to lose two years' seniority in my profession, but I scarcely gave that aspect a thought. My driving idea was to get to sea again, come hell or high water.

Ten days previously I had left London on that impulse and had travelled by train across England to Port Talbot, where, with what remained of my savings, I had booked in at a respectable boarding-house.

Day after day I had haunted the docks, looking for an opportunity to be signed on, but in most cases the Masters of vessels almost ready to sail were absent in Cardiff, where crews were usually picked up.

I had missed these opportunities, and now, as the *Caithness-Shire* entered the dock, I followed her in and asked a dock official where she would berth, and was soon standing by at a coal staith, ready to board her as soon as she made fast.

My experiences at Broughton's Nautical Academy in London rankled as an annoyance in my mind, which had caused me to leave London without waiting to pass for Second Mate.

I had enrolled at the academy, and for some weeks had attended classes there, in which instruction was given in mathematics, navigation and seamanship, under the direction of the principal of the academy, Captain Mense.

During my apprenticeship in the *British Isles* I had learned practical seamanship, I may say thoroughly, the hard way, by practical experience, having twice rounded the Horn to windward and twice to leeward, and also made passages, two eastward and two westward, across the wide Pacific Ocean, between the West Coast of South America and Australia, on voyages in total of some 80,000 miles under canvas within four years. But neither the Master nor successive First Mates had given me any systematic instruction in the theory and the practice of navigation, or in mathematics.

Consequently, my training as an apprentice had been chiefly physical, covering the many activities of keeping in order the maze of wires, ropes, blocks and tackles, spars, and many other components of the vessel's standing and running rigging, steering a compass course, or by the wind, occasionally, in the dog watches, and doing the pully hauly of trimming the yards and sails to take advantage of every breeze which would keep the ship moving towards her destination, and in port the heavy manual labour of shovelling coal, sand, or rubble, to discharge a cargo, or take in ballast.

But in the *British Isles*, as in most sailing-vessels, the practical navigation at sea was done by the Master, who supplied his own books, charts and chronometer, which were jealously guarded in his cabin, and seldom seen by the junior officers, or apprentices. He was assisted on occasions by the First Mate, but unless these officers had sufficient interest in the apprentices to teach them the finer points of navigation and mathematics, the apprentices were left to learn what they could from books supplied by their parents.

Fine seaman though Captain Barker was, he and the First Mate in the *British Isles* had shown little interest in the apprentices, except that the boys were physically able to do men's work, and were therefore a valuable, and at times necessary, compensation, in part, for the shortage of fore-castle hands in the continuous physical effort required to sail a large vessel from port to port.

I had been more fortunate than many apprentices, as during the whole of my fourth year I had been Second Mate in charge of a watch, occupying the Second Mate's cabin under the poop, and, on occasions, having access to the charts, chronometer, and sailing directions, when I had to stand by the chronometer, sometimes for half an hour, to take the time for the Master and Mate, when they were taking sights of the sun, and could collate some data for myself to work out the ship's position from the Mate's sextant reading, and occasionally take sights for myself with the Mate's borrowed sextant.

All this was useful practice and made me familiar with the use of nautical tables, books and instruments used in every-day practical navigation at sea, but in no way made me efficient in preparing diagrams to illustrate the theoretical positions of the data used, such as the rational horizon, observer's zenith, prime vertical and equinoctial.

In conversations with Captain Barker, who would talk freely with an officer who had gained his confidence, I had learned to take careful note of cloud formations, their direction and velocity of traverse at dawn and sunset, the run of the sea, and any swell making from a different quarter, which might portend a change of wind for fair or foul weather, and much more sea lore pertaining to the sailing of a ship by the motive power of the wind alone.

On enrolling in Broughton's Nautical Academy, I joined a class of some twenty men of various ages who were studying for the Second Mate's examination. We spent the mornings working through mathematical papers set by Captain Mense. In the afternoons we had lectures on seamanship, at which our tutor, with wooden ship models on a large table, demonstrated what most of us already knew, or thought that we knew, about rigging and handling a sailing-vessel, stowing and handling cargo, the rule of the road, and suchlike problems encountered from day-to-day in the many caprices of wind and weather which arise, often unpredictably, on a long voyage.

It was at these afternoon classes that I realised, with a sinking feeling, that the purpose of the instruction was not chiefly to impart knowledge of seamanship but to coach the pupils to give the answers to tricky problems which certain of the examiners were likely to ask, and to give those answers in a way which would please the examiners, a board of master mariners, some of whom had fads of their own on the best way of doing things, as all master mariners have.

In seamanship examination it would not be what I had learned by practical experience, even under the bitter conditions of a Cape Horn winter gale, that would constitute the correct answer to an examiner's question, but the examiner's own interpretation of how a special task on board ship should be done, in circumstances theoretically stated.

This was disconcerting on the eve of an examination. In practical seamanship I had been through a stringent tuition under a most exacting Master in one of the biggest and speediest sailing-vessels of Britain's mercantile marine. I now found that this experience might be useless to me in answering some questions to which a fixed answer favoured by a particular examiner would be the only one acceptable.

Even more disconcerting was the discovery that several of my classmates at the academy had failed, and some had failed several times. Most of these candidates were young, and just out of their apprenticeship, and were now wrestling in anxiety with textbook problems, perhaps in the hope of qualifying for employment in steamers, which offered easier work, shorter voyages, better food, and more prospects of promotion than working in sailing-vessels.

It was considered not a disgrace, but merely hard luck, if a candidate failed to pass at the first try. Those who were rejected by the Board of Examiners usually returned to Broughton's Academy and swotted some more, to try and try again, until the examiners let them through. In those days, when many hundreds of sailing-vessels still roamed the seas in a valiant endeavour to compete for cargo-carrying trade with the ever-growing fleet of steamers, a Square-rigged Foreign-going Certificate, either as an officer or Master in Sail, was respected, ashore and afloat, as a special mark of nautical competence, and was preferred, and even demanded, from officers seeking to join the large mail-steamship liners.

My ultimate ambition, to become a Master in Sail, was logical and natural after I had served my time as an apprentice in sail. To attain that, I would need to pass for Second Mate, then serve a further term at sea before going up for the stiffer examination for First Mate. Then, after a further term of service at sea, I would be eligible to sit for Master—an objective so far ahead that it was almost out of sight for a youngster of twenty struggling with textbook problems for the first time since leaving school five years previously.

Although I had been given, and had accepted, the responsibility of hounding some of the toughest seamen afloat I was out of my element in a classroom in London's murky atmosphere. I was innocent of some of the ways of the world, and suffering from what might nowadays be called an anxiety complex as my meagre financial resources dwindled. At last came the time when I felt confident enough to attend at the Board of Trade office, to lodge with the officials my indentures and other papers of service, and to enter my name and pay the fee for attending on the following Monday and subsequent days for examination as Second Mate.

Throughout that weekend I sweated at my books, and got myself into a nervous state of anticipation, not being able to envisage exactly what form the examination ordeal would take. I knew that on the first two days there would be tests in mathematical problems. If a candidate failed in these tests he was 'out'. If he passed he would be called on the third, and subsequent days, for oral examination in rule of the road, seamanship, signalling, cargo stowage, and general knowledge of pertinent matters.

The first day was, and probably still is, the most nerve-racking experience in a Second Mate's examination, especially when it is a candidate's first try. Having no previous knowledge of examination-room atmosphere and procedure, the horny-handed young mariner—who may have had little opportunity to set pen to paper during his four years' servitude afloat as an apprentice—felt more trepidation at this ordeal than he had astride a yardarm in a Cape Horn blizzard.

Such were my feelings as I entered the examination room, not knowing what to expect. When I was called to the examiner's desk to receive my first mathematical paper my mind was in a whirl. On returning to the desk allotted to me, I sat for some minutes staring at it before I felt steady enough to tackle the problems set forth.

The examination procedure in 1909 was one to test the candidates' nerves as well as their mathematical ability. Each candidate, after working out his first paper, was required to present himself at the examiner's desk, and to stand by while the examiner, there and then, checked the answers. If all the answers were correct he was handed, without comment, his second paper. But if any of the answers were incorrect the paper was handed back to him for correction, also without any comment or indication from the examiner of what error, or errors, he had made. This meant that the candidate had to return to his seat and check all his figures again, to discover for himself his mistake, or mistakes. If he was successful in this he was handed his second paper. If not, he failed, and the examination for him was over.

The system of obtaining a pass by an aggregate percentage of marks awarded for the whole subject-matter of the examination against a set total of perhaps 100 had not yet been adopted, and it was therefore sudden death—in or out—at each stage of the examination, with one chance, and one chance only. But those were hard days, when the lingering tradition of 'iron men in wooden ships' had not wholly been erased, and 100 per cent efficiency was the least which could be accepted.

Gaining confidence to some extent when I worked out the first paper successfully, I had tackled the second, but my confidence diminished as the hours went by, and one after another candidates disappeared from the examination room.

Yet somehow or other I survived the ordeal of that first day and duly received the acclamation of some of my classmates when I returned to Broughton's Academy at 4.30 p.m. to report progress.

Perhaps all would have been well if I could have relaxed then, but the principal hurried me into his office, and insisted on my writing out from memory all the problems I had worked out.

This would be valuable material for his instruction of future candidates, indicating tricky points that appealed to the examiners, but it was worse than useless to me, wearied as I was by the mental and nervous strain of the day's ordeals.

I returned to my lodgings near the academy and spent most of the night swotting up the problems which Captain Mense expected that I would encounter the next day. The result was that I arrived at the examination room with my mind utterly fatigued, and incapable of coherent thought. By 11.30 a.m. I was out in the street—failed!

It was a bitter blow, as my unaided finances would not permit me to continue at the academy for another try—and I had been eliminated without being asked even one question on seamanship. It was in this mood that I packed my sea-chest and took train for Port Talbot to look for a ship.

Now, as I watched the *Caithness-Shire* making fast under a staith, to take in a stiffening of coal before discharging her ballast, I hoped desperately that her Master would sign me on, to wherever she might be bound, at Second Mate's pay. Anything to recuperate my now almost vanished savings and to restore my somewhat damaged self-confidence far from the land and its restrictions!

2

THE CAITHNESS-SHIRE

THE *Caithness-Shire* was one of a fleet of sailing-vessels owned by William Law & Company, of Glasgow, some of which were named after shires of Scotland.

She had a steel hull and planked wooden decks, with hollow steel masts and yards, a spanker boom and gaff on the mizzen mast, and wire rigging. She had been built at Port Glasgow in 1894 by William Russell & Company, and was registered at Glasgow. Her length was 247 feet, breadth 37 feet, and depth in the hold amidships 22 feet.

Her gross tonnage (by volumetric measurement in units of 100 cubic feet of her approved enclosed spaces) was 1,641 tons: and after deducting 116 tons for crew, and other allowable spaces, her registered tonnage, net (or cargo carrying space by volumetric measurement), was 1,525 tons.

I was to learn these and other details in course of time, but at first glance I could see that she was considerably smaller than my previous ship, the *British Isles*.

As in all British sailing-vessels, the *Caithness-Shire* had a raised poop deck and forecastle head, with a main deck protected by steel bulwarks rising about four feet six inches above the main deck.

All these decks, and everything else in her, were smaller than I had become accustomed to, and I could see that the accommodation for the ship's people would be much more cramped than in my previous ship. But that prospect did not worry me. My only concern was whether there would be any chance of my being engaged as her Second Mate, or whether that position was already filled.

Seeing the Dock Master standing by the staith, supervising her berthing, I walked up to him and inquired where she was loading for.

'She's loading for Iquique on the West Coast,' he said.

'I've been there,' I told him.

'It's a hell of a hole, I've heard,' he remarked.

'Pretty rotten,' I agreed. 'It's like most of the other West Coast ports, just a few shanties, coal dumps, nitrate dumps, and bare earth. Nothing for sailors to do except work, work, work.'

'Yet you'd want to go back there?' he asked.

'It's not the pleasures of Iquique that makes me willing to go there again.'

'What is it, then?'

'After serving my time for four years it's the only way I know to earn a living, and I hope some day to be Master of a ship like this.'

As I stood near her bow, taking stock of everything visible about her, my eyes rested in admiration on her figure-head, the life-size figure of a beautiful woman, affixed to the bows under the jib-boom. It was a work of fine art and loving care, for this 'wooden angel' had obviously been carved by a master craftsman.

In a flowing white dress, with trimmings of red and blue, her figure was that of a well-nourished young woman of ample proportions, with a serene face and far-seeing eyes, crowned with auburn tresses, very finely carved and painted.

Looking up at the high side of the vessel I could see a number of elderly men on the forecastle head, and poop, making the mooring lines fast, and I surmised at once that these were runners, old sailors working ashore as riggers, or wharf labourers, who were engaged to work a ship in ballast from the port where she had discharged a cargo to the port where she was to load, and among them I noticed five apprentices, by their badge caps. This was comforting, as I knew at once that the crew had not yet been engaged for the impending voyage, but would join later, probably when the ship was nearly loaded. Then I saw something unusual. A mastiff hound and a bull-terrier were looking through the railings of the poop and growling at the people on the wharf. The Captain stirred them with his foot, and they sprang down the poop ladder to the main deck and disappeared from sight. They were fierce-looking brutes.

No sooner was the barque made fast than I climbed on board and made my way aft to the poop. The Captain, a tall, lean, clean-shaven, and youngish man, eyed me with a not unfriendly look as I approached. I was wearing a blue single-breasted suit, made to measure for two pounds ten shillings by a naval tailor in Fenchurch Street, London, which was a good price to pay in those days, as, no longer being an apprentice, or yet appointed as an officer, I was not entitled to wear any uniform, but apparently I had made a not unfavourable impression on the Captain, and no doubt he correctly surmised why I wanted to speak to him.

'Who are you, and what do you want?' was his greeting.

I told him my name and asked, 'Are you in need of a Second Mate, sir?'

'Yes. What are your qualifications?'

'I have served my time in the full-rigged ship *British Isles* under Captain Barker, on two voyages with coals from this port—one to Pisagua and one to Iquique—and two voyages from Newcastle in Australia to West Coast ports and to the United Kingdom and Continent with cargoes of nitrate, and wheat from Tecoma. My third and fourth years were served as Third Mate and Second Mate respectively in the *British Isles....*'

'Were you in the ship when she had that disastrous voyage round the Horn in 1905? I have heard the story; Captain Barker has a great reputation.'

'Yes, Captain. I was doing my first voyage then.'

'Have you passed for Second Mate?'

'No, sir, not yet, but I have a good reference from Captain Barker.'

'Come below,' he said, 'and let me see your papers.'

I followed him down the companion-way to the saloon. There he examined my papers and asked me many questions. At last he said, 'Very well, then. If you'll sign on at five guineas a month, I'll engage you as Second Mate. We're bound to Iquique, and you know what to expect rounding the Horn, and working cargo on the West Coast. We'll be loading here immediately, and I expect to sail one week from today. Be on board tomorrow morning at seven o'clock and report to the Mate, Mr. Laird.'

Captain Alexander Hatfield, as I subsequently ascertained, was twenty-nine years of age, and born in Liverpool. This was his first command. He had served in the *Caithness-Shire* on her previous voyage as First Mate, and held the highest qualification in his profession, the Board of Trade certificate of Extra Master. No doubt he could have easily obtained employment in one of the big mail-and-passenger lines of steamships that plied across the North Atlantic, or through the Suez Canal to Australia, India, and China, but having spent his years since first going to sea in sail, and passed through all the grades, he naturally wished to make at least one voyage as a Master in Sail, and it would be an advantage to him in his chosen profession to have done so. He was a man, I could see, who would not be flurried in an emergency, but could be tough if need be, for he was about six feet tall, and, though slim, was of wiry build. He could scarcely be anything else than physically tough after having served some years in sail. He spoke with a North Country accent. His home town, Liverpool on the Mersey, was, and had been for a hundred years, one of the busiest ports in Britain, handling the cotton trade with America, and much other seaborne commerce of the industrial Midlands and Northern counties of England. Liverpool had become the chief steamship terminal of the transatlantic routes to New York and Canada, but remained also a great sailing-ship port.

As we talked the mastiff and the bull-terrier I had noticed previously came frolicking down the companion-way and into the saloon, where they immediately jumped on to the settee. The Captain patted them indulgently. 'My dogs,' he said. 'I've signed them on for the voyage in the afterguard.'

I thought privately that they would be a confounded nuisance on board, but I knew better than to express such an opinion. Shipmasters were often known to take pets with them on long voyages, but these two fierce-looking dogs would scarcely be favourites with the forecastle hands, although sailors are kind-hearted and usually like animals. I wondered how the Captain's dogs would thrive on the Board of Trade scale of rations, including pantiles (ships' biscuits), salt pork and salt beef. If sailors could live on that, for months and years, so could dogs, I supposed; but each of these big animals would require a man's whack of hard tack and fresh water daily. A shipmaster of Captain Hatfield's alert intelligence and experience would be well aware of that fact. 'They won't bite you,' he said to me. 'They are clever dogs, and they know who's who.'

At that moment, feeling elated as I was at being appointed, I had another surprise, as the door to the Captain's sleeping compartment opened, and a pleasant-faced young woman entered the saloon.

'My wife,' said the Captain. Then he introduced me. 'This is Mr. Jones, who will be our Second Mate.' She smiled and shook hands, and he added, 'Mrs. Hatfield is a first voyager.'

'You'll enjoy it,' I murmured politely to her. I was thinking of my first voyage as an apprentice in the *British Isles*, when Captain Barker's wife and two children had voyaged with him on one of the stormiest passages in living memory round Cape Horn. The unfortunate lady had been seasick many times during that passage, and had been only too glad to leave the ship at Pisagua, and return home with her children by steamer.

Mrs. Hatfield was a much younger woman, a Liverpool lass, only nineteen years of age, and newly married. She had never been to sea before, and this could be a great adventure for her. The presence of a lady in the officer's domain was an agreeable prospect, as it presaged some peace and quietness, regularity with meals and little acts of kindness which would occasionally produce some delicacy at table to break the monotony of ship's rations.

On the other hand, the men in the forecastle would not look favourably on the idea of having a woman on board. To them it would mean some curtailment of their freedom. They would have to be decently dressed on deck, whereas in the tropics it was customary for the men to work stripped to the waist, and take baths standing naked by the saltwater pump, while shipmates poured buckets of water over them. Worst of all, they would have to avoid the unprintable words which are sometimes sung with gusto when they were at their daily tasks of hoisting or hauling yards around at every change of direction in the wind, and the obscenities and profanities which bespatter the speech of sailors beyond the hearing of the gentle sex.

The First Mate, Robert Laird, came into the saloon, and I was introduced to him. He was a braw Scot, from Dundee, aged thirty-four, and had been paid off from the ship *Purley*, at London, some weeks previously. Like myself, he was newly-engaged in the *Caithness-Shire*, but I could see at a glance that he was of the tough Cape Horn breed, who had learned his profession the hard way, and would stand no nonsense.

'Show Mr. Jones his cabin, mister,' said the Captain, thus getting us both out of the saloon smartly, for, like all ship-masters in port, he would have many other callers and much paper-work to attend to that morning, and until the vessel sailed. 'And get the hatches open,' he added briskly.

I followed Laird out of the saloon into a narrow alleyway that ran fore and aft under the poop on the port side. He pointed to the first door inside the alleyway, and said curtly, 'That's my cabin, not big enough to swing a cat in, but there's little space to spare under the quarter deck in this stumpy barque.' Then we crossed over to the starboard side and he opened a door at the fore end. 'This is your palatial abode, Mister,' he remarked, cynically. I saw a cabin which had been made by partitioning off six feet of the Master' sleeping cabin at the fore end. Two bunks were ranged athwartships, one above the other, and along the ship's side was a small settee extending from the lower bunk to the forward bulkhead, a length of about three feet six inches, with two drawers underneath, one for each occupant. In the forward corner there was a washbasin with a water pitcher underneath, also a hinged table, with an oil lamp above on the bulkhead, some hooks for hanging clothes on, and a coir rug on the floor.

'You'll be sharing this cabin,' said the Mate, 'with the Chinese steward. He has the top bunk, which will be easier for you as a watch-keeping officer, at night.'

My first reaction was to decline the job, and walk off the ship, but on second thoughts I realised that if I did so I might eventually have to accept a job as an A.B. in some other ship, and in such case would have to live in a forecastle with men of all nationalities, so, as beggars cannot be choosers, I decided to accept.

'What sort of a man is this Chink, Mr. Laird?' I inquired.

'Ah Cheong is his name, mister, and he's decent, sober, and clean in his habits, fifty years of age, a good steward and cook, judging by the food he has dished up so far.'

'Where do those big dogs sleep.'

'They are the Old Man's pet hobby, mister, they sleep in the saloon,' he added, with a wry smile, 'or anywhere else they fancy.'

'How many apprentices does she carry, Mr. Laird?'

'Nine, but four of them are still on leave, but will be rejoining in a day or two, and the four seniors have nearly finished their time. Their indentures will have expired when we arrive in Iquique, and they'll probably leave her there. The others are in their first or second years.'

In the much bigger *British Isles* we had had only four. The owners of this Scottish barque, as I could see, were willing not only to train youths to be officers but were also satisfied to have the labour-power of as many apprentices as possible, at apprentices' rate of pay.

'And how many seamen?'

'Eight, all able seamen, if we can get them.'

I knew, before he told me, that no matter how many boys were carried the regulations of the Board of Trade, under the Merchant Shipping Act of 1894, as applied to a vessel such as the *Caithness-Shire*, would require her to be manned with a minimum complement of twenty. But I had asked the question hoping to hear that there would be more seamen in the foc's'le than the minimum required. I knew we might get some no-hopers, and with four apprentices leaving in the next port the prospects for shovelling 3,000 tons of coal into bags were not encouraging. Having thus given me much information about my new ship, the Mate hurried out on deck through a narrow doorway at the break of the poop, for there was much for him to attend to.

I followed him out on deck, and saw there several people who had come on board, and were waiting to interview the Captain: port officials, stevedores, ship-chandlers, and the like.

The apprentices eyed me with curiosity, evidently surmising that I was the new Second Mate, as I wandered around the decks examining everything alow and aloft, secretly comparing my new ship with my last, which, to a sailor, was always the best, but to myself I had to admit that she was well found, and in the best ship-shape order.

Feeling satisfied with what I had seen I turned towards the gangway, and again encountered the stringent routine of a sailing-ship life as I heard the Mate roar out to the apprentices, 'Look lively there, lads, lay forrard and get the hatch covers off.' They obeyed on the run, a good sign.

I walked unhurriedly down the gangway, and away from the coal dust and grime of the staith, along the road and so to my lodgings, turning over in my mind the prospects which lay ahead, which added up to one word—Adventure!

3

CONDITIONS OF EMPLOYMENT

NEXT day, 2nd September 1909, I arrived on board the *Caithness-Shire* at 7 a.m. and reported to the Mate for duty at the same time requesting the assistance of two apprentices to get my sea-chest and bag from the four-wheeler cab waiting alongside.

'Never mind changing, mister,' was the mate's reply. 'You will be going to the shipping office with the Old Man to sign on, and the carpenter, sailmaker, cook and steward are also signing on this morning. Be back as soon as you can to relieve me. We can't both go now and leave the ship with only the apprentices on board.'

It was not required for the apprentices to sign the articles as they were indentured to serve in the ship to which they were appointed by the owners for four years, but their indentures would be produced by the Captain to the Shipping Master at the Mercantile Marine Office, for their names, ages, and other details to be entered in the articles, and, like the rest of the crew, the Master would certify they were all on board by a letter sent ashore by the tug after the ship had cleared port.

At 8 a.m., with the Master and Mate, I had breakfast in the saloon, and was able to endorse the opinion the Mate had given me that both the Chinese steward and his cook-assistant were efficient in their department, and at 9 a.m. I got a lift in the Old Man's cab to the Shipping Office and was signed on as Second Mate.

The law had been tightened up in regard to the engagement of crews in foreign-going vessels at British ports. The Merchant Shipping Act of 1894 had been amended in 1906, with many new regulations to protect seafaring men from exploitation by shipowners and shipmasters who, especially in sailing-vessels competing for trade against steamers, had to count every penny to make a voyage profitable; and consequently, in some, if not all, voyages in previous years, had economised in rations and pay, and in other ways had made the working conditions of seamen so unbearable that forecastle hands were chronically destitute.

In those days sailors worked their way from port to port, frequently deserting ships, earning little more than their keep on board and an occasional booze-up on shore in a crimp's boarding-house, from where they were shanghaied on board some other vessel ready to sail.

Those outrageous conditions, which I had seen for myself, had prevailed for many decades, and were in some respects a revised version of the press-gang methods employed to provide crews for British warships a century and more earlier.

This had led to the legislation of the Merchant Shipping Act in 1906 which was gradually becoming more and more strictly applied in 1909 and subsequent years.

It did not mean that conditions at sea had become suddenly perfect. The seaman's life continued to be a hard one, especially in sailing-vessels, and many forecastle hands of the older generation expected nothing else. But the Merchant Shipping Act of 1906 put compulsion on owners and masters to provide a scale of rations much more generous than previously, and in other ways regulated the conditions of employment laid down in the document known as 'the Articles' which was required to be signed by every man joining a vessel in British ports, in the presence of an official of the Board of Trade, and in foreign ports in the presence of an official of the British Consulate.

When compiling the present narrative, fifty years after the events described, I was able to obtain, by courtesy of the Ministry of Transport, Llandaff, Cardiff, a photostat facsimile of the Agreement and Account of Crew of the

Caithness-Shire on that voyage, from its beginning to its end. This has enabled me to check my own recollections and notes in most details, as concerns the crew and the barque's passages from port to port, and the conditions specified officially in the articles, to make this story as accurate as possible as a record of a voyage that was typical in most respects (except in its ending) of the working of a British cargo-carrying sailing-vessel in that period, prior to the 1914–18 war. Those years with some few lingering exceptions marked the finish of the great days of sail, and the victory of mechanical propulsion in ocean-borne commerce.

The Agreement and Account of Crew (Foreign-going ship) was a printed document of sixteen pages, issued by the Board of Trade, through the Mercantile Marine Office at Port Talbot. It was the legal form of a contract between the Master of the vessel (or his lawful successor) on the one hand, and 'every seaman whom he carries to sea as one of his crew' on the other.

The usual procedure was for the Shipping Master to read out to the assembled men all the clauses contained in the articles, including those of a standard form, such as penalties for misbehaviour, scale of provisions and maximum duration of the voyage, and those inserted by the Master, such as 'Crew to work cargo when required', and 'Shore leave only at the Master's option'.

The reading of the articles was usually gabbled through at express speed, and unless the Shipping Master had a clear and resonant voice the essentials were usually lost in an uninterrupted flow of unimportant detail. With the reading of the articles complete, the signing-on proceeded.

The signatories agreed to serve on board the vessel 'on a voyage from Port Talbot to Iquique, or any port or ports within the limits of 75 degrees North and 60 degrees South Latitude, the maximum time to be three years' trading in any rotation, and to end in the United Kingdom or Continent of Europe between the Elbe and Brest'.

This last-mentioned condition was due to the fact that cargoes of nitrates or guano from the West Coast of South

America, or of wheat and lumber from the West Coast of North America, or wool or wheat from Australia, were sometimes unloaded in German, Dutch, Belgian, or French ports, or at various ports in Britain or Ireland, all of which were considered to be 'home ports', where crews were paid off at the end of a voyage.

The crew agreed 'to conduct themselves in an orderly, faithful, honest, and sober manner, and to be at all times diligent in their respective duties, and to be obedient to the lawful commands of the Master and of their superior officers, in everything relating to the vessel and her stores and cargo, whether on board, in boats, or on shore'.

On the second page of the document was a printed list of the Scale of Provisions 'to be allowed and served out to the crew during the voyage'—a list extremely detailed, with rations much more generous than had been required on my previous voyages in the *British Isles*.

On page three of the agreement was a certificate of the vessel's permitted load line (the Plimsoll mark), stating that the centre of the disc was four feet six inches below the deckline (that is, of the main deck amidships). The Plimsoll mark is compulsory by law, and strictly enforced to prevent the overloading of ships which in earlier years had caused many vessels to founder, with heavy loss of lives and property.

The *Caithness-Shire*'s freeboard amidships when fully loaded was thus only four feet six inches from the main deck to the sea, in still water, with the added protection of steel bulwarks four feet six inches high, topped by a broad steel rail. This rail was only nine feet above the load waterline— no great height in stormy seas off Cape Horn, which can be fifty or sixty feet from trough to crest in long sustained gales, and was the cause of the decks being dangerously flooded in heavy weather. Hundreds of tons of water were frequently trapped by the high bulwarks, thereby reducing her free- board, and margin of buoyancy, until the washports and the scuppers could free the ship from the overload pressing her down in the sea.

B

In sailing-vessels, seas shipped over the rail poured out through the scuppers and washports, but in the meantime men working on deck had to wade up to their knees, and sometimes to their waists, through swirling water. It was no joke at any time, and especially in the icy latitudes, as rubber sea-boots, even extending to the thigh, gave no real protection against this discomfort.

The cargo hatches were protected by vertical steel hatch coamings, and at sea were covered by hatch-boards and tarpaulins, to prevent water entering the holds.

Everything else on the main deck, such as spare spars, chicken coups, coiled-up braces, halliards, and other working gear, was secured from the surge of water, except in the Doldrums and fine-weather latitudes, when for some weeks the decks would be dry.

The main deck was the working deck of the ship. There the officers and men had to stand to clew up sails when it was necessary to take them in during bad weather, before going aloft to furl them, and sheet them home from the main deck when they were again set.

All the braces for hauling the yards around were secured to belaying pins on the bulwark pin rail. The fife rail and the spider band around the main mast were used for belaying some standing and running gear.

Though the Plimsoll mark was a wise and necessary precaution of safety, it did not affect the fundamental design of steel sailing-vessels whose low freeboard and consequent 'wet decks' made their working in heavy weather not only difficult but at times dangerous to life and limb.

Page three of the articles also listed regulations for maintaining discipline on board. These had been a cause of much complaint in earlier years. The Merchant Shipping Act now defined the shipmaster's powers of discipline in regard to specified offences, and limited his power of punishment to fines (to be deducted from the offender's pay). He had a summary jurisdiction similar to that of a magistrate in the most common offences on shipboard, which were precisely defined in the articles as follows:

1. Striking or assaulting any person on board or belonging to the ship (if not otherwise prosecuted): *Fine, five shillings.*

2. Bringing or having on board spirituous liquors: *Fine, five shillings.*

3. Drunkenness, first offence: *Fine, five shillings;* second and for each subsequent offence: *Fine, ten shillings.*

4. Taking on board and keeping possession of any firearms, knuckleduster, loaded cane, slung-shot, sword-stick, bowie knife, dagger, or any other offensive weapon, without the concurrence of the Master: *Fine, for every day during which a seaman retains such weapon, five shillings.*

5. Insolent or contemptuous language or behaviour to the Master or officers, or disobedience to lawful commands, if not otherwise dealt with according to law: *Fine, five shillings.*

These were the only offences in which the shipmaster had a summary jurisdiction. For more serious offences under the Merchant Shipping Act, or under the Common and Statute laws of England, he had the power to put any member of the crew under arrest, in confinement and in irons if he thought it necessary, in order to bring the accused man to trial in a court of law on shore.

A statement of any offence committed on board ship was required to be entered in the ship's official log-book immediately after the offence was committed: this to be read over to the offender and his reply also entered in that log-book. Fines imposed by the Master, though deducted from the offender's wages account, were not appropriated to the credit of the ship's accounts, for the benefit of the shipowner, but were handed over to the Mercantile Marine Office, for the benefit of the Board of Trade, at the end of the voyage. (The same applied to wages due to deserters.)

At the foot of page three of the agreement form was a blank space ruled for a list of descriptions of the apprentices, whose documents of indenture were inspected by the officials at the M.M. Office at the outset of the voyage, and the necessary notations made.

On this voyage the four senior apprentices were James Smith, age twenty-six, born in Ireland; Robert Baird, age twenty-three, born in Scotland; Alfred Mowforth, age twenty, born at Hull, England; Joseph Brown, age nineteen, born in Scotland. All these were in the fourth year of their apprenticeship, and their indentures would expire at Iquique, or during the passage to that port.

The five junior apprentices were Frank Wilson, age eighteen, born in Scotland; John Murchie, age seventeen, who had been born of Scottish parents on board S.S. *Liguria,* at sea, in 1892; Alfred Jones, age sixteen, born at Greenwich, England; William Hamilton, age sixteen, born in Scotland; and James Bycroft, age fifteen, born at Grimsby, England.

The articles, indentures, official log-book, and ship's accounts comprised the ship's papers, in the Captain's safekeeping. He was required to deliver these papers to the Mercantile Marine Office at the end of the voyage in the home port of final destination.

The Master of a sailing-vessel had to be much more than a seaman and navigator.

When the ship had been chartered by the owners and an agent appointed at the port of discharge, the Master's duties were principally confined to making sure the quantity and quality of purchases made were correct, and to signing bills for disbursements sanctioned by him, such as towage, wages and advance to crew members paid off, or engaged.

In ports where the Master was his own agent, things could be very different. Here he had to rely entirely on his own judgment in dealing, at times, with not too scrupulous ships' suppliers, or exorbitant charges, quoted in foreign currency if he was not alert, drawing freight from the consignees or their agents for the cargo delivered, and transferring it to the owners by bills of exchange, after settling all local disbursements.

The law made the shipmaster responsible for everything that happened in the vessel under his command, at sea or in port.

At the signing-on of the officers and tradesmen of the *Caithness-Shire* our signatures were witnessed by the Deputy

Superintendent of the Mercantile Marine Office at Port Talbot. The ceremony, if it could be called such, took only a few minutes. First to sign was Captain Hatfield. His wages were not stated in the articles, as these were a matter between him and the owner. Probably he was paid twenty pounds a month, but that is a surmise.

Next I signed as Second Mate, at five pounds five shillings a month. I put my own age down as twenty-five, adding five years to it in the interests of discipline, so that the crew, to sign later, would not know that in fact I was younger than two of the senior apprentices. It would be difficult enough to control veteran seamen without letting them know that I was of immature years.

Next to sign was the fifty-year-old Ah Cheong, as ship's cook and steward, at wages of six pounds ten shillings a month. He held a Board of Trade Certificate as a ship's cook and steward, and was evidently regarded by Captain Hatfield as a find, since good sea-cooks were rare. Ah Cheong signed the articles in Chinese characters, the shipping office clerk adding his name in English spelling.

After him, as assistant, Chan Fai, signed on in Chinese characters at three pounds a month, stating that his age was twenty-seven years, birthplace Canton, home address Hong Kong. Both these Chinese had served in British sailing-vessels since their boyhood, and were well trained in their work.

The carpenter, James McCallum, aged twenty-four, from Govan, Scotland, signed on next at four pounds ten shillings a month. This was his first voyage.

Next was the veteran sailmaker, Tom Sutherland, who stated that his age was fifty-nine, and his birthplace and home address Glasgow. His wages were five pounds a month, the summit of ambition for such a man, after forty-five years at sea. He was an A.B. Seaman (able-bodied, able to steer, able to box the compass, able to splice, and able to do anything on board ship, as the saying went), and there were few ports in the world that he had not visited. Such a man would be a tower of strength in any emergency, when all hands were called on deck, as he knew exactly what to do; and in his work as sailmaker he would have an authority of his own among the forecastle hands and apprentices, and a prestige as a spinner of 'true' yarns, picturesquely exaggerated.

The four tradesmen had an advantage over everyone else in the crew, as they did not have to stand watches at sea, four hours on and four hours off, but worked only in daylight and could sleep uninterruptedly during the night, except at the emergency call, 'All hands on deck'.

This completed the signing-on for that day. The Mate and I, and the two Chinese, drew one month's wages in advance and Tom Sutherland two pounds ten shillings. As we would have a week in Port Talbot, with shore leave in the evenings, this cash advance would enable us to buy extra clothing and other necessities for the voyage, and to have a little recreation on shore before sailing.

4

MAKING READY FOR SEA

AFTER signing-on we returned immediately on board the barque to begin work. On the preceding day, after loading a few hundred tons of coal for 'stiffening', the *Caithness-Shire* had been towed by a steam tug to another berth to unload her ballast.

Towage and ballasting were two of the expenses which put sailing-vessels at a disadvantage as compared with steamers.

A sailing-vessel, with the weight of her top-hamper, including masts, yards, rigging, and sails, carried at a considerable height above deck, required cargo or ballast in her hold to counterbalance this top weight. Without sufficient weight down below she would be top-heavy, and could not safely set sail, or even proceed to sea under tow with no sail set.

Consequently, after unloading part of her cargo, a sailing-ship had to take in a quantity of rubble or sand ballast in her hold before she could discharge the remainder of her cargo.

In comparison, steamers required little, if any, ballasting. They were naturally ballasted with the weight of their engines, bunker coal, and fresh water, and had little top-hamper. They could proceed under their own power from berth to berth, or to an adjacent port for loading, but where they had to make a long ocean voyage to another port to load a cargo their double bottom tanks could be filled with sea water for ballasting.

The towage of sailing-vessels was another great expense. At some ports they could sail in from the open sea to anchorages and load or unload into lighters, but the time had long gone when they could proceed under sail to berths alongside wharves, as had been the practice in the centuries before steam engines were invented and installed in tugs. In those times ocean-going sailing-vessels were comparatively small, and could be worked to a berth under sail, or towed alongside by rowing-boats, but a sailing-vessel of 1,000 tons or more usually furled her sails outside her port of destination and was towed into harbour by a steam tug to her berth for loading or unloading.

There and then, if in a home port, her crew, with the exception of the officers, apprentices and tradesmen, were paid off; the carpenter and sailmaker usually being kept on if they wished to do another voyage in the ship, and given such leave as they might require while the vessel was in either the discharging or loading port. The apprentices were usually sent on leave to their homes, at their parents' expense, one half being retained on board until the other half returned, after perhaps three weeks at home, before commencing another voyage of twelve or eighteen months' duration.

On arrival at a loading-port, such as Port Talbot for coals, she had to take in a few hundred tons of her new cargo as 'stiffening' before being towed or warped to another berth to unload her rubble or sand ballast: then to be hauled back again to her loading berth to complete her cargo.

When she was ready to put to sea she could not set sail at her berth, especially in an enclosed dock, but required the services of a tug to tow her clear of a harbour busy with shipping before she could set sail in open water. All this implied not only much expense, but also a slow turn-around of sailing-vessels in ports, especially in home ports before a new voyage began, whereas steamers could be in and out of a port in a few days, their cargoes unloaded and loaded by steam winches and cranes.

Radio signalling at sea was in its infancy, at a crude experimental stage in some few passenger-steamers and warships in 1909, and quite unknown and unthinkable in sailing-vessels. The owners could estimate to within a few weeks the expected date of a sailing-vessel's arrival in a home port, which was usually at Queenstown in Southern Ireland or Falmouth in Cornwall, 'for orders'. From there she would proceed under sail or in tow to an unloading port; but their first positive intimation of her arrival at any home or foreign port was when she actually arrived there, this being telegraphed to the owners by the local agents, or published in the shipping news in the press. In these conditions steam was winning easily in the competition with sail for ocean-borne trade, and the windjammers were doomed to extinction, though we who worked in them could not, or would not, acknowledge that fact. Their owners had a dwindling asset, but they too stubbornly continued to make the best use possible of their vessels, until they were forced, by the hard logic of their balance-sheets, to acknowledge defeat.

The ballast from the *Caithness-Shire*'s hold was discharged by labourers from the shore, under the supervision of the Mate and myself

The ship was then towed again by a tug to the coal loading berth, and the serious work of loading her with 3,000 tons of coal, began.

The coal trade from South Wales to the West Coast ports of America enabled many a windjammer to survive.

Best-quality hard coal could be bought in South Wales at about ten shillings and sixpence per ton, at the pit mouth, and sold in the ports of Chile and Peru for about four pounds ten shillings per ton, the profit constituting the main reason for the trade, combined with return loadings of nitrates or guano, similarly bought cheap, and sold dear.

The coal trade was the last resort of windjammers to operate successfully, and many famous sailing-ships which had traded regularly to Australia, and the east, with clean general cargoes, ended their days in the lowly trade of a Cape Horn coal-carrier.

In this trade sailing-vessels had one advantage over steamers: they could 'keep the seas' for months on end without putting in to intermediate ports for bunker coal and fresh water, as cargo-steamers had to do. The distance from South Wales to the West Coast of South America, via Cape Horn, some 10,000 miles, was far beyond the range of steamers without rebunkering *en route*.

On the other hand, they could provide a passenger-and-mail service to supplement their earnings, and also carry general merchandise. Steam colliers had a huge trade in carrying export coal from Britain to naval and other coaling-stations at Gibraltar, Malta, Suez, and to ports in the Baltic, Spain, and elsewhere within easy range. Not content with this, some steamship-owners had invaded the sailing-ship trade to the West Coast, taking return loadings of nitrates which could be arranged for them conveniently because they could arrive at stated times, to within a day or so: whereas agents for nitrates (and also for guano) from the islands off the coasts of Chile and Peru could make arrangements to load sailing-vessels only after each vessel had actually arrived, with a delay in loading of weeks, or sometimes months.

So steamers were killing the trade of the sailing-vessels even in the last rendezvous of the windjammers: and there too progress was inevitable.

The actual loading of coal at Port Talbot was accomplished in two or three days. Long trains of rail-waggons, each waggon containing about ten tons of coal, were shunted by a locomotive adjacent to the staith. There each waggon in turn was hauled on to the base platform of the staith by a hauling rope and capstan, the bogie secured to the platform with chains, and the platform then hoisted up inside the staith structure to the desired height, where the whole unit was overturned on its side to cascade the coal down a broad metal chute into the ship's hold.

Careful trimming of the cargo was essential to avoid shifting at sea, when the vessel rolled heavily, and also to put the vessel in her best sailing trim.

Unlike a steamer which, day by day, alters her trim at sea by consumption of fuel for the furnaces, and water for the boilers, a sailing-vessel, once trimmed at the loading berth on an even keel, remained nearly so throughout her passage of perhaps four months to her next port.

To maintain trim was perhaps the most important single item of technical skill and knowledge a Master required to sail his ship from port to port under the several conditions of wind and weather which could be encountered.

This applied not only to the stowage of cargo, and consumable stores, but to the trim of the sails under all conditions to maintain that perfect balance which enabled a ship to steer easily with the rudder amidships, instead of across the stern, acting like a drogue, while exerting the maximum thrust of driving, or lifting power, to carry the ship forward at her best speed under the conditions prevailing.

While the loading was in progress, the decks were smothered in fine coal-dust. Smoking or striking matches or taking naked lights into the hold, or anywhere below the main deck, or near the open hatchway, was strictly forbidden.

The men down below worked in semi-darkness, half smothered in coal-dust. As the ship neared her loaded draft, the Captain and the Mate frequently went ashore on the dockside, carefully watching the draft marks on the stem and stern posts, and the Plimsoll mark amidships, to get the ship into her best sailing trim.

At intervals loading stopped, while all hands available manned the capstans on the forecastle head, or main deck, to haul the vessel ahead or astern, to enable a waggon to be tipped in this hatch, or that, where the Captain or Mate required it.

As the loading went on from day to day, the Captain had gone to the shipping office, and had signed on nine sailors, each at a wage of three pounds per month.

Each man was given an advance note for one month's pay and was ordered to be on board at 7 a.m. on the 5th of September, four days before the barque was due to sail.

They were experienced seamen, and were required for the work of getting the ship ready for sea and embarking stores and provisions for the long voyage.

The forecastle hands were all engaged at three pounds a month, irrespective of previous experience, but with different ratings, two only of them being rated as Able Seamen, Frank Patier (known as Frank Parker) aged fifty, a Frenchman, born at Nantes, who had served many years in British ships: and John Stocken, age thirty-four, a native of Guernsey in the Channel Isles. The other seven forecastle hands were all rated only as seamen but they had recently been discharged from different ships, and were therefore all strangers to one another at the outset of the voyage.

The working hours in port were from 8 a.m. to 6 p.m., with an hour's break for midday dinner. Rations in port, as required by law, included fresh beef, fresh vegetables, and soft bread. The Chinese cook and his assistant knew their work, and the forecastle hands could keenly estimate the prospects ahead of them in regard to food, accommodation, and working conditions—the last-named depending on their estimate of the characters of the Captain and officers.

If she was a 'hard case' ship, it was not unusual for men to 'skin out' (desert) once they had been on board and had a few meals, and sized up the prospects of the impending voyage from a survey of the ship, her Captain, officers, and their fellow-seamen. For this reason, some shipmasters deferred signing on the forecastle hands until sailing-eve, and put to sea immediately after they came on board; but Captain Hatfield had shown his confidence by engaging good men and ordering them on board a few days before sailing.

The crew was now complete with Captain, First and Second Mates, nine apprentices, cook-steward, assistant cook-steward, carpenter, sailmaker, and nine forecastle hands; twenty-five all told. Actually there were twenty-six, as the Captain's wife signed articles as 'stewardess', at wages of one shilling a month: a nominal procedure, to comply with the law, since the vessel was not certified to carry passengers.

The First Mate and I, after washing coal-dust from our hands and faces, and changing from dungarees into more suitable clothes, took our meals with the Captain and his wife at the saloon table, waited on by the Chinese stewards, and found this a pleasant experience.

When the loading of the *Caithness-Shire* was nearly completed, the Captain and the Mate took extra care in supervising her trim, and there was much heavy work for all hands, trudging around the capstans to warp the barque ahead or astern for careful placing of the load. Those were the days when sailors sang at their work, the rhythm of the shanties ensuring united pulling or heaving; their words and tunes known to sailors all over the world. Usually one of the men, would strike up the words of the shanty, telling the tale with all joining in the chorus, which was the signal to haul or heave as required, in unison.

A typical hauling shanty was 'Sally Brown', with solo and chorus in its alternating lines:

SALLY BROWN

(Solo)   Sally Brown she's a black Mulatto.
(Chorus) *Way! Oh! Roll and go!*
        She drinks rum and chews tobacco.
        Spend my money on Sally Brown.

        Seven long years I courted Sally.
        Way! Oh! Roll and go!
        She said, 'My boy, why do you dally?'
        Spend my money on Sally Brown.

        Seven long years she wouldn't marry.
        Way! Oh! Roll and go!
        I said, 'I can no longer tarry.'
        Spend my money on Sally Brown

        Off I sailed across the water.
        Way! Oh! Roll and go!
        And now I'm courting Sally's daughter.
        Spend my money on Sally Brown.

If that was not enough to finish the task in hand, some one else would strike up another, usually with sailors' additions of forecastle wit, carefully censored as these had to be when there was a lady on board.

So the work, aloft and alow, of getting ready for sea, proceeded smartly. Provisions and stores were embarked, including casks of salt beef and salt pork, biscuits ('Pantiles' as they were well named), and also flour for making soft bread on board, as now required by law. The stores included rope and wire, and bolts of canvas (the breath of life in a sailing-vessel). All this material was checked as it came on board by the Mate or myself, and the provisions by the cook.

The provisions were then stowed in the lazaret, and two 'harness casks' filled—one of salt beef and one of salt pork, before being lashed in place at the forward end of the poop where they would be accessible to the cook and well away from the living quarters.

Bolts of canvas were stowed in a special locker in the sail room aft, and cordage in the forward tween-deck, while all the small gear, such as hanks of marline, spunyarn, seizing wire, marlin spikes, serving mallets, thimbles, and other items much favoured by the thieves which infest the docks, was kept under lock and key.

Filling the fresh-water tanks was easy, as this was done with a hose from the town supply. The law required four quarts (that is, one gallon) of fresh water to be issued daily for each member of the crew.

On a voyage of, say, 120 days to Iquique, the water consumption for twenty-six persons would be 3,120 gallons.

In all these preparations at the outset of the voyage the Captain's main concern was to avoid having to put into any intermediate port on the route for replenishments of provisions, fresh water, or gear,

His duty was to 'keep the seas' until he reached his port of destination. At any intermediate port he might enter, either to obtain stores, or make good damage sustained during heavy weather, he would enter in distress, and would be easy prey for local suppliers, who usually soaked such a vessel to the limit.

Shipowners were severe in their private Instructions to Masters in this regard, suggesting that even with a loss of spars such course, if possible, was to be avoided.

At last everything was snug, and our sailing-day arrived, 9th September 1909.

The hatches had been battened and covered, each with three good tarpaulins, truly secured with locking bars and wedges.

The decks had been washed down, and most of the grime removed, the owners' house flag hoisted to the main truck, and the red ensign to the mizzen gaff.

At 9 a.m., just before the Master left for the agent's office on his way to clear the ship outwards, it was discovered that two of the seamen had skinned out, deserted, immediately after their breakfast.

It was now imperative to find two more men who would be willing to join a vessel at an hour's notice for a voyage which might last for three years.

While a search was being made for two men by the agents and ship-chandlers, the Master cleared the ship and returned on board. By early afternoon he decided he could wait no longer or we would lose the tide for undocking, so the mooring lines were cast off, and with a tug alongside, and a pilot on board, we proceeded towards the lock, the Master's intention being to anchor outside to prevent any more men deserting. As we entered the lock our agent arrived alongside in a cab with two men, who climbed over the rail, and so joined the ship while she was actually under way, in what was known among seamen as a pier-head jump.

5

OUTWARD BOUND

When the lock gates opened we towed slowly out into Swansea Bay, away from the grime and smoke of that coal-loading port, outward bound down the Bristol Channel for a voyage around Cape Horn. There were unpredictable perils ahead, and perhaps some pleasures in the ports we would visit if the voyage was to last the three years covered by the articles of agreement.

Port Talbot is towards the western end of the Bristol Channel. It had become one of the principal Welsh coal-loading ports many years previously and in suitable weather conditions sailing vessels could sail into anchorages in Swansea Bay.

Outward bound, loaded from the Bristol Channel, sailing-vessels were towed fifty or more miles, depending on the weather conditions, to a safe offing in the vicinity of Lundy Island. Owing to the strong tides in the Bristol Channel, where the rise and fall of the tide was around thirty feet, and unless a sailing-vessel, leaving the dock at high water, had a strong fair wind, and could gain a safe offing in the open sea under sail with the ebb tide behind her, she might be swept back up the Bristol Channel by the strength of the new flood tide, in a congested lane, with little room for manœuvre if the wind changed against her. An additional risk was that of having a new crew, unfamiliar with the gear, and not yet accustomed to working together as a team.

We had left the dock about 3 p.m. and therefore would have about seven hours of daylight in which to pick the watches, secure everything about the decks and, make all preparations for getting sail on the ship before darkness set in.

As soon as we were well clear of Swansea Bay, and towing down channel, the Master ordered the Mate to send the two pier-head jumpers aft to the poop to sign on.

With the two men in the chart-house, and myself as a witness, the Master looked the men over.

They were both of average size, with plenty of beef and brawn which would be an asset in hauling the yards around, and shovelling coal when we reached the West Coast.

Addressing one of the men, the Master inquired, 'What was your last ship?'

'I have never been to sea before, Captain.'

'What, and you come on board my ship as a *seaman*?'

'The agent said it would be all right, sir.'

'Did you tell him you were not a sailor?'

'Yes, sir, but he said he would take me as there was no one else.'

'What was *your* last ship?' He turned to the other man.

'I have forgotten her name, sir; she was foreign.'

'What's that you say. You don't know her name? Where is your discharge book?'

'I lost it, sir.'

'Well, m'son, we'll soon find out if you are a sailor, or not, when we get down to the Horn! But as you both have no discharges I will only sign you on as Ordinary Seamen, until I consider you capable of being rated as Able Seaman.'

After reading the relevant details from the articles the Master signed the two men on as Ordinary Seamen at three pounds per month and dismissed them to various duties.

In those days it was common practice for destitute seamen, and sometimes fugitives from justice, or casual workers ashore, to try to join foreign-going ships as pier-head jumpers, a course which was only possible when a ship was on the point of sailing and no other men were available, or willing, to join at such short notice.

It was also common practice to have lost the last discharge particularly if it was a bad one, and seek employment under an assumed name, perhaps after months of unemployment, or a glorious spree ashore. But even the worst men after three or four months at sea under the iron discipline of capable Masters and Mates usually emerged as useful hands by the time they reached the next port.

If a Cape Horner had a full complement, and stowaways were found before the tug was cast off, it was seldom that they were sent back to port in the tug, as, with many vessels undermanned, work could always be found for extra men, and, as they received no pay, they provided a cheap source of labour for the shipowner.

It was a fine autumn day, with a gentle northerly breeze, when we towed down channel towards the open sea, making about six knots.

The Mate and I had picked our watches, and I was keeping the eight to twelve, when about 10 p.m. the Master came out of the chart-house, where he had been plotting our position, and ordered me to set the lower topsails.

Sending two apprentices aloft, one on the fore mast, and one on the main mast to cast off the gaskets, we sheeted the sails home from the main deck, as the clewlines and buntlines were let go, and then trimmed the yards more finely to a freshening breeze from the starboard quarter. This eased the strain on the tug, and we made better progress, and by midnight were sufficiently clear of the land to make all sail.

At one bell, 11.45 p.m., the fore and main topsail halliards were led to the capstans, and the gaskets cast off by apprentices aloft, while one seaman loosed the jibs and made all ready to set the sails.

As an apprentice struck eight bells, Midnight, the Old Man roared out from the poop, 'All hands on deck, heave away your topsail halliards! Some hands forrard, Mr. Mate, and set the fore-topmast staysail and inner jib', and, to the man at the wheel, 'Follow the tug, m'son; watch your steering.'

By 1 a.m. under the four topsails and jibs we were over-running the tug, and the order was given to cast off. Taking some men forrard the Mate cast off the towing hawser from the mooring bitts, after telling the tug master to slow down.

The tug sheered away to port, and hailed the ship as we passed with a '*Bon voyage*, Captain', and several toots on his whistle, before setting a course back to the dust-laden atmosphere of the coal ports.

On the main deck all hands now sheeted home the lower t'gan'sls, hoisted the upper t'gal'nt yards by tailing on to the halliards to the rhythm of the shanties 'Sally Brown' and 'Rio Grande'. By 2.30 a.m. on the morning of September 10th, 1909, the *Caithness-Shire* was under all sail, set to a spanking breeze from the nor'-west'rd, logging about eight knots into the vast stretches of the North and South Atlantic oceans, which lay between her and the dreaded Cape Horn.

The system of picking the watches was that all hands, including the apprentices, were mustered on the main deck, at the break of the poop, where the Mate, as senior officer, had the first pick, and, being a man of wider experience than the Second Mate, usually took the best man. After that, the Second Mate picked a man, and so on until all had been separated into two groups, or watches, the Mate's watch being the port watch, and the Second Mate's the starboard watch. The latter was really the Captain's but kept by the Second Mate.

In *Caithness-Shire* the senior apprentice was to act as Third Mate, more or less as a glorified bosun, on duty all day supervising the crew's work on deck. One experienced seaman was also assigned to day work to assist the sailmaker in repairing old sails, and making new ones. These day-men slept all night, when there was no call of 'All hands on deck', leaving a total of four apprentices and four seamen in each watch, with two additional men available on deck for any urgent work required throughout the day.

The living accommodation for the seamen was structur-ally divided into two compartments, port and starboard, by a fore-and-aft dividing bulkhead which did not extend the full length of the forecastle but left an intercommunicating opening at the after end. In it was set a bogie stove, to warm the compartments.

Inside each of the forecastles the bunks were ranged in tiers, upper and lower, shallow box-like structures consisting of plain wood shelves about two feet wide and six feet long supported by iron stanchions against the bulkheads, with a lee board about eight inches high along the outer side to prevent a man being thrown out by the rolling of the ship. In the centre of the compartment there was a mess-table, and benches, with hurricane lamps suspended over the table, and portable oil lamps on the bulkhead.

After we had picked the watches, the seamen of the Mate's watch had moved their gear into the port foc's'le, and consequently were known as the port watch, while the men of my watch settled into the starboard foc's'le.

This arrangement allowed the watch below at any time to sleep, and take their meals in company, without much disturbance from the comings and goings of the men in the watch on deck. Their mess-kits, tin plates, pannikins, and other eating utensils were stowed in wood lockers and their sea-bags suspended from the iron bunk supports or in any spare bunks.

Ventilation in the forecastle was chiefly through the doors, and by port-holes, which had to be kept closed in heavy weather with seas breaking on board, and at times the atmosphere was foetid with human breath, tobacco, and smoke from the lamp. Conditions were similarly overcrowded in the apprentices' deckhouse, where the nine boys also had bunks in tiers, and a mess-table. The wonder is that seafaring men and boys could keep healthy in such primitive living-quarters, but they were used to it, and expected nothing better.

Before leaving port the cook had served the midday dinner, which on this first day consisted of fresh beef stew, flavoured with onions and carrots, and soft bread, washed down with sweetened black tea. The luxury of fresh beef could not be sustained for more than a few days after leaving port. Refrigeration in sailing-vessels was unknown, unimaginable, and impossible at that time.

Under the articles they had signed the seamen were required to keep their forecastles clean, and could be fined five shillings per man for any gross neglect or refusal to do so. It was seldom necessary to enforce this rule as the seamen themselves dealt by direct action with any lazy or slovenly man whose turn it was to be peggy for the day.

The Captain and officers rarely entered the crew's forecastles, except to visit a man who was sick, or perhaps pretending to be sick, or on occasions in port, or soon after leaving port, to raid for grog or weapons.

There was no washroom provided for the forecastle hands, or the apprentices. Their ablutions were done on deck, with buckets of salt water drawn from the pump, or using their skimpy ration of fresh water.

Some fresh water was saved for washing clothes, after they had shaved, if they shaved, and for drinking purposes.

The sanitary arrangements consisted of two lavatories, one on each side under the forecastle head, one for each watch, known as 'the heads', and one aft under the break of the poop, for the officers, but no bathrooms, except one in the Master's quarters, where his wife did her washing.

After breakfast, with the crew settled into the sea routine, and the ship, under full sail, listing to the pressure of a fresh breeze from the starboard quarter, the Mate was discussing with me a programme of work to be undertaken as opportunity occurred during the next few days, and the most suitable men to be allotted to particular duties, when the Master came up from his cabin and joined us.

After a discussion on various matters Captain Hatfield informed us of some sailing peculiarities of the ship, which were well known to him from his previous experience in her as First Mate, and impressed upon us the necessity of, at all times, attending strictly to the set of the sails, to reduce to a minimum the carrying of lee or weather helm.

This was my first time as an officer of the watch in a barque, but I knew from experience in the full-rigged ship

British Isles, and some bawling out from her Master for neglect of this seamanlike action, the effect on the vessel's speed of having the rudder acting as a drogue at an angle to the line of the vessel's keel.

This peculiarity, if it can be called such, was present in some full-rigged ships, and its presence, in greater or lesser degree, depended in most cases on the balance, or lack of balance, in the area of sail set, and the trim of the sails on each mast, in the weather conditions prevailing.

Crowding on every stitch of sail did not necessarily mean more speed through the water.

Fore and aft staysails between the masts could, in certain conditions, reduce the power of the square sails.

With the wind aft, the crojic, the largest square sail on the mizzen mast, in a three-masted, full-rigged ship, would be hauled up, or its clews, corners, only, to give more power to the larger mainsail it was blanketing, and the fore and aft sails would be hauled down.

The correct set of the sails was another factor affecting the speed through the water.

To drive a vessel in the early stages of an approaching gale, when it was possible to carry a press of sail, while the sea was still moderate, the flatter the sails were, the more driving power they exerted, but as the sea increased, and cut the speed through the water down, carrying the press would bury her bows deep in the seas, and even under shortened canvas, in a well-sailed ship, it was customary to ease off the lower topsails sheets, and lower the upper topsail yards a foot or two, to put more belly in the sails to create lifting power, particularly with the sails on the fore mast, to lift the bows.

In a barque, with only a spanker and gaff topsail on the mizzen mast, near the stern, the effect on the rudder was less, which is perhaps one of the reasons, if not the principal one, why a barque rig was adopted by the shipowners, and favoured by most masters in the era of iron and steel sailing-ships.

The comments of Captain James S. Learmont, a famous

Master, who commanded sailing ships for many years, says, in this regard, in his book, *Master in Sail*: 'Yards at, or near the stern of a ship, are no good. In the *Bengairn*, a four-masted barque, you had the benefit of the driving power of the mizzen yards, that were in the *Brenda*, a full-rigged ship, not helpful but a hindrance.'

These remarks apply more particularly to sailing in fine or moderate weather. In bad weather, with great seas rolling up astern, with the rudder half out of the water one moment and buried deep the next, the action of the sea would cause the ship to yaw, first to one side of the course being steered, then to the other, even against the restraining action of the rudder, which could result in the ship broaching to, and laying dead in the trough of the sea.

As the Master impressed upon us his methods of getting the best speed out of the vessel, the thought occurred to me of the possible reaction of our small crew to the pully-hauly involved in these evolutions, more particularly in light variable winds, and the calms and squalls of the Doldrums.

The prospect of a tranquil passage, with perhaps harmonious relations existing between the forecastle hands and the afterguard, did not seem promising if the Mate and I were to interpret our orders literally, and keep the crew on the jump all the time, day and night. Among the many duties of forecastle hands in a sailing-ship, none was more hated than this pully-hauly, which to the men meant nothing more than useless labour, but to the Master and owners possibly a shorter passage between ports, with additional freight earnings, and minimised expenses showing in the yearly balance-sheet.

Making sail after leaving port, with a new crew, was an opportunity for the Master and officers to size up the seamanlike capacity of the men.

As was usual, some of the seamen were more expert than others, and the senior apprentices even more expert than most of the men we had shipped on this voyage.

Both the Mate and myself had carefully watched the different men's reactions to orders, whether they turned immediately to the right tackles, or ropes, or whether they fumbled about at the pin rail, waiting for another man to put his hand on the right gear. From these and similar observations we were later able to tell off suitable men for seamanship jobs, such as splicing wire or rope, putting seizings on the doublings of the shrouds or stays, parcelling and serving, when the time came for overhauling the running gear and standing rigging, in the trade-wind latitudes, and allotting the casual work of chipping, painting, greasing parrels of the yards, and blacking down, to the inexperienced men.

During night watches, no work was done by the crew, except that required to keep the ship moving.

The helmsman, and an apprentice, were stationed on the poop, a lookout man on the forecastle head, while the other men and boys of the watch stood by on the main deck, usually under the forecastle head, where they could hear any blasts on a whistle from the officer on the poop.

Among the men on watch, one usually stayed awake, while the others sat around, or lay down on the deck and dozed, but they were awake instantly, and going aft on the run, when a bellow from the poop of 'Lee fore brace' or 'Square the main yard' rang out.

At any change in the direction or force of the wind they were required to trim the yards, or, if necessary, to shorten sail, or make more sail, but while the breeze was steady there was little for them to do.

As officer of the watch, I kept the weather side of the poop, and an apprentice the lee side, keeping an eye on the set of the sails and on weather signs, and occasionally glancing at the compass by the wheel, to check the course. At each half-hour the apprentice sounded the bell, with the appropriate number of strokes. The clock consulted for this purpose was not the chronometer but a brass wall clock in the chart-house near the head of the companion-way.

When the bell sounded, the lookout man—to prove that he was awake—was required to answer at the top of his voice after looking at the navigation lights, easily visible from the bows: 'All's well and lights burning brightly'. If at any time he sighted anything ahead he would sing out, 'Light on the port bow'—or starboard bow, or dead ahead, as the case might be—and the officer of the watch would sometimes go forrard to verify, or send an apprentice forward or aloft into the rigging, to examine the vessel or object ahead in order to decide if any alteration of course was necessary to avoid collision.

These cries from the lookout man were frequent in the coastal waters of Britain, where it was necessary to exercise special care, as traffic was heavy, and to avoid trawlers, drifters, and other small craft engaged in fishing, which showed lights to indicate where their nets and lines were set.

Apart from these mild distractions, the tranquillity of a night watch in a large sailing-vessel at sea in fine weather is something that has no counterpart in any other way of life. The silence of the night is disturbed only by the pleasant caressing sound of the bow-wave as the stem parts the water which falls away along the vessel's sides, leaving a creaming wake astern, while aloft may be heard a gentle creak or groan as the parrel of a yard chafes against a mast, and the sighing of the breeze in the maze of rigging and vast spread of canvas. So the half-hours pass, with the sounding of the bell, and the cry of 'All's well', beneath the stars, while the watch below slumbers and the dark waters that stretch away to a distant horizon lie still and silent below the canopy of starlit heavens, and man is indeed in harmony with nature.

6

THE LIFE

THE romance of life in a sailing-ship was an elusive thing, which was always present in the sub-conscious mind and brought vividly to life by a spontaneous reaction to the beauties of nature as revealed in abundant measure by the ever-changing pattern and conflict between sea and sky, while the vessel passed from one zone of climatic conditions to another in an ever-widening field of adventure which encompassed the globe. The expectancy, the urgency, of everyday life, as, alone, beyond succour in his own little world, the sailor might see the apparition of impending doom as his ship battled for life in a terrible gale, the mental picture fading to insignificance when a new day broke clear and cloudless over the torn and troubled sea, shorn of all menace with the passing of the great wind.

With the disappearance of windjammers from the world's regular ocean routes, much of the romance of seafaring also vanished, to become only a memory. Never again will it be the privilege of large numbers of men, in their daily lives, to pit their strength, unaided by mechanical devices, against the wrath of the Almighty on those vast oceans where storm and tempest so often set at naught the efforts of brave men to conquer every adversity and bring their sorely battered ships to their destinations in havens of refuge. Never again will those old shellbacks be seen, hardened and toughened by many years of exposure to the heat of the tropics and the icy blasts of the blizzards and hurricanes that rage to the south Horn, their hands gnarled and misshapen by grappling frozen canvas, their faces seamed by the weather, and, beyond that, by the anxieties of battling for their lives, and for the lives of their shipmates, to save their ship from foundering in the terrible seas. The old-time forecastle hand was sometimes a drunken, brawling sot on shore, but, in his own and natural way of life afloat, brave beyond understanding, and with a heart of gold.

And what shall be said of the Masters and officers whose duty it was to control the complicated fabric of ropes, wires, spars and canvas extended aloft to dizzying heights, and to bring it into submission to their skill and judgment as they forced the long, glistening hull through fair weather and foul across the oceans to far-distant ports? Every movement of the barometer, change of temperature, bank of cloud on the horizon, glaring sun rising over a high dan—all these and many more signs and portents had a meaning for men traversing the oceans by the power of winds alone—and woe betide the shipmaster or officer who failed to take heed of those warnings of impending change that Providence supplied as foreknowledge for the observant, enabling sail to be shortened in good time to avoid disaster.

These men had one thing in common. To them a ship in full sail was the summit of perfection. In most, if not all, other ways they were as varied as the winds they strove to use or conquer, sometimes benevolent, sometimes obstructive and hostile. They, like the men and ships they commanded, belonged to that era of seafaring which had contributed so greatly for 2,000 years to the building of civilisation by ocean-borne trade, only to disappear, almost like a light snuffed out, within the short historical term of one lifetime.

Now our first daylight routine on this voyage would begin. We were free of the land and its dirt and worries, and would not see England again for a year or two, or maybe longer—who knew? At least it would be four months before we would set foot on shore again—at Iquique, if we weathered Cape Horn without mishap.

Soon we would be out of the shipping lanes and alone on the ocean, out of sight of all other vessels, except very occasionally, without wireless or any means of communicating with the shore, or other ships, except by visual signals with flags of the international code.

Our route would take us far away from the usual tracks of steamers, and if any man became sick, even requiring surgery, his life might depend on such skill as the Master and officers possessed in making a correct diagnosis, and their ability to treat the patient effectively from the meagre contents of the medicine chest, and the instructions contained in the *Shipmasters' Medical Guide Book*.

Very soon we would pick up the north-east trade wind which would bowl us along merrily until we lost it in the Doldrums of the tropics.

There were many things that could be predicted, almost with certainty, on the route we would take to Cape Horn, and beyond, and among these were the trade winds and the Doldrums, and the dreaded Cape Horn storms: but the essence of adventure is in the unpredictable, and no man on board could foresee how, when, or where our voyage would end.

Under normal conditions, hoisting and hauling was done on deck by a watch of six or more men and boys tailing on to a rope, and pulling in unison to the rhythm of a shanty. In such work brawn was essential, and each additional hand on the rope made the work less heavy.

In fine or steady weather the sails could be handled by the officer, apprentices and sailors of each watch in succession, but in storm and stress both watches might be kept on deck, sometimes until the men and boys were at the point of exhaustion. The two-watch system, with its ingenious alteration of the dog-watches, meant that seamen worked and rested, under normal sailing conditions, in what would be described on shore as 'broken time'. The sailor's twelve hours a day off duty was broken into short periods for sleeping in cat-naps at various hours of the day and night. For months on end, while the vessel was at sea, he would never have one full night's uninterrupted sleep.

The interposing of the dog-watches had originated some

centuries previously, and had become traditional, as a method of alternating the periods of duty and of rest equitably in rotation within each forty-eight hours, the watches being set and relieved as in the following example:

First Watch	8 p.m. to midnight	First Mate
Middle Watch	midnight to 4 a.m.	Second Mate
Morning Watch	4 a.m. to 8 a.m.	First Mate
Forenoon Watch	8 a.m. to noon	Second Mate
Afternoon Watch	noon to 4 p.m.	First Mate
First Dog-watch	4 p.m. to 6 p.m.	Second Mate
Second Dog-watch	6 p.m. to 8 p.m.	First Mate
First Watch	8 p.m. to midnight	Second Mate
Middle Watch	midnight to 4 a.m.	First Mate
Morning Watch	4 a.m. to 8 a.m.	Second Mate
Forenoon Watch	8 a.m. to noon	First Mate
Afternoon Watch	noon to 4 p.m.	Second Mate
First Dog-watch	4 p.m. to 6 p.m.	First Mate
Second Dog-watch	6 p.m. to 8 p.m.	Second Mate

Thus in every forty-eight hours, each watch had seven turns on duty, namely five full watches of four hours and two dog-watches, making a total of twenty-four hours on deck and twenty-four hours (in theory) below. This completed one mathematical cycle of watch-keeping.

This system of unremitting vigilance was required only while the vessel was at sea. When in port, all hands worked in daylight hours, and had time off for rest or recreation at night, and also on Sundays, like any other daily workers. In some ports the crew were allowed shore leave in the evenings and on Sundays, but the articles signed at the outset of this voyage of the *Caithness-Shire* specifically stated: 'No liberty granted abroad otherwise than at the Master's option.' (In West Coast ports sailing-vessels were not berthed at wharves but were anchored half a mile or more offshore, unloaded or loaded from lighters, and the only recreations on shore were of a distinctly dubious character.)

During daylight hours at sea it was the duty of the Mates to keep the men and boys of their watches hard at work, at tasks such as washing or holystoning the decks, chipping rust, sanding the teak rails, renewing the paintwork, polishing brasswork, or repairing the standing and running gear of the rigging—and countless other tasks to keep the vessel shipshape in a never-ending struggle against the corrosive effects of salt water, spray, tropical sun, or Antarctic snow and icicles.

All such extra work on deck and aloft was stopped temporarily when it was necessary to adjust the trim, or areas of sail set, in the weather conditions prevailing, but was resumed as soon as that imperative demand had been met. Meals were served on board at stated times, to correspond with changes of the watch, but varying in bad weather when working conditions made it necessary for all hands to be on deck, and in such case all the men and boys, except the man on lookout, and at the wheel, were sent below together for a meal when the urgent work on deck was finished.

During the four-hour watches the helmsman was relieved by another seaman at the end of the first two hours, except when all hands were on deck for any purpose, when the wheel would be relieved when the watch was sent below.

It was rightly considered that two hours' concentration on steering was a sufficiently sustained mental and physical effort. The wheel was connected by chain gear to the tiller on the rudder head, and the tiller operated the rudder by direct leverage, so that it was necessary to exert physical strength to steer and keep the vessel on her course, and if steering 'full and by the wind' to keep an eye on the weather leech of the main upper t'gan'sl, or the upper square sail set, to keep it close to the wind's eye, and consequently the ship as close-hauled as possible.

This was indicated by a trembling of the leech of the sail, and any relaxation of vigilance in steering could put the sails aback and cause the ship to lose steerage way, with the wind blowing against the forward side of the sails, instead of the after side. The helmsman's responsibility was a heavy one, particularly in bad weather, and it was sometimes necessary to have two men at the wheel, when the ship was yawing about in a heavy following sea and a great strain was being put on the rudder.

With one seaman at the wheel and one on lookout, the man-power available for handing sail aloft, and for other tasks on deck during the night watches in the *Caithness-Shire*, comprised four apprentices and two sailors in each watch, with two additional men, the Third Mate and sailmakers' assistant, during daylight hours.

This would be enough brawn-power for trimming the sails in fine weather, and while the barque was proceeding on a steady course, but to tack or wear ship during the night required all hands. She had five square sails on the fore mast and five on the main mast, plus the spanker, and a triangular gaff topsail, with the staysails between the masts, and jibs forrard, when all sail was set.

This meant ten yards to be hauled around at any change of direction of the wind, which could be done by the watch on deck at night fairly quickly: but if the wind came in heavy squalls, or a gale was making, so that it was necessary to clew up and furl heavy topsails or courses, it may be well understood that both watches might have to be kept on deck for that purpose at the change of the watch, or the watch below called out to help in the work.

Consequently, the officers, apprentices, and sailors worked longer hours than the eighty-four-hour week indicated theoretically under the two-watch system.

Because of the 'broken time' and interruptions of rest during watches below, the men and boys, whose duty it was to work the ship to her destination regardless of their personal convenience and comfort, sometimes turned into their bunks fully clad, even in wet clothes and with their boots on, ready to answer instantly the all-too-frequent call of 'All hands on deck'.

Small wonder, then, that workers in secure jobs on shore considered that a sailor's life must be a dog's life: but the sailors themselves were accustomed to the hardships of a life at sea under sail, and eased the burden of their fate by growling and grumbling through the long-continued struggles against the elemental forces of nature.

They were, in general, a breed of their own, hard-bitten, as their calling demanded, constantly comparing their ship with the last one they had served in, and, by such condemnation of their present environment, sought to console themselves with the thought that their present purgatory was only for a few months, and then they would get another real ship.

The daytime routine work in fine weather in the *Caithness-Shire* began at four bells (6 a.m. precisely) in the morning watch. Some officers in sailing-vessels, in order to get a little extra work out of the crew, were not above pushing the clock hand forward ten minutes, and then putting the clock right again after work had begun.

When four bells had sounded, the officer of the watch instantly blew a long blast on his whistle, the signal for all hands of his watch to muster at the break of the poop, and to put an end to their dawn reveries. He then sang out, in a voice strengthened by singing out orders down wind, or across wind, or against the wind, '*Relieve the wheel and lookout!*' This was followed immediately by '*Wash deck. Tub and buckets aft!*'.

The next few minutes saw intense activity not only by the seamen and boys but also by the officer, for he had to keep an eye on many things happening at once. The seaman who was to relieve the helmsman sprang up the companion-way to the poop and hurried along the lee side to the wheel. The officer closely supervised the change, listening carefully as the man taking over the wheel repeated the course to be steered, given to him by the man going off duty. Helmsmen were required to be able to 'box the compass'—that is, to know by heart the thirty-two points marked on the compass card in their correct sequence, each point covering $11\frac{1}{4}°$, making a complete circle of 360°, through the four cardinal points of north, east, south, and west, each quadrant divided into eight named points, which were further divided into quarter-points.

The course laid down by the Captain was steered until he gave orders to alter it. The helmsman going off duty had only to speak in loud and clear tones the course he had been steering. The relieving helmsman repeated this loudly and clearly, and took the wheel, while the officer glanced at the compass-card to satisfy himself that the course was being correctly steered.

That done, the officer cocked an eye forward to make sure that the lookout on the forecastle head had been duly relieved and, descending the poop ladder to the main deck, walked forward, and, from the fore side of the square sails on the two masts, noted if any buntline stops had been broken during the night and sent apprentices aloft to renew the stops on any of the buntlines which needed overhauling.

This was very necessary to prevent the canvas of the sail being chafed by the rope buntline, a bight, loop, of which about two feet was left to hang below the foot of the sail.

The *Caithness-Shire* had no boatswain leaving Port Talbot, but later in the voyage, when the senior apprentices finished their time and left the ship, an experienced seaman was signed on as bosun, in Callao.

The leadership of work on deck therefore devolved on the two Able Seamen, Frank Parker and John Stocken, one in each watch: or, if they were at the wheel, one of the other seamen was put in charge by the officer of the watch, or perhaps one of the senior apprentices, until the officer himself was free to take charge of the work in hand.

In fine weather, when the decks were dry, it was a daily routine to wash decks as the first task each morning.

This was not only a matter of cleanliness. It was also a precaution to prevent the pitch in the seams of the deck planks from melting, and oozing out in the heat of the day, which would open the seams.

In heavy weather, when seas were shipped over the rail on the main deck, or when there had been heavy showers of rain during the night, the morning routine of washing down decks was not necessary. Also, in bad weather, all available manpower might be required for other tasks, such as hauling

C

in and untangling braces, and other running gear washed out through the washport doors in the bulwarks, or through the scuppers, by seas breaking on board during the night.

Washing down decks was one of the least-liked tasks in a sailor's life. A large tub was brought aft and placed alongside the bulwarks in the waist of the ship. Then a spar was rigged to project a few feet over the side, with a small block attached at the head, through which a handy line was rove, and shackled to a deep canvas bucket, for pulling up water from overside.

Standing on the pin rail, a seaman threw the bucket, mouth down, into the water a few feet forward of his position. By the time the bucket had filled, the forward movement of the ship had brought it directly under the projecting spar. It was then hoisted up by two men tailed on to the hauling end of the line, and tipped over into the tub by the man standing on the pin rail.

Four men stood by with brooms. When the tub was filled, water was passed in buckets along a line of two or three men and boys, to the officer of the watch, or a man detailed by him, who stood at the head of the line, and threw the water over the deck before him, as he advanced along the deck, supervising the men with brooms as they scrubbed the planks.

In fine weather all hands in a watch, except the man at the wheel, and on lookout, were busy at this work, most of them barefooted, with trousers rolled up to the knees. It was a regular opportunity for the officer to hound the men, as he could throw the water over the decks faster than it could be pulled up from overside. Failure of the three hands in the waist to keep the tub filled was regarded as a bad dereliction of duty, and was usually corrected by a free application of fluent sarcasm, and perhaps abuse, which some officers were wont to consider an essential part of their professional knowledge.

The *Caithness-Shire* had a small salt-water pump on the main deck forward, but this did not give a sufficient volume of water for washing decks. Near the time when the day's work started, depending on the geographical position of the ship, the officer of the watch had to keep in mind the time when the sun would rise. A few minutes before that great daily event was due to occur he would station himself at the standard compass on top of the apprentices' deckhouse, in order to take an azimuth bearing, and so to calculate the deviation of the magnetic compass on the course that was being steered, and then to compare the standard compass with the steering compass aft by the wheel, and, after reporting any change to the Master, alter the course to allow for the new deviation.

That task was one which could not be postponed, even though he had many other observations to make, as his eagle eye scanned the decks, taking note of the workers, and shirkers.

When the Captain was not on deck the officer of the watch was the directing brain of the barque's safety and efficient working towards her destination—a fact which was usually recognised by the common sense of the crew. The mysteries of navigation were not understood by the forecastle hands. The Captain and officers, when sights were possible, knew exactly where the vessel was at any time, but the men in the fore-castles had only vague ideas of her position as a pinpoint pricked out on charts of the immense oceans, on courses towards shores and ports that only superior knowledge could find.

It was therefore not for them to question orders but only to obey the decrees of that superior knowledge. This applied in small details of daily routine not less than to orders to turn out both watches for the heavy work of shortening sail on some indication by the barometer that stormy weather was imminent or to set more sail at the first indications of finer weather.

This being understood, seamen not only obeyed orders unquestioningly and promptly but tolerated and expected rebukes, and sometimes sharp rebukes, as the Mates unre-mittingly hounded them on to efficient efforts. They well knew that these orders and rebukes were not given officiously, even by young officers, but had experience and knowledge, as well as lawful authority, to back them, since every officer in sail had learned seamanship the hard way, and was no gilded popinjay promoted by favouritism. The officers worked not only mentally but physically as hard as the men, and never hesitated to go aloft to lead them when there was difficult or dangerous work to be done, or to handle ropes and wires on deck, up to their waists in swirling water, and also when the decks were dry.

The so-called 'bully mates' or 'bucko mates', who enforced discipline with their fists or a belaying pin, to work a ship with sullen, mutinous, and inexpert crews containing a proportion of men who had been shanghaied aboard in a drunken or drugged condition, had become rare, at least in British sailing-vessels, in 1909; but occasionally an officer might be required to show his toughness if there was a trouble-maker in his watch. Seamen were disciplined by being hit in the pocket rather than on the jaw. They could be fined by the Captain for disobedience or for 'insolent or contemptuous language or behaviour' to himself or the officers. The Captain could order any seaman to be arrested and locked up on board, and put in irons, to be brought to trial on shore, for assaulting an officer.

In short, discipline on board a sailing-ship depended on commonsense recognition of the need for lively obedience to orders, the necessity for which was only too apparent to a good seaman, whose daily routine was resolved into maintaining the intricate maze of rigging in efficient order, and effectively using it to master the vagaries of wind and weather, on which self-preservation might depend. The necessity for discipline was acknowledged by most forecastle hands while at sea, but occasionally a practised malingerer, or self-opinionated sea-lawyer in a forecastle, would cause discontent, and passive resistance to an officer's interpretation of his duties, and in such case the Captain would intervene with such action as the circumstances dictated to enforce obedience.

Sailors at sea were teetotallers for months on end—except on very rare occasions when the Old Man served out a tot of rum to all hands as a reward for some special effort or ordeal. Their enforced sobriety contributed to the peaceful order and discipline of the crew. The articles they had signed made it an offence to bring hard liquor on board, and also stipulated that any member of the crew who considered himself to be aggrieved should make his complaint to the Captain 'in a quiet and orderly manner'. The Captain was bound to listen to and to deal with such complaints as he considered the facts required.

In all these circumstances the authority of the officers of the watch was exercised chiefly by spoken orders firmly given, and with forthright rebukes for slackness, but never with any undertone of weakness, uncertainty, or attempts at ingratiation. An officer's duty was to see that all work on shipboard was well done. He was the judge of what was necessary to be done, and of how and when it should be done, and the men knew it.

When the decks had been washed, and the tubs, buckets, whip gear, and brooms put away, the officer of the watch— if no sail-trimming was necessary—told off the men and boys to various work to be done before breakfast, such as getting the day's supply of coal for the galley-stove, mixing paint in tubs under the forecastle head in preparation for the day's tasks of painting masts, yards, bulwarks, or other steelwork and woodwork; or hauling sails up out of the sail-locker for the sailmaker to repair.

At seven bells a seaman from the forecastle mess of the watch below, and an apprentice from the half-deck mess, went aft to the door in the break of the poop from which an alleyway led into the officers' quarters, and the stewards' storeroom. At the door they waited with the bread barges and other receptacles for Ah Cheong and his assistant to hand out the day's ration of bread and other rations, which would not be included in cooked food to be handed out from the galley.

Under the Merchant Shipping Act of 1906 the bread ration was defined as one pound of soft bread per man on Sundays, Tuesdays, and Thursdays, and one pound of ships' biscuits (pantiles) per man per day on the other four days of the week. The baking of soft bread on board a sailing vessel at sea depended on the weather, and on the cook's skill as a baker, besides other factors such as weevils in the flour and yeast that went mouldy in the tropics. The law provided that when soft bread was not available an equivalent weight of biscuits must be issued as a substitute for it.

Other rations handed out at the door under the poop were weighed or measured for each mess, according to a weekly allowance or 'whack' per man, as required by law, of $1\frac{1}{4}$ lb. sugar, $\frac{1}{2}$ lb. of tinned butter (which became oil in the tropics), 1 lb. of jam, $\frac{1}{2}$ lb. of syrup or molasses, half a pint of pickles, 5 oz. of dried fruit, 2 oz. of salt, $\frac{1}{4}$ oz. of mustard, $\frac{1}{4}$ oz. of pepper—each of these quantities being per man per week, less a deduction which the cook might make in his own wisdom in items such as sugar, salt, pepper, and dried fruit, to be included in cooked food. There was also a ration of one 1 lb. tin of condensed milk per three men weekly, and finally the compulsory issue of one fluid ounce of lime juice per man per day, to prevent scurvy, for which British sailors were known (to Americans) as 'lime-juicers' or 'limeys'.

From the cook's galley the remaining provisions were dished out in cooked rations at the rate of 3 lb. of salt beef and 2 lb of salt pork per man per week, plus $2\frac{1}{4}$ lb. of tinned beef (bully beef), and $\frac{3}{4}$ lb. of tinned fish per man per week; and—while they lasted—6 lb. of potatoes and $\frac{1}{2}$ lb. of onions per man per week, plus small quantities of dried peas and haricot beans ('calavances'), and also, while it lasted and weevils permitting, 2 lb. of flour (used by the cook for thickening stews, or for dumplings and on rare occasion for making johnny cakes), $\frac{1}{2}$ lb. rice, and $\frac{1}{2}$ lb. of oatmeal per man per week.

The oatmeal was supposed to be served as 'skilly' (porridge) on Tuesdays and Saturdays. On other days the breakfast menu was bread (or biscuits) and tea or coffee. The law prescribed an allowance of $1\frac{3}{4}$ oz. of tea, and 4 oz. of coffee, per man per week. All these weights and measures were intended to be a guide to shipowners, shipmasters, and ship-chandlers, in provisioning a vessel at the beginning of her voyage, the quantities to be multiplied by the number of persons in her complement, and that quantity multiplied again by the number of weeks that the voyage, or a passage to another port where replenishments could be obtained, was expected to last.

It would have required a mathematical ability far more highly developed than that possessed by Ah Cheong, or most other sea-cooks, to calculate, weigh out, and apportion to the various messes the exact quantities of provisions stipulated by legislators who, in their wisdom and benevolence, and in response to the pressure of public opinion, had attempted to improve the living conditions of seamen which had been described in the press for years as a public scandal, in more ways than one, but especially in regard to rations at starvation level.

Ah Cheong, like other sea-cooks, had the responsibility of making provisions last as long as possible, on a voyage of indefinite duration. The food which he cooked in the galley was calculated on the ration for the entire complement of the barque, daily or weekly. It was quite impossible in practice for a cook at sea to measure cooked food in fractions of a pound or ounce per person. Consequently the rules and regulations of the Merchant Shipping Act of 1906, however satisfactory these may have seemed to lawmakers, officials, and humanitarians on shore, could not be enforced on board a vessel at sea in all circumstances.

The food served in the saloon was the same as that served to the crew in the main items on the menu each day, with a few extras, such as scones or cakes baked to please the Captain's wife, or stewed or tinned fruit added as dessert. With only the Captain and his wife, the First Mate, or myself at the table (one officer being always on deck, and consequently taking his meal alone before going on watch or after being relieved), there was no need in the saloon for the careful portioning of 'whacks' which prevailed in the fore-castles and the half-deck. The table in the saloon was nicely laid with cloth, cutlery, and crockery, a touch of refinement due to the presence of a lady, and highly appreciated by Laird and myself.

After drawing the dry rations the mess delegates drew the cooked ration at the galley door, this consisting at breakfast time usually of nothing more than a billy-can of tea or coffee. Breakfast was then served in the mess to the watch below at 7.30 a.m.

The watch on deck had their breakfast after being relieved at 8 a.m.

Such was the situation when I took over the 4 a.m. to 8 a.m. watch on 10th September, our second day at sea, and my first daytime watch since we cast off the tug some hours previously.

On the fourth day we picked up the north-east trade wind in Lat. 45°N. Ahead of us was the prospect of ideal sailing in the fair-weather latitudes, beneath clear skies with a steady breeze from aft on our south-westerly course— Europe's oncoming winter left astern, and sunny days ahead.

7

FINE WEATHER AND FAIR WINDS

BOWLING along in the north-east trade wind, with a steady moderate breeze from astern or on the port quarter, the *Caithness-Shire* ran to the south-westward in the bright sunshine by day and beneath the unclouded starry heavens by night, in perfect sailing conditions. This breeze blows steadily in most seasons of the year in this zone of the North Atlantic, from Europe towards the Equator in the direction of Brazil. It was the breeze that wafted Christopher Columbus and his three little ships across the Atlantic in 1492, to the island he named San Salvador (later named Watling Island) in the Bahamas, and so to 'discover America'.

That same breeze had favoured many a mariner thereafter, Portuguese, Spaniards, French, Dutch, and English, at the outset of their adventurous voyages to explore and map those large parts of the world which had been unknown to Europeans; and then for four centuries the trade winds, north and south of the Equator, in the Atlantic and Pacific Oceans, had marked the routes for ships innumerable in the great days of sail.

We in the *Caithness-Shire* knew what to expect, but the fair breeze was nonetheless pleasant when it lived up to expectations; for we knew, too, that the trade winds would end in the Doldrums, and then it would not be plain sailing, and beyond in the South Atlantic there would be the ordeals of Cape Horn before we could reach our destination.

On deck the men and boys of each watch were kept at work at their various tasks overhauling gear in preparation for the stresses and strains to be expected later in the passage. On the poop the sailmaker sat on his bench making a new sail, or repairing an old one. In the carpenter's shop 'Chips' could be seen making wooden buckets or wooden shells for blocks.

As the sails bellied out in the gentle or moderate breeze there was little work of handing sail to be done, sometimes for several days, except when a worn or torn sail was clewed up and sent on deck for repairs, and another sent in its place, the usual practice being to hoist the sail aloft in a few minutes by tailing on to the rope gantline, which had been rove through a lead block on deck, and walking, tug-of-war fashion, along the deck to the rhythm of the shanty, stamp and go, such an occasion usually being followed by 'freshening the nip'.

This meant tightening or 'sweating up' the braces, which stretch and become slack when they are dry, and under tension from the vessel's rolling and the wind's pressure in the sails. 'Freshening the nip' meant hauling in a short length of all the braces through the bulwark leads, and securing them anew around the belaying pins to which they were made fast. To do this, after hoisting a sail aloft, required fifteen or twenty minutes' work for all hands of both watches, with a consequent loss of that amount of time for the watch going below. This was a routine that seamen disliked.

With that exception, there was an easy life for the crew while the barque was running before the trade wind.

In these conditions the mind of a sailor is at peace. He is isolated in a world of his own, far from the turmoil and smoke or fog of cities, and able to move about the deck, or rest in his bunk, undisturbed by the incessant clang, clutter and pulsation of the engines in a steamer.

In a sailing-vessel in fair weather men are in harmony with nature. Then, many hundreds of miles from land, the diverse interests, habits, and reactions of the ship's company, few in number in comparison with the crews of large steam-driven vessels, converge towards a bond of fellowship, since the safe working of the ship to her destination depends on the willing co-operation of all, each man doing his best: but sometimes the association for months on end of men living and working together in a restricted shipboard space may tend towards self-pity in an individual, with antagonism to others—and upon that issue the ultimate fortunes of the voyage of combined adventure may depend.

Men who would become surly in ideal sailing conditions —for example when called upon to freshen the nip in the trade winds—would in all probability be malingerers in harder conditions to be expected later in the passage, and their demeanour would be duly noted by their shipmates, and especially by the Master and officers, in anticipation of that development.

Occasionally we sighted other vessels—full-rigged or steamers—on the horizon, outward or homeward bound. Their hulls might be below the horizon, and only the upper sails, or a trail of smoke drifting to leeward, indicated the stranger's course; but if perchance a full-rigged ship came within full view, either homeward bound or overtaking us on a parallel course, as the famous flyers could do, we had then for some hours in sight the most beautiful object ever designed by the brain and made by the hand of man, a sailing-vessel with all sail set in a fair breeze, perfectly balanced perfectly rhythmical, the product of centuries of experience made for a purpose: poetry in action.

In the clear waters schools of porpoises frolicked around the barque, swimming under the bows and effortlessly keeping pace with the stem as it gently parted the water. At other times shoals of dolphins took over the escort, but, for some reason best known to themselves, preferred to take their station astern, swimming in the barque's wake, their light-coloured skins catching the refractions of the sun's rays and making them seem to be of variegated colour. Schools of flying fish sprang from the surface and skimmed over the crests of the sea, probably to escape from enemies pursuing them, but it seemed that they were practising their aerobatics in sheer joy of life. Sometimes they collided with the sails or rigging and fell to the deck, to end in a frying-pan.

The antics of the porpoises, dolphins and flying fish were a pleasure to watch. It was otherwise with the sharks frequently to be seen cruising tirelessly round the barque, but usually astern, waiting for morsels of garbage to be thrown overboard, or perhaps for a sailor to lose his hold in the rigging and fall into the water. Those ferocious sea-brutes were hated by sailors with a ferocity equal to their own. The presence of a shark cruising astern was a reminder and constant warning to men aloft of the value of the old saying, 'One hand for the ship and the other for yourself'.

Sometimes when a large shark was sighted, persistently following in our wake, the men would ask permission to set a line to catch him. For this purpose a stout line with a shark-hook was kept with other assorted gear in my cabin. The hook was baited with a piece of salt pork, thrown with the line over the stern free of the patent log, and paid out ten fathoms more or less. Officers and men on the poop would watch the shark, his every movement visible in the clear water, swim up and nuzzle the bait, turn away as if in doubt, then change his mind, and in a swift rush snap his jaws on the bait and begin wildly thrashing the water in attempts to get free.

As soon as he was hooked, the cry of 'Shark!' resounded on deck from stern to stem. This always brought the watch below out on the run, eager to share in the sport. There was never any shortage of volunteers to tail on to the line when it was manned and passed along to the main-deck rail amidships, the hooked brute struggling violently and tiring himself but providing a heavy resistance to the men hauling on the line. To attempt to haul him up to the poop deck, where the planks would be soiled with his blood and entrails, would have been nothing less than sacrilege, and would never have been permitted.

When he was at last brought alongside, a noose was lowered down the hook line and pulled tight around his body. With this he was hauled up to the bulwark rail, and fell with a flop to the deck, lashing his tail and snapping his jaws, the seamen nimbly dodging around with cries of excitement and warning as they watched for opportunities to kill him. One man thrust a capstan bar down the brute's gaping throat, others stunned him with blows on the head, and the carpenter, with one blow from an axe, severed his tail, after putting a billet of timber under it, to avoid damaging the deck planks.

Next, the shark's head was cut off, to be stripped of its flesh and the jawbones and teeth preserved, and to be presented at the end of the voyage, perhaps, by one of the sailors to his sweetheart as a memento of his travels. Then, with a butcher's knife borrowed from the cook, the shark's belly was ripped open, to see if any human bones or trinkets were inside. Blood and guts were spread around on the deck planks in profusion, as the seamen took turns in cutting up the carcase and throwing the pieces overboard, where other sharks, attracted by the prospect of a cannibal feast, appeared from all directions and devoured the remains of their late brother as the pieces slowly sank in the water.

The sport or recreation of catching a shark, occupying an hour or more of time, with its accompanying excitements, was a welcome break in the monotony of sea-routine.

Another diversion on board the *Caithness-Shire* was sometimes enjoyed by the crew, but not always appreciated by the Mate. The antics of the Captain's mastiff, Crokie and bull-terrier, Bozo, as they roamed the decks freely in the fine-weather latitudes, sometimes caused consternation, and sometimes amusement, but they were fierce and powerful dogs, and their presence could not be disregarded by men at work on deck, especially by men with pots of paint, since the dogs nosed into and frolicked over everything, and their fierce appearance, combined with the Captain's authority, made it difficult for some of the more timid seamen to rebuke or chastise them.

It was a matter of wonder how such big dogs could be kept healthy on a diet of salt beef and pork and biscuits, and a special ration of precious fresh water, on a lengthy passage at sea, including some weeks in the heat of the tropics, and there seemed always the possibility that one or the other or both of them might go mad and attack somebody without warning, or so some of the seamen thought.

Sometimes when I went below after a watch on deck I would find Crokie or Bozo comfortably asleep in my bunk, and the Mate had similar experiences. The dog would not be at all pleased at being roused out and chased on deck, growling and looking as mournful as only a dog can when he feels he is a victim of persecution.

The dogs were a constant worry to the Chinese cook and his assistant, as they would squat on their haunches outside the galley door, begging for scraps, or licking their chops as they eyed the salt beef or pork on the bench ready for cooking. At such times Ah Cheong dared not leave the galley to go aft in his capacity as steward until the meat was safely on the boil and everything else edible in the galley stowed away.

The dogs had soon learned the contents of the water barrel which stood inside the galley door, containing the 'cook's whack' of fresh water for culinary purposes and making tea and coffee.

As the weather became warmer, whenever Ah Cheong and his assistant left the galley unguarded Crokie and Bozo would make a raid on the water barrel, nose its lid off, and drink their fill. On seeing this, some seaman would report it to the officer of the watch. The Captain then had no option but to approve of emptying out the polluted water, cleaning out the barrel, and refilling it from the fresh-water pump—a waste of precious water and working time.

The dogs had another playful habit of raiding the quarters under the poop, or the apprentices half-deck, in quest of whatever they might be able to find for their amusement. It was not unusual for the peace and quietness on board to be shattered as someone in the afterguard emerged from slumber and bounded out on deck in pursuit of the two hounds racing away along the deck with perhaps a shirt or a pair of trousers in their teeth, worrying the garment with loud growls, as, with a firm grip at each end, they shook and tore it to rags.

This was amusing to everyone except the owner of the destroyed article of clothing.

One morning in my four to eight watch on deck, while I was drinking the cup of tea on the poop which the steward always brought up to the officer on watch at 5.45 a.m., I heard a commotion below, and shortly afterwards saw Crokie and Bozo bound out of the main-deck door and race forward together snarling and growling in their usual manner as they worried something between them. They made their way forward to where the watch on deck were drinking tea and smoking before beginning the day's work at 6 a.m. Then I heard raucous laughter intermingled with the savage growls of the dogs. I walked along to see what was happening.

In the midst of a circle of men the dogs were worrying and tearing to shreds a lady's dainty undergarment which they had apparently purloined from the Captain's sleeping cabin. With a few blows of a belaying-pin on their ribs, I made the dogs let go, and salvaged a few pieces of linen and lace, while the men looked on, grinning broadly. At that moment four bells sounded, so I blew a long blast on my whistle and sang out, 'Relieve the wheel and lookout! Wash-deck tub and buckets aft!'

An hour later, while I was supervising some work on the main deck, I noticed that the Captain's wife was walking about the poop with a worried expression on her face, furtively looking for something that she had lost, while the man at the wheel—who had been present at the 'killing'—sought to hide a smile by staring fixedly at the horizon instead of at the compass. I felt lacking in courage to tell the lady what had happened to her garment, but fortunately the Captain came on deck at that moment, and I evaded a difficult situation by handing to him unobtrusively the tattered piece of linen and lace that I had salvaged, being careful not to smile as I did so, and remarking only that I had taken it away from the dogs. He needed no further explanation.

On suitable occasions in fine weather, when the barque was sailing steadily, the Captain would set his dogs fighting.

This was a thrilling, and even bloodcurdling, sight, which he regarded, with the eye of an expert, as a sporting encounter. He would bring them on to the poop, and set them at each other in fierce combat. These were no half-hearted affairs, as the dogs, with growls of anger or yelps of pain, flew at each other, rolling on the deck with gaping and foam-flecked jaws, biting and tearing one another and spattering hair and blood on the carefully holystoned white planks to the unconcealed annoyance of the Mate.

But the Old Man—for so every shipmaster was called, whether he was young or old—could do whatever he liked in his ship, within legal limits, and if he chose to have a dog-fight on the poop the decision was his and his only. It was obvious that in his youth he had acquired a special interest in the breeding or training of fighting dogs, and, as this was his first command as a Master in Sail, he had taken Crokie and Bozo with him to engage in his hobby, and to study its finer points whenever opportunity occurred.

When the dogs, like pugilists between rounds, disengaged themselves temporarily and stood apart, eyeing and growling at each other, the Old Man, excited and eager, 'sooled' them on until, with a rush and fierce snarls, they were at each other again, while he walked around them, or leaned over them when they were locked together, watching every point of attack and defence, like a referee at a prize-fight. When he was satisfied he called off the fight and the dogs obeyed him. Then for several days they remained together quietly in the sail-locker under the poop, licking their wounds and recuperating, until they emerged on deck again, frolicking together and making a nuisance of themselves, as previously.

With these various incidents the north-east trade wind bowled us along merrily until one morning, in 10°N. Lat. the barque was becalmed. We had entered the Doldrums the belt of equatorial calms and light variable winds, between the north-east and south-east trade winds. Blazing heat and occasional downpours of torrential rain could be expected in this part of our passage. At that season of the year the Doldrums extended for a distance of approximately

360 miles, from 4°N. Lat. to 10°N. Lat., more or less. It was no great distance for a steamer, but for a vessel under sail an ordeal that frayed the tempers of all on board, since constant vigilance and hard work at all hours of the day and night were required to take advantage of every puff of wind in the light and variable airs, in order to make any headway at all. So, when the north-east trade wind ceased to fill our sails, and the barque lay becalmed, rolling gently in the easterly swell, all the seasoned sailors on board knew what to expect. They were prepared for the worst, but hoped for the best.

8

IN THE DOLDRUMS

PASSAGE through the Doldrums is a nerve-racking experience. The frequent flat calms are interrupted at irregular intervals by light swirling airs which suddenly ripple the surface of the ocean in catspaws, then die away. As wind is the breath of live in a sailing-vessel, its absence means stagnation, but capricious light airs are baffling and irritating, raising hopes of making headway, and dashing those hopes almost as soon as they are born.

In the calms the vessel lies broadside on to the ocean swell, rolling easily but otherwise inert. Her sails hang lifeless from the yards, and slat against the masts with a bang and slap as she rolls. In the humid and breathless atmosphere the brassy sun shines fiercely with dazzling light and scorching heat, a ball of fire in the cloudless and vivid blue sky. It softens the pitch in the seams of the deck, which sticks to the bare or shod feet of men and boys as they move listlessly at their work, while those unfortunate enough to be working aloft shuffle carefully and painfully along on wire footropes suspended from steel yards that are heated and burning to the touch, as are the hollow steel masts and all the wire rigging.

On deck there is little shelter from the pitiless sun, but aloft there is none. The crew suffer discomfort from thirst, and from sunburn wherever their skins are exposed. On the poop the Captain paces from side to side, gazing over the taffrail, and quietly whistling for a wind. He is expected by the crew to perform this traditional ritual, and perhaps he partly believes in it himself. His efforts will certainly be rewarded, sooner or later, but not necessarily with a breeze from aft, for the wind-gods are sometimes deaf, and in the Doldrums they play a cat-and-mouse game.

Suddenly a faint breath of air is felt by the officer of the watch, or perhaps he notices the ripple of a catspaw breeze approaching on the glassy sea. At the order 'Lee for brace', or 'Square the main yards', the men and boys aloft scramble down the heated rigging to join the others on deck in manning the braces to haul the yards around. The breeze fills the sails, which belly out, and the vessel moves almost imperceptibly forward, as the helmsman hopefully steadies her on course.

She makes perhaps a mile, perhaps less, of headway; then, as suddenly as it came, the breeze dies away. The clews of the foresail and mainsail are hauled up again, with muttered curses, and the vessel once again lies becalmed on the glassy sea.

Every effort was justifiable to make even a little headway through those accursed Doldrums, in which the barque seemed to be crawling like a fly on treacle, and the hours of inertia seemed eternities. By taking the utmost advantage of every puff of wind we could make headway of from twenty to fifty miles, on some days, but tempers became shorter, and nerves frayed, as the crew, their skins wet with perspiration, were driven without respite to haul around the yards and trim the sails to the capricious and short-lived 'cap-fulls' of variable zephyrs.

At times the crew, exhausted by hours of pully-hauly, and by the heat, would not pull their weight, when tailed on to a brace, but would only appear to do so, by going through the motions of responding with pretended gusto to the forehand's shanty-rhythm. Such malingering was difficult to detect in an individual, but was apparent in the result achieved, and the experienced officer would know that the limit of possible effort had been reached. There was nothing then to do except fume inwardly and hope for more headway in the next zephyr's puff. The constant vigilance and frequent trimming of sail continued throughout the night watches, in conditions a little more agreeable than those under the burning sun, but scarcely less exhausting and disappointing in the slow headway achieved with strenuous effort.

At sunset on our fifth day in the Doldrums a dense black cloud was spreading gradually across the sky, and preparations were made to meet whatever this phenomenon might portend. A heavy downpour of rain seemed certain, but whether it would be accompanied by strong winds, who could tell? The Captain gave his orders; the courses were hauled up snug in the buntlines and clewlines; the staysails were hauled down, and the spanker brailed in; the topgallant and topsail halyards were flaked on deck in readiness to lower the yards if need be. The atmosphere was heavy, with no breath of a breeze, and the barque was at a standstill as she lay in an eerie silence beneath the dense black cloud which blotted out the stars and seemed to be pressing down upon her, like an encompassing void.

In anticipation of a heavy rainstorm the Captain had decided to attempt to replenish the fresh-water tanks. A large square sail was got up from the sail-locker and suspended horizontally above the after hatch, its corners, sides, and ends made fast with ropes to the rigging to catch the pure water from the skies.

Normally, in this situation, with the weather hot and stifling, and the imminence of heavy rain, some of the crew would frolic about the decks almost naked, and during the downpour actually naked, as they indulged to the full the pleasure of shower-bathing with unlimited warm water, but with a lady on board this pleasure was denied them, and in trousers and singlets they were to see this heaven-sent opportunity for a real fresh-water bath fade away, except for a few bolder spirits whose stations on deck forrard were concealed from the poop by the deck structures.

At the change of the watch at 8 p.m. all hands were kept on deck. Whatever was to happen was now imminent and awe-inspiring. The sea appeared to have turned milky white as it lay smooth beneath the dense black pall of cloud which now pressed down and appeared to touch the surface of the water at a short distance from the barque on all sides.

In the stillness the Captain and the Mate were quietly talking near the man at the wheel, who stood holding the spokes firmly to counteract an occasional convulsive kick of the rudder as a swell brushed it. I was stationed with most of the crew on the main deck, standing by, with the yards squared in, ready to haul them on the backstays when the first breath of an impending wind might indicate from which direction it would come. In the eerie silence the men spoke not a word as they gazed apprehensively around them.

Suddenly the dense black cloud was split by a vivid flash of lightning, which revealed the stark outline of white canvas, hanging limp overhead, and the pattern of spars and rigging silhouetted against the black celestial concave, while a rumble of thunder announced the approach of the tropical rainstorm. Again and again the darkness was rent by searing flashes of lightning, all around and above us, momentarily making visibility as clear as daylight, and then the darkness more intense in contrast, while the peals of thunder rose to the volume of a cannonade, reverberating to stun the senses, but with no breath of wind to disturb the stillness of the sea and air.

On the main yard a corposant, or St. Elmo's Fire—a ball of 'static' lightning—formed a bluish glow and rolled along the yard to cling for a moment on the yardarm before it flickered and disappeared. Others of these ghostlike apparitions formed on the mastheads and yards to frolic like will-o'-the-wisps in the steel fabric aloft, and vanish like visitors whose curiosity is satisfied. It seemed that the steel masts and yards had in some way become electrified by the lightning that now forked and branched in incessant searing flashes, splitting the darkness asunder and raging in fury down to the sea.

It appears that very few, if any, vessels at sea have been struck or destroyed by lightning, but this was no comforting thought in a barque with metal hull and spars in the midst of a violent electrical storm, with St. Elmo's Fire dancing eerily aloft, and at such a time the survival of puny men on deck seems to depend on luck, or fate, or the mercy of Providence.

Suddenly a vivid flash of lightning, with a simultaneous loud clap of thunder, seemed to tear open the dense cloud above us, which poured a deluge of torrential rain upon the barque and the surrounding sea in which she continued becalmed with not the slightest breath of wind. The rain fell vertically, and not in scattered drops, but compacted like a cataract poured over a cliff. This deluge cleared the humidity and cooled the temperature in which for two hours the crew had waited restlessly for the storm to break. Within minutes we were all soaked to the skin; the horizontally slung catchment-sail was full to the brim with some 500 gallons, and brimming over, as were the tubs and buckets and other utensils which the crew had placed on deck to catch water for their own use; and fresh water from the skies was swirling ankle-deep on the decks and pouring out through the scuppers.

Rain such as this is known only in the equatorial zone, where the fierce suction of the sun's heat draws the water from the immense evaporating basin of the ocean, to form clouds of such heaviness and density that they are impermeable by light, and so show black on their under surface. The drops of moisture in the clouds, swept upwards by a rising current of heated air from the surface of the ocean, increase in size, it is said, to a quarter of an inch in diameter, when they disintegrate and fall as rain. The massive disintegration of the globules within the clouds liberates an electrical charge which accumulates as flashes of lightning.

This scientific explanation, which satisfies meteorologists, does not take into account the awe-inspiring effect of a tropical thunderstorm at sea upon the minds of men in a sailing-vessel who are caught in its throes. The sailor's life is dominated at every moment when he is on the high seas by the weather, in its benevolent and malevolent moods, which he must anticipate by careful observation in order to take timely measures to ensure the safety of the vessel and her progress towards her destination. With that requisite, every seaman cocks his weather eye on sky and sea at the moment he steps on deck. Yet there are times when observation and practical knowledge and experience can do nothing to avert the unleashed furies of nature in her violent moods. Many a sailing-vessel has disappeared at sea 'without trace', with the loss of all on board, from causes unknown, the unnamed perils of the deep. In no other profession is puny man in such direct contact with the ferocities of nature as in an ocean-going vessel on a lengthy passage across the hemisphere of the globe, traversing all the known zones of the weather's vagaries, and likely to meet at any time with unpredictable conditions which may leave him powerless.

Many people on land as at sea have experienced the violence of a tropical thunderstorm; this does not make it any the less awesome while the storm rages; but even though the searing flashes of lightning and the detonations of thunder numb the senses, the downpouring of the rain eases the tension in the air which had been working up for hours and perhaps for days previously to this cloudburst which comes as a climax to the drama of the skies, and as a long-wished-for relief.

For half an hour the deluge continued, so solidly that it was scarcely possible to see through its curtain, from the main deck amidships to the bows or the poop. It was not a rain-squall with driving wind, but a vertical deluge with not a breath of wind accompanying it. The barque remained inert under the flood that poured upon it directly from overhead; she was on an even keel, her rolling having ceased as the torrential downpour flattened the ocean swell.

Although there was not the slightest breeze on or near the surface of the ocean to fill the limp sails, there was evidently a strong air-current at an altitude of 1,000 feet or more, driving the cloud masses in scuds, for presently the downpour eased on the barque, as the clouds and their storm centre slowly receded, with more distant flashes of lightning and growls of thunder. Intermittent showers of rain continued to fall on the decks, but between the showers lighter patches of cloud could be glimpsed in the illumination of the 'sheet lightning' that was a reflection of the more distant forked lightning at the storm centre. Those cloud masses were flying overhead under the impetus of winds in the sky which had in no way disturbed the flat calm of the ocean's surface during the storm or when the storm receded.

It is a common experience of seamen to observe clouds travelling at a great velocity in a direction opposite to, or different from, that of the winds at the surface-level of the ocean; or in the Doldrums to see the black flat-bottomed cumulus storm-clouds scudding in the sky with their base not more than 1,000 feet above the masthead, while not a breath of air from any direction fills the sails.

The calms of the Doldrums are in all probability due to the upcurrents of heated air rising uniformly from the surface of the warmed waters, causing the north-east trade winds of the Northern Hemisphere and the south-east trade winds of the Southern Hemisphere to be diverted upwards in the atmosphere when they impinge on the heated equatorial air, at the Doldrums' fringe, so that the air near the water's surface remains undisturbed, except by occasional eddies.

The rain ceased entirely as the storm centre receded, and gradually the residual clouds dispersed, the sky lightened, and the myriads of stars appeared. The surface of the ocean lay dark and silent again, stretching away to a distant horizon, its swell flattened by the deluge that had fallen upon it. The barque lay becalmed as previously, her sails hanging limp but now dripping wet. The rain had cooled the air, and relieved the humidity for the time being; but on the morrow, we knew, we would be sweltering again.

Towards 11 p.m., the storm having then expended itself, the men and boys of the Mate's watch were allowed to turn into their bunks for an hour before being roused out at midnight. Under my supervision the watch on deck formed a chain gang, to hand buckets of fresh water from the canvas catchment to be poured into the tanks abaft the main mast.

For the next two days men of the watches below were to be seen washing their clothes in the fresh water that they had caught in tubs and buckets for their own use. The sun beat down on us as mercilessly as previously, as we slowly made headway, with laborious effort, to the southward, striving to pick up the south-east trade wind.

At long last there was a light but steady breeze from the south-eastward, which was almost certainly the fringe of the trade wind, since slight rippling seas were running before it, and there was a long and low swell also from that direction, caused by a stronger wind at a distance.

'The trade wind! The trade wind!' The joyous cry resounded, and was followed by the order, 'All hands on deck.' But this time the watch below turned out with alacrity, to assist in carrying out the orders which now came in rapid succession from the Captain on the poop.

'Lee fore brace.'

'Keep the yards off the backstays, mister.'

'Fore and main sheets aft.'

'Set all jibs and staysails.'

'Sweat up the topsail sheets and halliards.'

With her sails bellied out to a steady freshening breeze, the *Caithness-Shire* gathered way on the port tack. The taffrail log was soon ticking over slowly, to register some miles made good; and under her bows 'a bone in her teeth' showed that she had come to life again.

9

TOWARDS THE ROARING FORTIES

THE south-east trade wind in the South Atlantic blows steadily in all seasons of the year, from the direction of the Cape of Good Hope towards Brazil. It prevails in a belt of the ocean as wide as approximately 1,500 miles, extending from the vicinity of the Tropic of Capricorn to Lat. 4°N. of the Equator, with seasonal variations of its northern limits, and also its southern limits which can extend across the Equator into the South Atlantic Ocean when unusual conditions prevail.

It blows in the fine-weather latitudes, corresponding to those of the north-east trade wind in the North Atlantic.

The Doldrums lie between the two trade-wind regions, caused by their converging pressures.

Sailing-vessels which were bound for the Indian Ocean or for Australia, round the Cape of Good Hope, usually crossed the Equator further east than vessels bound for Cape Horn, so as to enter the south-east trade-wind belt in a more advantageous position for sailing full and by the wind, on the port tack, or even with the wind free if it was coming from more easterly, especially in the case of the old-time passenger-carrying clippers which bore up for St. Helena and Cape Town as ports of call.

The subsequently developed cargo-carrying windjammers which plied on this route, perhaps under owners' orders not to put in to intermediate ports, were able to keep away and make a leading, or even a fair wind, in the south-east trades, in order to get to the southward with all possible speed, to pick up the westerly winds of the Roaring Forties, encountered between 40° and 50°S. Lat., which would drive them down to the south of the Cape of Good Hope where they could begin to 'run the easting down' to Australia.

All that was ancient history in 1909, when steamers had captured the passenger and mail trade to Asia and Australia, mostly using the much shorter route of the Suez Canal, though some steamers and occasional sailing-vessels continued to use the route round the Cape of Good Hope. But as the Panama Canal was not then opened, the only route from the Atlantic Ocean to the Pacific shores of South and North America was round Cape Horn, or for steamers via the Strait of Magellan. It was the Cape Horn route which gave the large steel-built sailing-vessels, chiefly of the British, German, Scandinavian and French Mercantile Marines, but also some surviving Down Easters of Yankee Clipper build, their last opportunity of demonstrating their ability to sail to windward, in weathering the westerly gales off Cape Horn.

The American Down Easters had been developed in the 1850s, sailing from New York to California, at first with passengers and trade goods for the Californian gold-diggers, and later trading for wheat and lumber from the West Coast ports of the U.S.A. and taking out cargoes of general merchandise to those West Coast ports, before railways development had surmounted the obstacle of the Rocky Mountains.

More numerous on the Cape Horn route in 1909 were British, German, French and Scandinavian sailing-vessels, usually carrying—as we were in the *Caithness-Shire*—coal from Europe to the ports of the West Coast of South America, with return cargoes of nitrates or guano.

It happened that Chile and Peru had no coal-mines, but required coal for railroads and other purposes, including copper-mining. These countries had an export trade in the nitrates (saltpetre) mined in Chile, which was used in Europe for the manufacture of gunpowder, and also in the guano (deposits of the droppings of sea-birds) on the offshore islands and mainland of Peru and Chile, used in Europe as farm-fertiliser.

Coal, nitrates and guano were unromantic but profitable cargoes for the beautiful windjammers that sailed from and to Europe on the Cape Horn route, defying the fierce westerly gales and blizzards, mountainous seas, rock-bound shores and icebergs of the world's stormiest ocean passage; but men of the merchant marine, whether in sail or steam, cannot be choosers of cargoes or routes. So it was that these queens of the ocean had become drab at the end of their long reign of glory, but the spirit that drove them on, and inspired the men who sailed them, was that of the mariners of centuries gone by, to whom sailing was an art and a science, and a great adventure, undimmed by the ravages of time.

The track of the Cape Horners, in the south-east trade wind after emerging from the Doldrums, was in a south-westerly direction, more or less parallel with the east coast of South America, and this was maintained for ten days or more of steady sailing until the trade wind died away in about 22°S. Lat.

In these conditions, while the wind remained steady and moderate to strong in velocity, as it usually did, life on ship-board was again pleasant. The breeze dispelled humidity, and the heat of the sun, though tropical, was no longer oppressive but enjoyable and friendly.

Heeled over to starboard, our barque required very little attention to the set of the sails, to maintain the maximum driving power from them, except for the routine of freshening the nip at the changes of the watch.

But now all on board knew that this would be our last stretch of assured fine weather for many a day. The Mate and I inspected the standing and running rigging and gear alow and aloft, and kept the crew at work overhauling wires, ropes, tackles and brace blocks, and reeving off new running gear where necessary to withstand the stresses and strains of bad weather. The sailmaker overhauled the heavier canvas hard-weather sails which would be set before we reached the Roaring Forties. It was a task for several men and boys to carry up these heavy sails from the sail-locker to the deck for his inspection and repair if required.

The masts were greased and the chain sheets of the lower topsails carefully inspected for flaws—more difficult to detect in a chain than in a wire cable, since the strength of a chain is proverbially only that of its weakest link, and the insidious effects of rust and of wear in steel links may lie hidden at that weak point.

The men in their watches below were busily engaged in re-coating their oilskins coats and sou'-westers and those with leather sea-boots worked oil and grease into the leather to make it soft and pliable, in anticipation of flooded decks and swaying footholds aloft in the gales to be expected further to the southward.

Soon after we had crossed the Tropic of Capricorn, in Lat. 23°S., the trade wind died away, and we were in the region of light and variable breezes known to sailors as the Horse Latitudes, and in official nautical terminology as the Variables of Capricorn. The sailors' term had probably originated in bygone days because this is where they had to work like horses, hauling around the yards, as in the Doldrums. This belt extends in the western part of the South Atlantic Ocean from 600 to 900 miles wide more or less according to the season of the year, southward from the vicinity of the Tropic of Capricorn to the vicinity of Lat. 40°S. where westerly winds blow strongly and consistently in the Roaring Forties. Those westerly winds prevail in the high latitudes of the southern oceans of the globe, between 40°S. and the fringe of the Antarctic ice in Lat. 60°S.

The breezes of the Horse Latitudes are as variable as their official name indicates, and frequently veer around, or drop to a calm, then blow suddenly from an entirely different quadrant. The air is cooler here than in the Doldrums, but otherwise the variable breezes resemble the capricious light airs of the Doldrums, and are equally exasperating in delaying a vessel's headway over a more lengthy stretch of the ocean (off the eastern shore of South America) than that of the

Doldrums. On some passages, vessels took two or three weeks to work through the Horse Latitudes.

One fine day the Captain decided the time had come to change the suit of sails, replacing the fair-weather canvas with 'No. 1 storm' canvas of heavier texture. This was a full day's work, with all hands on deck throughout the daylight hours. My watch took the fore mast, and the Mate's watch the main mast, in a competition which aroused little enthusiasm from the men aloft as they eyed the progress of their rivals on the other mast.

This was hard work. Each sail when sent down was rolled up snugly, tagged, labelled, at each end for easy identification when stowed in the sail locker, and carried aft on the shoulders of a file of men and there stowed away: while also the hard-weather sails were carried up from the sail locker to the poop and forrard on the main deck to the foot of the mast. There was much activity on deck and aloft as sail after sail was replaced, while the barque, with as much sail set as possible, was steered on various courses in the variable breezes, or lay becalmed.

Towards sunset the laborious task was completed to the Captain's satisfaction, and the wearied crew had a respite, as they sat down to a long-delayed evening meal.

Next day further preparations were made for the coming battle with the elements. Extra lashings were put on the two lifeboats, which were under davits aft, and on the pinnace and the Captain's gig forward. Relieving tackles were rove off to check the violent kicking of the wheel in a heavy sea, and the hatch covers were reinforced with heavy planks of wood bowsed down with wire lashings to ringbolts in the hatchway coamings. Life-lines were rigged fore and aft on the main deck, to give a handhold to men wading there.

A few days later we entered the Roaring Forties. A fresh north-westerly breeze was blowing offshore from the coast of Argentina, some 200 miles distant, raising a lumpy sea, in which we drove on to the southward, running with the wind on the starboard quarter, beneath grey skies of lowering cloud. Now, for the first time in many weeks, the barque shipped seas abeam as she rolled, flooding the main deck. The wind increased with squalls of rain, and we made all ready to shorten sail. Beyond doubt we had arrived in the bad-weather latitudes, and severe ordeals might lay ahead. Our course was shaped for Staten Island, some 900 miles to the southward.

I now approached what would be my third beat to windward round Cape Horn as an officer with more confidence than on the previous voyages in the *British Isles*, having learned by bitter experience, both physical and mental, what to expect and how to deal with emergencies which arose so frequently in these storm-swept southern waters as to become almost a routine in the latter-day windjammers under the British flag, in which sailing qualities were sacrificed to cargo-carrying capacity, and the vessels were manned with a minimum crew, often reduced in number by illness, feigned or real.

The rounding of Cape Horn under sail was reckoned from Lat. 50°S., in the Atlantic Ocean, to 50°S. Lat. in the Pacific Ocean, a distance of approximately 1,200 miles, when the head winds encountered necessitated making westing to 80° or 84°W. Long to gain a safe offing from the dangerous lee shore of the rock-bound and uninhabited Patagonian coast of Chile, before setting a course northward to 50°S , and beyond through the Roaring Forties into fine weather and the approaches to a nitrate port in Chile. The time taken to sail from 50°S in the Atlantic to 50°S in the Pacific varied greatly with the winds encountered. Sailing ships have doubled Cape Horn in as little as five days, covering much less distance than 1,200 miles, while many others have taken two and three months, sailing and drifting in a series of long-sustained ferocious gales to cover two thousand and more miles before arriving in 50°S in the Pacific Ocean, often reaching as far south as 60°, thereby traversing from north to south the 10° of latitude known to sailors as the Howling Fifties, and this was certainly the most severe part of the passage. Bad weather could also be encountered from 40°S in the Atlantic, to 40°S in the Pacific, but on the Atlantic side of the South American coast, good progress could usually be made with the westerly winds coming off the land, and the seas, although heavy, not rising to the proportions of the Cape Horn greybeards.

On the Pacific Ocean side the vessel was so far to the westward by the time she crossed the parallel of 50°S., and entered the Roaring Forties, that the westerly winds between north-west and south-west could be made a leading, or even a fair wind, to drive the ship rapidly northward into fine weather.

Tactics of weathering the Horn varied with the knowledge, judgment, experience, and temperament of the shipmasters, some of whom felt impelled to drive on at all costs, to make a good passage, while others played for safety, content to arrive eventually at their destinations with as little damage as possible to their vessels.

Cape Horn, the most southerly point of the South American continent, is on an island in Chilean territory, in Lat. 55° 58′ 28″ S. and Long. 67° 17′ 20″ W. but to clear it with ample sea-room, in adverse weather, it is necessary to stand well to the southward also of the San Diego Rocks in Lat. 56° 27′ 20″ S. and Long. 68° 44′ 0″ W.

These rocks are a formidable danger to shipping, being unlit and situated in surroundings in which visibility can be obscured for days or weeks on end by incessant gales from the westward, bringing hail, snow, sleet and rain, to mingle with streaks of foam torn from the crests of the mountainous seas, and with spray and spindrift driving as densely as smoke over the labouring vessel, beneath low scudding clouds which obscure the sun, moon and stars, making navigation and fixing of the vessel's position extremely difficult, if not impossible.

In those conditions shipmasters stood well to the southward of Cape Horn and of the San Diego Rocks, sailing up to 58°S. Lat., or sometimes, according to the direction and velocity of the wind, proceeding up to 60°S. and even further south.

There they were on the fringe of the Antarctic icefields: but the hazard of collision with an iceberg was less than that of piling up on a rock-bound, storm-swept, uninhabited and unlit shore, which might eventuate if they attempted to beat around the Cape in close proximity of the land. Some ship-masters navigated through the Strait of Lemaire (between Staten Island and the mainland), but most of them avoided those narrow waters, where strong currents and tiderips prevailed, and a ship was likely to be becalmed under the lee of the precipitous rocky cliffs, and kept to the eastward of Staten Island, to round it at its eastern extremity, Cape San Juan, in open water.

On rounding Staten Island, the course would be altered to the south-westward on the starboard tack, to make every mile of westing possible while the barometer was falling, and the wind remained to the northward of west. On this course the full blast of the westerlies was to be expected, with high running seas and winds of gale, storm, or hurricane force that sweep around the glove in the far south, unimpeded by any continental land masses. This problem would require sailing into the teeth of the westerly winds until the baro-meter ceased to fall and the wind hauled into the south-west quadrant, the vessel perhaps reaching as far south as sixty degrees before the change of wind came, when the ship would be in a favourable position to put about and stand away to the north-westward, well clear of the land, with the wind gradually hauling more southerly.

In this region the gales were likely to rage for days, weeks, or even months, on end, in the winter season, with running valleys between hills of water crested up from thirty to sixty feet from trough to a creaming torrent of overfall as the crest was torn asunder by the screaming wind as it vented its fury on the tortured sea. These Cape Horn greybeards, which could be anything to 2,000 feet long, were termed by sailors 'mountainous', but were officially described as 'precipitous', and were usually accompanied by blizzards of snow, sleet and hail, as they rolled forward in endless procession, awe-inspiring in their grandeur, merciless in their devastating strength.

The course steered depended on the force and direction of

D

the wind and the height of the seas, which frequently were so formidable as to necessitate heaving the vessel to, under storm canvas, to lay with the helm hard down, and the wind six or seven points on the bow, wallowing in the great seas under a deluge of water, drifting, always drifting, to leeward, away from the direction in which her destination lay, losing in a few hours as much westing as she had gained in days of strenuous effort previously. When headway was possible, the shipmaster had to keep well to the westward of the rocky and uninhabited Patagonian coast of Chile, which was under his lee. Many a fine vessel was lost with all hands, perhaps after being dismasted in the violent gales, by drifting help-lessly into the grip of the Antarctic ice, or being driven on to the lee shore of Patagonia: or in some recorded cases by foundering in a gale after being dismasted and the hatches stove in by the terrible seas.

After battling for weeks in long-sustained gales in these waters, some shipmasters, with their ships battered and damaged, sails blown away, and crew members sick or injured, put their vessels about and ran for shelter in the lee of Staten Island to lick their wounds until the weather moderated, while others entered ports of distress, and, in some rare cases turned, eastward for the Cape of Good Hope, and after running the easting down to beyond Australia hauled northward a little and made their port in Chile after circumnavigating the southern sea.

On some rare occasions, more particularly in the summer months, November to March, there were Cape Horn calms, and even easterly breezes and sunshine, which enabled the Horn to be rounded in a few days in ideal conditions, but such good fortune was exceptional, and among Cape Horn sailors was spoken of as such.

One writer has stated that some British shipmasters were 'afraid of Cape Horn'. This could not have implied any lack of personal courage, but may have referred to the refusal of some to press on, regardless of consequences—a matter of caution, even good seamanship, rather than fear. The tactics of rounding the Horn, and the measures taken, varied in different vessels according to the judgment of individual masters, who always had to keep in mind the owners' printed book of instructions, the condition of the vessel, the state of sails and cordage, and the amount of spare equipment carried, and, most of all, the crew they commanded, both in numbers and quality.

It was not unusual in some of the last British windjammers to find masters harassed by their owners' orders, which usually included avoiding the loss of sails, and spars, and putting into foreign ports for repairs, or to purchase replenishments of stores, provisions, or fresh water, *en route* to her destination.

With the vessel perhaps uninsured, or the owner carrying a portion of the liability, of which the Master would have been made well aware, and a cargo below hatches being freighted for about nine of ten shillings a ton, there was nothing to spare, and, among other things, a Master's competence was apt to be judged by the profit or loss accruing for the voyage, and to play safe in such circumstances was no more than an obvious necessity.

If he put in to any port of refuge, the shipmaster would have to meet the lawful demands of the crew for fresh beef and fresh vegetables daily, while the vessel was in port, as required by the Merchant Shipping Act. In all probability he would be soaked to the limit in prices demanded for provisions, stores, repairs, towage, harbour dues, and other expenses, by the devious ruses practised on shipmasters unfortunate enough to require such assistance, and in addition would perhaps find his vessel undermanned by the desertion of some members of his crew. In these conditions vessels were sometimes sold where they lay, on owners' orders, to meet debts incurred in port.

British shipmasters who, in those last days of sail, were cautious in their methods of rounding the Horn, were not 'afraid'. Their feelings of caution, rather than of fear, were not engendered by doubts of their own competence to overcome the hazards of storm and tempest in the far south, but only by concern for the safety of the living fabric beneath their feet. In ageing vessels, undermanned, usually with crews representing many nationalities—some not able to understand orders given by the officers, and others unfitted, by age or infirmities, or by inexperience, to work aloft or on deck in heavy weather—shipmasters knew that, unless they shortened sail to the minimum before the wind reached gale force, they would never shorten at all; and then the storm canvas, their only means of survival and irreplaceable, would be blown from the yards and shredded to fragments, to disappear in the scud and spindrift to leeward.

There were also some shipmasters who shortened sail and hove to, in order to ensure a night's rest for themselves and their crews. Their vessels made slow passages round the Horn, but in relative comfort, and were 'good homes' for all on board.

Other Masters were different. They carried on with a press of canvas to the utmost before giving orders to shorten sail. They 'made passages', to earn perhaps some admiration by arriving in a remote South American port earlier than expected, or more speedily than other vessels; but in many such cases this triumph was achieved at the expense of death, injury, or utter exhaustion for their crews battling aloft for hours to hand frozen canvas, balancing themselves on the footropes, on yards reeling high above a half-submerged hull that was tearing along, rolling and pitching in mountainous seas which threatened to engulf it.

As we headed southwards in the Roaring Forties, on our course shaped for Staten Island, some of our crew, noticed previously by the Mate and myself as possible malingerers, remained in their bunks, complaining of illness. During bad weather the cry 'All hands on deck' was frequently heard, especially at the changes of the watch, when all the men and boys of both watches were required for the heavy work of clewing up and stowing the courses or t'gan'sls in a gale of wind, or to wear ship, which required all the yards to be hauled around quickly. The small number of men and boys in one watch, with one man at the wheel and another on lookout, were unable to reef, or stow the larger sails in a rapidly rising wind which required this to be done quickly, especially when one or more men were sick or malingering in their bunks below.

Malingering was one of the most difficult problems with which the Master and Mates had to deal in handling men, some of whom had no intention of staying in a vessel longer than it took to reach the next port, where they would desert and put themselves in the hands of crimps for a glorious spree, before being shanghaied in a drunken or drugged condition on board some other vessel that was in need of men to make up a full crew.

The crimping racket flourished in many ports, though efforts were being made in 1909 to suppress it. The articles signed by the crew of the *Caithness-Shire* at the outset of the voyage specified: 'No liberty granted abroad otherwise than at the Master's option.' This was an attempt to circumvent crimps, who enticed seamen on shore leave to indulge in a spree at the crimps' expense, which was more than reimbursed by the blood money paid by shipmasters for delivering drunken or drugged sailors on board a few hours before the anchor was hove up.

Many sailors, and men who pretended to be sailors, worked their way from port to port in foreign-going vessels, not for cash wages (which they forfeited when they deserted), but in a desperate quest for adventure, or to escape from some personal entanglement in their home country, or for the satisfaction of bragging in the forecastles of their skill in skinning out and of the glorious sprees that they had enjoyed on shore as guests of crimps.

In the crews of some sailing-vessels there were men with this irresponsible or carefree outlook, who had no steady home life, or were dodging the police for some minor offence, or simply joined a ship because they were unemployed and starving on shore. To them, shipboard life was only a means of getting food and a bunk, a transport to some other place, no matter where. These were the ones who were most expert in dodging hard work on board, and consequently in making the work of all other members of the crew proportionately harder, and the working hours longer, since certain tasks had to be done by combined efforts in which the willing horses carried the heaviest loads.

Sailors were not paid their cash wages weekly, fortnightly or monthly like workers on shore, but only in a lump sum when they were discharged at the end of the voyage, or on being paid off on leaving the vessel in a port abroad with the Master's consent. Some of even the steadiest seamen seldom remained in a vessel throughout a voyage of two or three years' duration.

They would endeavour to be discharged when they arrived at some civilised port with a useful amount of accrued wages due to them, or on the prospect of obtaining employment in a steamer or some other vessel which took their fancy.

In consequence of desertions, and the legitimate discharge of men in foreign ports, by mutual consent due to illness or other cause, few British sailing-vessels, after the turn of the century, completed a lengthy voyage with the same crew throughout, except for the nucleus of officers, apprentices, and perhaps two or three of the veteran sailors, also the sailmaker, bosun, and the carpenter, who had better working conditions and pay than the forecastle hands of the watches.

Malingering by feigned illness occurred chiefly in the bad-weather latitudes. Then, when a sailor lay groaning in his bunk, and complained of pains in his innards which only a qualified medical practitioner could diagnose, the Captain had to take a difficult decision as to whether the man was malingering or not.

On shore, an employer had the protection of medical opinion, and could employ a substitute for a man who was genuinely ill; but, at sea, on a passage of several months, without any means of communicating with the shore, and only a remote possibility of sighting a steamer which carried a doctor, the Captain, equipped only with the knowledge obtained from a book, *The Ship's Medical Guide,* and a limited supply of medicines kept in his saloon, had the responsibility of making a diagnosis of the patient's true condition.

Practised malingerers knew well how to describe symptoms to baffle the Old Man, who, as a matter of conscience, could not compel a really sick sailor to work on deck or aloft, with possibly fatal consequences. But the invalid's shipmates in the forecastle, and also the officers and apprentices, who had ample opportunities to observe his character and attitude to his work, could more readily diagnose the cases of 'Cape Horn fever', which frequently occurred, by something more than coincidence, in cold and rough weather.

In hard-case ships, with brutal Masters and Mates, a dose of 'belaying-pin soup', or a hammering with fists as a preliminary to booting the malingerer along the deck to work, was the recognised cure for Cape Horn fever, but in vessels in which such curative measures were not countenanced a strong dose of Black Jack (jalap purgative), or of Epsom salts, cured most of the sufferers, but only after they had succeeded in evading one or two watches on deck.

As the *Caithness-Shire* bore to the southward in the Roaring Forties and entered the Howling Fifties, with her storm sails set, her lee rail frequently under, and the main deck flooded, the routine order to the watch on deck was to 'stand by'. This routine prevailed throughout the passage round the Horn, and in some vessels it meant what it said, namely, no tasks to be done except working the ship, and the men to be ready at instant call for any such work required.

In hard-case ships men standing by on the poop were put to work at the futile tasks of holystoning the poop deck and cleaning off varnish from the teakwood stanchions, rails, and skylight frames, while fully exposed to the freezing weather. There, they were under the eye of the Captain or officer of the watch, available instantly if any emergency arose on deck or aloft, when sails or cordage were carried away, or if it were necessary further to shorten sail.

In the *Caithness-Shire* men standing by were allowed to shelter under the forecastle head, and were usually put to work making sennit mats and chafing-gear from old rope or junk, a light task. This was good treatment and probably appreciated as such, but at any real emergency the call of 'All hands on deck' resounded and was essential, though not the less resented on that account by the men of the watch below, although they were well aware the manpower available was insufficient for heavy tasks in bad weather, without calling out the watch below, and even then she was undermanned for any serious emergency.

Of the nine forecastle hands only two were rated as A.B. One of these was fifty years of age, and the other thirty-four. The other seven forecastle hands, though rated as Ordinary Seamen, included some of limited or no prevous experience in sailing vessels or without experience of Cape Horn sailing. The manning scale, as laid down by the Board of Trade and the Merchant Shipping Act, conveniently overlooked the quality of seamanship or experience of men engaged as sailors, but stipulated only, in the case of the *Caithness-Shire*, 'the crew shall be deemed complete with twenty hands all told, of whom not less than eight shall be sailors'.

Among the seven of our sailors rated as Ordinary Seamen, one had signed on stating his age as fifty-two and another forty-four. These older men were limited in their agility for working aloft in heavy weather.

Of the two men who had joined at the last moment by a pier-head jump, one, aged thirty-two, had admitted that this was his first voyage, and the other, aged thirty-six had stated vaguely that he had served in a 'foreign' ship, of which he could not remember the name. Another of the Ordinary Seamen, aged thirty-eight, had stated that he had been in 'an Italian ship'. These three would not be of much use aloft in Cape Horn weather.

Of the seven Ordinary Seamen, therefore, only four could be expected to measure up to the standards of seamanship and agility required for working aloft in a vessel forcing a passage round the Horn.

The nine strong, able, willing, and reliable apprentices we had on board, whose average age was nineteen years, were the hard core of efficiency in a crew in which some of the forecastle hands were of such limited seamanlike quality.

One apprentice in each watch was required to be stationed on the poop, but the other eight worked on deck or aloft in watches with the forecastle hands, and without them the working of the ship in heavy weather would have been practically impossible.

With their youthful exuberance, and ambition to succeed in their chosen profession, the apprentices set an example when any of the seamen hesitated in dangerous situations on deck or aloft, and could always be relied upon to stand fast, as members of the afterguard, to support the officers, if any signs of insubordination threatened the routine discipline of instant obedience to orders. Among themselves, they maintained a loyalty and cheerfulness of spirit which was apt to find expression in hilarious songs and laughter in their quarters in the half-deck, occasionally disturbing my rest in my watches below, as the door of my cabin was near their deckhouse.

Despite the problems caused by undermanning, and some malingering, inefficiency, and lack of agility among the forecastle hands, the *Caithness-Shire* stood on to the southward in the Howling Fifties, and at last Cape San Juan on Staten Island hove in sight.

All Cape Horn sailing-vessels, except those which were navigated through Lemaire Strait, made for the rounding mark of Cape San Juan, to get a fix of their position and check the rating of their chronometers and there were several of them in the offing, outward or homeward bound, when we rounded the island. As soon as we were beyond the lee of the land, we felt the full force of a westerly gale, into which we headed on a south-westerly course, hoping for the best, but without any good reason for that hope, as far as the weather signs portended. All the indications were that our passage to the westward would be a stormy and difficult one.

With vivid recollections of my previous experiences off Cape Horn, especially those of my first voyage as an apprentice in the *British Isles* in the terrible winter gales of 1905, I wondered how we would fare if Captain Hatfield intended to try to press on, to make a passage.

He had rounded the Horn as an apprentice and as an officer and knew what to expect. The stumpy-top *Caithness-Shire* was no flyer, but she could sail well enough even though she was deep-laden, with very little freeboard. She was manned in accordance with the Board of Trade scale, and a little more than that, as far as numbers were concerned; but beef and brawn alone do not make a sailor. It remained to be seen what the reaction of our forecastle hands would be under the severe test of the world's most angry waters.

10

A CAPE HORN WARNING

WHEN we rounded Staten Island and set course to the south-westward, it was late afternoon. A pale sun was setting behind banks of scudding cloud, its rays weirdly gleaming on the foam-capped crests of the high running seas, in which the *Caithness-Shire* rolled and pitched violently, her main deck occasionally flooded with swirling water, as the wind whistled and screamed in her rigging.

It was strange but true that vessels on the passage to the southward of Cape Horn seldom sighted each other. They were usually obscured in driving rain, sleet, or snow and hail, which, combined with the spindrift and spray whipped by the wind from the crests of the 'greybeards', reduced visibility practically to nil beneath heavy and low clouds that blotted out the light of the sky to a total blackness at night and a thin ghostly grey in the daytime; and also passing vessels were partly concealed in the troughs of the precipitous seas.

Vessels on westward courses were frequently hove to and drifting, and at other times labouring to make headway on one tack or another. They crossed each other's tracks, sometimes perilously near but invisible, and they also crossed the tracks of the numerous east-bound vessels which ran free but blindly before the gales, at speeds of from ten to twelve knots; all trusting to luck to avoid collision. If perchance another vessel was sighted, that fact in itself would indicate urgent danger within one mile or less. The stranger would be glimpsed for only a few moments, poised on the crest of a comber before disappearing from sight into the trough of the seas. Then, as if by act of Providence, manœuvre to avoid collision might be possible.

If any collisions occurred, either between vessels or with an iceberg, they would probably never be recorded. The impact would be such that no one would live to tell the tale, as lifeboats could not live in those tremendous seas. Likewise if any seaman fell overboard in a Cape Horn gale, he was gone forever, and would be swept away beyond help in a few minutes.

When darkness closed in, the *Caithness-Shire* laboured on to the south-westward into an approaching storm, with only her foresail, upper and lower topsails and a staysail set. The Captain was closely watching the weather signs, to make as much headway as possible before giving the order to shorten sail further. The barometer, which all day had been falling, now remained steady at a low level, and the air temperature was falling rapidly towards freezing point.

At eight bells (8 p.m.) my watch was due to be relieved, but the Captain, as expected, gave the order 'All hands on deck', followed by 'Get the upper topsails off her, mister.'

The Mate and I went forward with all available men and boys of both watches, to man the downhauls and buntlines of the upper topsails on the fore and main masts.

Next it was my duty to lead the men aloft, to hand the sails on the yards, which were rising and falling through an angle of perhaps 30 or 40 degrees as the vessel rolled in the heavy sea, with the clewed up sails bellied out above us. It was usual for an officer to go aloft in such conditions, not only to lead the men and to work with them, but also because orders given from on deck could not be heard aloft in the howling wind.

The only way to go aloft in a strong wind rising to gale force was to climb the rigging on the weather side, a laborious effort in itself as the roaring wind pressed our bodies against the ratlines, while we held on grimly to preserve our balance against the heavy rolling which from time to time left us suspended above the foaming seas as we climbed.

When all were aloft without mishap, we lay out along the yard, balancing on the wire footrope and leaning over the yard with our bellies pressed against it, while, using our hands like claws, we forced our fingers into the canvas to make a crease in it, leaning forward as far as possible over the yard, and so rolling up the sail in fleets, after which the gaskets (short lengths of thin rope, used as bands at intervals around the rolled sail) were passed over and under the yard, and secured.

This operation, safe enough in fine weather, though requiring seamanlike skill at all times, was much more difficult with the handing of heavy and frozen canvas in a Cape Horn gale, and dangerous when some of the men laying out on the yards were inexpert.

Nearly two hours of effort were required before the barque was snugged down to lower topsails, foresail, and fore topmast staysail at 10 p.m.

I made my way to the poop, where the Old Man asked me how the crew had behaved aloft. My report could not have been very comforting to him, as I told him that some of the men had clung to the jackstay with one hand while trying to muzzle the canvas with the other, the weight of their bodies being useless in this attitude to hold down the fleets of canvas gathered in on the yard, while the gaskets were passed around it.

After reporting to the Captain, I went to my cabin, to empty the ice-cold water out of my sea-boots, change my socks and wet underwear, and turn in to my bunk for a catnap of ninety minutes or less, before I was called to relieve the watch at midnight, in which the Second Mate acted as the Captain's deputy when the Captain himself was not in personal control of the poop.

The Mate, or Chief Officer, was second-in-command, and would be delegated to take over and navigate the vessel if the Master was ill or otherwise incapacitated.

In *Caithness-Shire*, and many other vessels, the Mate was consulted by the Master on various matters. His designation was originally 'Master's Mate' and that was exactly what he was supposed and expected to be, namely the Captain's right-hand man, standing watch alternately with the Captain, and vested with sufficient authority to voice an opinion when a course of action ordered seemed unwise in the conditions prevailing.

The Second Mate was in a somewhat different position, keeping, officially, the Master's watch, but nevertheless he was responsible for his own actions, and at an official inquiry could be so held if an accident occurred due to any dereliction of his duty.

All Masters were not alike, however, and there were some who kept aloof from their officers, and assumed an unapproachable attitude which allowed no discussion of relevant matters pertaining to the working or navigation of the ship, and an order from them, right or wrong, had to be obeyed. Others, and they were the majority, having engaged an officer, and found him competent, were content to invest him with sufficient authority to take necessary action in any emergency which might arise when the Master was below, and until he appeared on deck after being called.

The usual procedure in *Caithness-Shire* was, when the Master was going below at night to sleep, with the barque perhaps under full sail in a strong breeze, to say to the officer on watch, 'If the wind freshens any more, mister, get the upper t'gan'sls in, and call me if necessary, or at any time.' Conversely, he would say, 'Set the upper t'gan'sls, mister, if the wind takes off.' In bad weather the Master frequently remained on the poop for many long hours when the officers had to be on the main deck, or aloft supervising the men handing or reefing sails, or other necessary work, and when rounding the Horn in bad weather he usually had less rest below than anyone else on board.

When such conditions prevailed, a precious five minutes, more than long enough for the vessel to be caught aback, dismasted, or thrown on her beam ends, might elapse before a Master in a heavy sleep, after a long period on deck, be woken and again be on deck with a full appreciation of what was happening, and a tacit approval of the action taken by the officer on watch did much to engender confidence, which could be undermined where the Master abrogated to himself absolute authority to issue orders in regard to the sailing of the ship, but such orders as when to wear, or tack ship, or alter a set course were always the prerogative of the Master, and executed under his personal supervision at his chosen time.

The midnight to 4 a.m. watch was known as the Graveyard Watch, probably because, under normal sailing conditions, the vessel was more silent at that time than at any other period of the twenty-four hours. The watch on deck stood by only to work the vessel as required, not engaged in the routine tasks that occupied them during the daytime, and the watch below were then usually deep in well-earned slumber, with silence and probably the lights dowsed in the forecastle and apprentices' half-deck.

But a Cape Horn gale is no respecter of silence or of seamen's slumber, even in the Graveyard Watch. When I came on deck at midnight I found the barque labouring heavily, with the deck awash as seas broke in over the rails. The wind was now from the west-south-west and increasing rapidly with frequent heavy squalls of sleet and rain. Through the darkness to windward the white crests of the oncoming seas towered and curled, poised high above the bulwark rail for a moment until the barque was rolled to leeward by the advancing avalanche of water and then lurched violently to windward as the sea passed beneath her keel.

The Captain remained for some time on the poop, with myself, an apprentice and the helmsman, carefully checking the course and eyeing the weather signs, while the other men and boys of the watch stood by under the forecastle head, with one man posted on the forward deckhouse as lookout.

When he was satisfied that everything was done that could be done in the circumstances, the Captain said to me, 'Keep her up to the wind, mister, and call me if anything unusual happens.' He then went below.

Soon after five bells (2.30 a.m.) a heavy squall struck the barque, and I sent the apprentice to call the Captain, who came up instantly on deck. At that moment, with a sound like a pistol shot, the chain sheet of the fore lower topsail broke at a weak link halfway along the yard. This left the sail flogging violently in the wind with some twenty feet of chain hanging from the clew iron at the yardarm, thrashing through the air like a huge and menacing whip.

'Lay forrard, mister. Call out the watch below. Clew up the sail and secure the chain,' the Captain ordered, leaving the further details to my initiative.

'All hands on deck! All hands on deck!' I sang out, as I sprinted along the sloping but drier lee side of the main deck while the barque rolled to windward.

The men and boys who had been standing by under the forecastle head leaped into action to tail on to the clewlines and buntlines, joined soon by the watch below, who were rubbing sleep from their eyes, but livened up as they found themselves wading to their thighs in the icy water swirling on deck from the seas shipped abeam. The Mate also emerged from his cabin, and hauled himself forward by the lifeline stretched on deck, to lend a hand and assert his due authority.

Our intention was to haul the sail up snug under the yard, to prevent the canvas from being flogged to pieces in the wind and by the flailing of the chain, but, before we could get the slack in, the flying chain fouled the clewline.

This left the leech (side edge) of the sail bellied out, with the broken chain whipping up under the yard, and continuing to flail in the air and against the sail, as the barque rolled violently in the heavy sea.

It was now my duty again to lead the men aloft to lay out on the yard and secure that chain before the sail was flogged to pieces. I had led them aloft in the previous watch, but in five hours since that task had been completed, the wind and sea had increased. The masts were now raking through an arc of sixty degrees, and the topsail yard was rising and falling jerkily as it rode up and down with a creaking and groaning sound at every half-minute with each violent roll of the barque. It looked like certain death for anyone who might be struck by that flailing chain while laying out along the yard to furl the sail.

Was such a risk worth taking, to save a piece of the ship-owner's canvas, worth a few pounds, from being shredded and blown away from its fastenings. No man or boy, trained in the hard disciplines of the sea, would ask such a question. When gear aloft had carried away, it had to be secured without delay. That was the only thought in our minds. The lives of all on board might depend on clearing up any mess in the top-hamper, and in preserving our storm-canvas from damage, great or small.

The task could not wait for daylight, for in that interval the sail would have been shredded to fragments; or, worse than that, with no sail set on the foremast the steering of the barque would be difficult, with a tendency to yaw, possibly causing further damage aloft, or even causing the vessel to broach to in the trough of the seas.

I led the way, followed by the four apprentices and the four most agile and experienced forecastle hands. As previously, we climbed the weather rigging with laborious effort, our bodies pressed against the ratlines by the force of the wind. We carried a gantline aloft to secure the flying chain, which would be heard but not seen in the pitch blackness of the night. As we lay out along the yard, we knew that there was a risk that the flying chain might strike any one of us at any moment, but our first task was to furl the sail before an attempt could be made to secure the chain which had fouled the clewline. In the freezing wind, with driving rain and needles of hail, as we reached forward over the yard to hand the sail our oilskin coats were blown up over our backs, though secured with 'soul-and-body lashings' of ropeyarn around our waists.

The sail on the weather side was ballooning up and crack-ing like a whiplash as it was flailed about by the terrific force of the wind, the heavy canvas frozen and seeming to the touch as hard as iron. With numbed fingers we clawed at the canvas, as far forward as we could reach, balancing our bodies on the heaving yard with our legs braced far apart on the footrope.

This was not a case of 'one hand for the ship and one for yourself', but of both hands for the ship, and hold on by your feet, legs, and belly-muscles.

Only when a slight lull in the squall momentarily eased the pressure of the wind on the sail was it possible to force our fingers into the canvas and make a crease to obtain a grip; but time after time, when we had gathered in a part of the sail and lay on its folds with our bellies to hold it down, while we reached out to gather in another fleet, a sudden blast of another squall tore it from under us, and the sail ballooned out, giving the men on the yard only a moment's warning to grasp a jackstay or anything else handy, to prevent themselves from being thrown off the yard into the raging seas.

Meanwhile, the length of broken chain was whipping up under the yard, its clang of metal on metal resounding as an urgent menace amid the wail and dirge of the wind scream-ing in the taut fabric of steel masts, yards and rigging. We seemed to be in the grip of demoniacal forces, so that not only physical but also sustained mental concentration was necessary to preserve us from destruction.

After a bitter struggle, the sail was gathered in, and made fast in the gaskets during a lull between squalls. The broken sheet-chain was then hanging free from the yardarm, swinging to the roll of the barque. We dropped a running bowline down its half-length, weighted with a hand lead, and then scrambled down to the deck to haul its bight up under the yard, while one man on the yardarm unshackled the end from the clew iron of the sail to enable the chain to be lowered to the deck.

Fortunately there was a spare chain on board. This was now sent aloft, and shackled on, and the sail was reset, and sheeted home. These operations had taken more than an hour of strenuous and dangerous effort.

When all were safely on deck again, soaked to the skin

with freezing water, eyes bloodshot from salt spray, and weary in every limb, there were no congratulations, no medals or mentions in despatches. An emergency had been dealt with, and the task was forgotten as soon as it was completed.

It was now 4 a.m., and my watch was due to be relieved, but all hands were kept on deck, as another task now awaited us. The Old Man had been fretting and fuming silently on the poop, impatient for the work aloft to be completed, as the wind had now hauled to the south-south-west, and was blowing with gale force across the direction of the great rollers from the north-westward and the heavy swell from the westward.

The new direction of the wind, which had not yet had time to heap up a cross sea, made it necessary to change the barque's course from the starboard tack to the port tack, a manœuvre extremely difficult in a gale, which could not be begun while men were aloft securing and resetting a topsail. The wind and seas were setting the barque to leeward, as witnessed by the wake streaming from her stern to windward. As the last man from aloft safely reached the deck, the Captain's order was heard above the roar of the wind:

'*Wear Ship!*'

11

OFF CAPE HORN

In fine weather, with moderate seas and a steady breeze, a vessel beating to windward could wear ship, with no great difficulty, simply by putting up the helm while the main yards were squared in, as the vessel fell away and brought the wind astern, and the fore yards were hauled around to conform with the vessel's movement as she rounded up to the wind on the other tack. In a full gale, in mountainous seas off Cape Horn, the manœuvre is both difficult, strenuous, and dangerous enough in daytime, but much more so in the darkest hours before the dawn, and is an experience not easy to forget.

The barque was now sailing and drifting to the eastward, before the great rolling seas coming from north of west, whose direction had not yet been changed by the force of the gale now blowing from the south-south-west. Overhead the black shapeless void of the sky seemed to reach down and mingle with the flying spray and spindrift.

Presently there was a lull. The wind moaned and wailed on a more subdued note as the maze of rigging aloft alternately fell away from the wind, or was compressed against it when the barque rolled in the tumult of the confused seas. A rift appeared in the wall of darkness around us, and we glimpsed dense masses of cloud on the horizon piled high into the heavens, with an ever-changing vista of snow-laden hills and dark valleys, poised and threatening, as their contours were thrown into relief by a gleam of light from hidden celestial bodies. This moment of radiance was quickly obscured by masses of low-flying cloud and smoke-like spindrift, as the screaming wind in another squall tore the curling overfalls from the huge and menacing seas, to drive another deluge of water over the labouring barque, and again clothe her in a wall of darkness.

When the squall had spent its fury we saw the Mate hauling himself forrard along the main deck by the lifeline, up to his thighs in water, bawling out, 'Haul the foresail up'.

The time for strenuous action had come. The barque was sailing close-hauled into the wind with only her foresail, two lower topsails, and the fore-topmast staysail set, all the other square sails were furled and fast in their gaskets. It was now necessary to haul the foresail up before she was put about on to the port tack.

The Mate took his station at the main deck capstan, where the wire sheet of the foresail was led to it from a sheave in the bulwarks, so that he could slack it away gently to ease the pressure in the big sail, while I stood at the capstan on the forecastle head, to slack away the tack (lower forward corner of the sail), as both watches tailed on to the buntlines and clew garnet on the weather side, to haul up that side of the sail.

This is not an occasion when the rhythm of a shanty can be used by the seamen when hauling on a rope. Manning the clew-garnet, which hauls up the leech, or side of the sail, and the three buntlines which haul up the foot of the sail, on one side, simultaneously, the sail was hauled up by the men and boys with four on each rope, reaching above their heads, as they stood under the right fairlead in the rigging, hauling with a downward pull, one boy taking in the slack around a belaying pin to which that particular rope is always belayed, so that it can easily be found in the darkness of night. With the weather side snugged up, the lee side was similarly hauled up, and the sail left hanging in its gear, to be set again later, or secured in its gaskets as conditions might require after the barque was rounded to on the other tack.

She then had only two square sails set, the fore and main lower topsails, to give her steerage way during the impending manœuvre, and the fore-topmast staysail to assist her head in paying off before the wind, when the helm was put up. The next stage was to square the yards, beginning with the main yards as she came before the wind.

There were five yards on each mast, so that all had to be hauled around or squared together, whether sail was set or furled on one or more of them at that time.

Wading aft through the water swirling on deck, and holding on with one hand to the lifeline as we waded, we stood by the braces, the seamen and apprentices on the weather side, to haul in, and the Mate and myself on the lee side, to slack away. The men and boys on the weather side were in a dangerous position, threatened every few minutes by the towering walls of water rearing up high above them when the barque rolled to windward into the trough of the seas and her weather rail was under the water, until she was lifted and rolled violently to leeward as each sea in succession passed under her keel. Torrents of loose water rushed across the deck at each roll, immersing the men to their waists, as they held on grimly to the brace, which the 'Tail End Charlie' swiftly made fast by giving it a few quick turns around a handy belaying pin in the pin rail. Woe betide a man who panicked and did not take a turn with the brace quickly enough, or perhaps not at all, leaving the men and boys to be swept away across the deck, or even over the side.

At last the Captain on the poop saw his opportunity and roared out, '*Square away, mister!*' at the same time jumping to the wheel to assist the helmsman to put the helm hard up against the pressure of the seas on the rudder.

Instantly the Mate bawled to the men at the weather braces, '*Haul away, lads!*' while we on the lee side, slacked away, carefully watching the yards, and ready to make fast instantly whenever the men hauling in on the weather side belayed as a sea broke on board.

When the main yards were squared, the barque came before the wind and forged ahead at three or four knots.

On deck we waded to the fore braces and began to haul the foreyards around. As the seas were now running from aft, the gigantic greybeards reared high over the poop, and we, in comparative safety at the fore braces, did not envy the solitary figure of the Master as we saw him standing in stark relief against a dark and menacing avalanche of water poised above him. We could not see the helmsman from our stations at the fore braces, as the wheel house hid him from view, but we knew, from our own experience in similar circumstances, that he would be casting apprehensive glances over his shoulder at the towering seas when the barque's stern sank into the trough, until he felt the upward thrust of the deck under his feet as she lifted to the onward rush of the next great comber. In these conditions, many a vessel has been pooped by a sea from astern crashing on to the poop, sometimes to destroy the wheel or the binnacle, and to injure or wash overboard the helmsman or officers, unless with a split second of warning they could cling to the mizzen rigging, or some other support, to save themselves.

With the fore yards hauled around there was a brief respite as all hands sheltered for a few minutes under the lee of the forward deckhouse awaiting further orders. On the poop the Old Man, in his yellow oilskin coat, sou'-wester, and thigh-long rubber sea-boots, was carefully watching the seas astern while keeping the barque running before them.

We were now on a reverse course to that which we had been steering away from Staten Island. It was imperative to put the barque about with the least possible delay, in order to get her on to the port tack and headed westward again: but 'rounding to' is the most dangerous phase in the manœuvre of wearing ship in a gale and requires excellent judgment of the right moment.

Even with only the two lower topsails set, we were being carried by the wind, the run of the seas, and the currents and 'scend' of the ocean to the east-north-eastward, and therefore losing the little headway to the westward that we had laboriously gained on the starboard tack since rounding Staten Island some twelve hours previously.

The Captain was waiting for a 'smooth'. This is a relative term, and well understood by Cape Horn sailors.

During a prolonged gale in those waters, a series of seas from forty to fifty feet high roll onwards in endless procession, culminating at intervals in a monster or rogue sea considerably higher than the others, its approach visible at a distance, even in the darkness of the night, by a luminous effect in its frothing curled crest.

In the wake of a rogue sea there is an apparent lessening in the height and speed of the following undulations, and this short interval is known as a 'smooth'.

Suddenly the Captain roared out, '*Hands to the braces! Stand by to haul away.*' The Mate and I ordered our watches to man the fore and main braces on the starboard side which would be the lee side when the barque came up to the wind, while he and I, in the usual duty of officers, took station on what would be the weather side, to slack away the braces on that side while the men hauled the yards around.

As we stood by the braces on the main deck, the monster sea rolling up astern, lifted the barque aft, so that her bows sank into the trough until water flooded in over the forecastle head. Then, as she surged forward and righted herself, the Old Man's voice bellowed '*Haul away the lee braces!*', as he put the wheel over, and the barque began to swing up on to the port tack towards the wind and sea.

This was the most dangerous moment, as there was a risk that a heavy sea might strike the vessel forward of her beam while she was rounding up towards the seas, causing her to lose her way and fall back into the trough, broadside on, where possibly she could be overwhelmed by the weight of hundreds of tons of water crashing on to her decks. In such a predicament hatches have been stove in and vessels have foundered as their holds filled with water, to sink to the bottom of the ocean and never to be heard of again.

On this occasion the *Caithness-Shire* was turned deliberately into the wind as a planned manœuvre, but it was all-important that the yards should be hauled round quickly as she rounded to on the new tack, so that she would not lose her way through the water.

The men and boys on the lee side, hauling in on the braces as the yards came around, were in comparative safety; but the Mate and I, now alone on the weather side, slacking away the braces, were in continual danger of being swept away if, during the turn into the wind, a heavy sea broke on board over the weather rail, against which we stood with a precarious foothold amid the surging water. That danger was surmounted without mishap, as the barque was safely brought up to the wind and sea on the port tack.

In the grey light of dawn, she was riding the seas with her bows about six points off the eye of the wind with the curling greybeards rolling down from about two points before the port beam. An occasional sea broke against the ship's side in a smother of water which cascaded over the decks, while others hove her up and over in a sickening lurch to starboard, to roll back violently into the trough before the next on-coming sea.

It was now 5 a.m. and my watch had been due to go below an hour previously, but it was for the Captain to decide whether the clewed-up foresail would be set again, or secured in its gaskets—in either case both watches would be kept on deck for that further work.

The wind and sea continued to rage in unabated fury, with all the signs of further tempestuous weather, and in this situation the Master decided not to set the foresail again, but to lay hove to and ride out the gale under the lower topsails. Battling his way forrard along the lee side the Mate ordered, 'Up aloft and stow the foresail', and to me, 'See they make a good stow of it, Mister, and get the bunt tight up on the yard.'

Climbing aloft with the men and boys I stayed at the bunt, the centre, from where I could direct operations on both sides of the yard. The canvas was wet and half frozen, but after much laborious effort we at last got the sail rolled up snugly and secure in its gaskets.

That task completed, we scrambled down to the deck. My

watch was now sent below and the Mate's watch set to work disentangling the loose ropes which had become fouled during the night as they were washed around in the swirl of water on deck, and secure the main upper t'gan'sl, which was becoming loose in the gaskets.

The men and boys of my watch had to dry out their sodden clothes as best they could at the bogie stove in the forecastle, where water swirled ankle-deep, forced through the door-jambs during the night by the seas breaking on board. They would have little more than an hour's rest before being roused out for a breakfast of tea and pantiles and going on watch again at 8 a.m. to relieve their shipmates of the Mate's watch.

The wind whistled and screamed, and the seas reared up and roared in unabated fury, but the barque was now riding out the gale in comparative safety, and headed a little towards the westward, where we wished to go: but, hove to as we were, we were making no headway in that direction.

12

TURNED BACK

Hove to on the port tack, headed to the north-westward, but making little headway, with the wind a 'dead muzzler' and squalls of intermittent gale and hurricane force, we were carried to the eastward by the drift of the currents and the scend of the seas, and found ourselves edged back to the vicinity of Staten Island.

There it was necessary to wear ship again, to stand to the south-westward once more on the starboard tack. Day after day these conditions prevailed, in a wearying and futile sustained attempt to make westing, which resulted only in our losing as much headway as we gained. Occasionally the weather improved, the wind and seas died down for a space, and we made sail (that is, set more sails), only to be disappointed when the wind increased to gale force and persisted in coming from a western quarter, compelling us to shorten down to lower topsails again, while the ocean current accelerated our drift to leeward.

The baffling task of trying to work the barque to windward became a routine to induce a feeling of hopelessness, increased by sickness or malingering among the forecastle hands. They knew only too well the discomforts of a four-hour watch on deck in wet and salt-encrusted clothes. Some had painful boils on their wrists, caused by the chafing of the oilskin coats, of which the sleeves were tied at the wrists with rope yarns, and many had chilblains on their fingers and toes, caused by frost and ice. In their watches below, they took such rest as they could in the smoke-befogged atmosphere of the forecastles, where a dim yellow light from the blackened glasses of swaying oil lamps illuminated the damp and desolate surroundings, with steam rising from wet and dirt-grimed clothes hanging between the tiers of bunks, to be partly dried by the smoking bogie stove. In those surroundings the sailors turned in to their bunks to take such sleep as they could on straw palliasses ('donkeys' breakfasts') already flattened by months of use since we had left port, and covered by grey blankets of shoddy quality which were usually found in the forecastles of sailing-vessels.

Under the poop the Captain's wife—who was known as 'the Old Woman', though she was only nineteen years of age—was cheerful company for the Mate or myself when we took our meals with her and the Captain in the saloon, which was warmed by a well-tended bogie stove. A courageous lass, on this, her first voyage, she must have been at times terrified by the rolling and pitching of the barque in the stormy seas, but she showed no signs of fear.

The Captain's dogs had been confined in the sail-locker since we ran into the bad-weather latitudes, but at times they were brought on leashes into the saloon, to be fed and to warm themselves at the stove. They would in all probability have been washed overboard if they had been allowed to roam on the main deck.

For day after day we made little headway to the westward. The men and boys of the watch on deck stood by, but were seldom idle for very long. Again and again the howling wind tore loose part of a sail stowed on the yard, and they were ordered aloft to make it fast. At other times, ropes on deck were washed off the belaying-pins and trailed out through the washports, or became tangled; it was uncomfortable work to secure them again. Frequently, too, the movement of the yards, straining against the braces, caused the ropes to stretch and the yards, to 'range' out of alignment, with an inevitable order from the Old Man, 'Sweat up the weather braces, mister.' These and other tasks kept the crew on the jump. When not otherwise working on deck or aloft, the men and boys of each watch stood or crouched out of the wind and spray under the forecastle head, wherever they could find a dry space, and were occasionally sent aloft to renew some chafing-gear in the rigging, as it became worn away by the continual movement of the masses of wire and rope under the pressure of the screaming winds.

As day followed day, some of the crew became more and more despondent.

With haggard, unshaven faces, they moved about painfully with boils and chilblains, as they obeyed orders, wading through the icy-cold water on deck, or climbing aloft in a surly silence, but never refusing to do what they knew had to be done, except for those who were malingering or perhaps were really too ill to move from their bunks.

In the *Caithness-Shire*, as in most other British sailing-vessels beating to windward round the Horn, the daily task of drawing water from the fresh-water pump was one of the many ordeals to be expected, but not the less exhausting and worrying, even if it might seem to a landsman a fairly simple procedure. The importance of fresh water in a sailor's life may be better appreciated by anyone who might try to live for months, or even for a year or more, on an allowance of one gallon per day for all purposes, including cooking, drinking, ablutions, and washing clothes, in climates ranging from the blazing heat of the tropics, to the freezing cold of the polar regions, and doing hard physical work, with an eighty-four-hour week as the minimum, frequently extended to 100 hours a week or more.

In the sailor's life, there was a glut of salt water, as the poet said, 'everywhere', but fresh water seemed as precious as diamonds. When salt water got into some of this precious fluid, to ruin it, the mishap was almost unbearable; but it was no use grumbling. Any man who went to sea on long voyages under sail expected hardships, and had to take them as they came.

The winter gales of the year 1905 had been the most prolonged and violent that had been recorded in living memory until that time, and became recognised as such in nautical history. In May, June, and July of that year, no fewer than 130 sailing-vessels had left European ports, bound for the Pacific Coast ports of North, Central and South America, by the route round Cape Horn. At the end of November the records showed that only fifty-two of these vessels had arrived at their destinations. Four had been wrecked, twenty-two had put into ports in distress after Cape Horn damage, and fifty-three had not arrived, or were unaccounted for. (Quoted by Captain James Learmont in his book *Master in Sail*, London, 1950, from an article by an historian, Mr. Huycke, in *Sea Breezes* magazine, October 1947.)

It must be assumed that the masters of these 130 vessels were able, experienced, competent, and courageous men, fully qualified in their profession, and aware of the theory and practice of rounding Cape Horn. According to that theory, a vessel would stand from Staten Island or the Strait of Le Maire, to the south-westward, on the starboard tack, across the westerly gales, to the vicinity of 60°S., then would go about on to the port tack, to stand to the north-westward, hauling off the dangerous lee shore of the rock-bound shore of Tierra del Fuego.

During those winter months of 1905 the majority of the shipmasters attempting the westward passage had found that skill and courage were of no avail to prevent their vessels from being battered into submission by the incessant fury of gales which raged continuously against them. The sun, moon, and stars were obscured for weeks on end by dense masses of cloud, which, with hail, rain, sleet and snow, in gales and squalls of hurricane force, made it impossible to ascertain the vessel's position by reliable astronomical observations and calculations.

Those shipmasters who refused to be beaten, and, defying the wrath of sky and sea, continued to claw to the westward, and eventually battled their way to the Pacific Ocean, and to their destination ports, had paid dearly for their courage and tenacity. The German ship *Susannah* and the British ship *British Isles* had left Port Talbot on the same day (11th June 1905), both loaded with coals. *Susannah* took 188 days to reach her destination port, Caleta Buena. On that passage she took ninety-nine days to round the Horn from 50°S. in the Atlantic to 50°S. in the Pacific, and arrived at Caleta Buena with most of her crew suffering severely from scurvy.

The *British Isles*, in which I was a first-voyage apprentice, took 139 days to reach her destination port, Pisagua, and was seventy-one days rounding the Horn 'from 50 to 50', during which she encountered headwinds of gale force for fifty-two days in succession. Four of her seamen perished—three lost overboard and one died of injuries received on deck—and eight others were incapacitated by injuries or frostbite, while the ship was heavily damaged aloft by loss of sails, and cordage, and the fracturing of both the fore mast, main mast and jib-boom.

The gales in that season were of exceptionally long duration, but severe weather was usual in the winter months every year.

Despite many recorded experiences such as these, the weather off Cape Horn was not always hostile. On my second westward passage, in the *British Isles* in 1908, during the winter months, we had met at first with strong headwinds, but then, it seemed miraculously, we had been favoured by a moderate easterly breeze, and had made the passage 'from 50 to 50' in seventeen days! Those milder conditions sometimes occurred, especially in the summer months, so that instances have been recorded of ships doubling Cape Horn with all sails set to the royals, with fair weather all the way, within five or six days. Such good fortune was rare, and, as a rule, headwinds could be expected in all seasons of the year.

Much has been written of the brutality of some masters and bucko mates of Cape Horn vessels in hounding men aloft during gales, especially in the earlier years of the Down Easter, when crews sometimes included men of many nationalities and races kidnapped by crimps in low dives along the waterfront, some with no previous seagoing experience. When emergencies arose, in which the safety of the ship and all on board required strenuous efforts by every man, it was necessary to enforce instant obedience to orders by whatever means were at hand—frequently a belaying-pin wielded by a burly Mate as a truncheon.

In the military code cowardice in the face of the enemy, or refusal to obey orders to advance, was punishable by death; but in a sailing-vessel, battling for her life off Cape Horn, against the bitter enemy of the elements, a refusal of men to go aloft, in the terrible conditions prevailing, to do work on which their own lives, and the lives of everyone on board, might depend, was punishable in British vessels, under the Merchant Shipping Act of 1894, by a fine of five shillings.

In those circumstances it was not surprising that ship-masters and officers sometimes dealt with shirkers in a forthright manner, especially when provoked by insolence.

The individual shirkers of dangerous work that is necessary for the preservation of a group working together at risk of life and limb have usually a streak of cowardice in them, but that same fear can become a dominating force to make a coward perform extraordinary feats of valour under the influence of hot rage.

The fear of being manhandled by a bucko mate or iron-fisted shipmaster was the only force respected by some birds of passage in the forecastles, who habitually malingered in dangerous situations, on deck or aloft, in the working of a sailing-vessel in a storm; but when they were cowed into submission with a punch on the jaw or a clout with a belaying-pin such men have been known to perform feats of reckless valour as a consuming rage and hatred obliterated within them, for the moment, all thoughts of the risks that they were then willing blindly to take.

Cape Horn was living up to its reputation. What were the natural conditions which made that comparatively short stretch of open water so formidable that its dreadful power to destroy ships and men had become legendary? It is the only open strait in the world connecting two great oceans.

Southward of Cape Horn, the stretch of open water

A three-masted barque

Above   In dock: a forest of masts
Below   Cape Horn

Right   The author, 1914
Below   *Caithness-Shire*
at anchor

Above   Callao
Below   Iquique

Fine weather and fair winds

A dolphin makes a
welcome change of diet

Heaving the log

Right   Running before a
gale
Below   Decks full of dead
water

The figure-head of
Caithness-Shire at Nassau
—still facing the
Atlantic

between the southernmost outlying islands of South America (in approximately 56°S. Lat.) and the outlying icebound islands off the shores of Antarctica (in 62°S.) is approximately 360 miles wide. Into that channel are compressed the elemental forces of tides, currents, winds, running seas, and oceanic swell, accelerated by the rotation of the earth on its axis, as the immense pressures of the Pacific and Atlantic oceans meet in turbulent adjustment of their gigantic natural forces, to equalise the interoceanic levels. For such a purpose a channel even 360 miles wide, when viewed in global perspective, is a relatively narrow conduit or bottle-neck, but, to the mariner on the deck of a sailing-vessel storm-tossed in the throes of its turbulence, the ocean immensity to westward and to eastward is unlimited, while always he is aware of being compressed between rocky shores on one side and the ice of Antarctica on the other.

The passage where the oceanic waters meet 'in a most large and free scope' is fitly named Drake Strait, after the intrepid navigator who had discovered it, on its western side, but without sailing through it. Unfortunately this name was not in common use among latter-day sailors, who usually referred simply to 'rounding Cape Horn'. It is the widest and most unsheltered strait in the world, and for this reason was not thought of as a 'strait' but as an ocean stretch.

Thirty-eight years after Drake had proved the existence of that passage, the first Europeans to sail through it were the Dutch navigators, Schouten and Lemaire, in the ship *Eendracht*, 220 tons, from the seaport town of Hoorn in the Netherlands. They were seeking a mercantile route from Europe to the Dutch East Indies, as an alternative to the route round the Cape of Good Hope, which was infested by pirates, and, in time of war, by enemies.

They discovered and named Staten Island, in honour of the 'States' of the Netherlands, and on 29th January 1616, in fine midsummer weather, while sailing to the westward through Drake Strait, within sight of the shore, they sighted 'all high hilly land, covered with snow, ending to the

E

southward with a sharp point which was named Cape Hoorn'.

The name of the Dutch town, as applied to that 'sharp point', soon became altered in usage to 'Cape Horn'. As such, having regard to the general configuration of the southern tip of the South American continent, it is one of the most appropriate and romantic names to be found anywhere on the map of the world.

The British Admiralty charts of the coasts of Patagonia and Tierra del Fuego were made in the years 1826–30 by H.M.S. *Adventure*, commanded by the Australian-born Captain Philip Parker King, R.N., in company with H.M.S. *Beagle*, in which the later-to-become-famous Charles Darwin voyaged as a young naturalist.

The position of Cape Horn and its adjacent islands being thus well fixed on the charts, mariners gave the Horn a wide berth, and seldom sighted it, preferring to keep 100 miles or more to the southward of those dangerous shores.

In Drake Strait the massive movements of the Southern Ocean (a name applied to the conjoined waters of the South Atlantic, South Pacific, and South Indian oceans in the high latitudes) are not obstructed by any continental land-masses as they girdle the globe on the fringe of the Antarctic ice-fields. The winds frequently attain tremendous velocities, caused by a flow of ice-cold air from the Antarctic regions to take the place of warmer air rising elsewhere, or by a flow of air from regions of high barometric pressure to regions of lower pressure, the direction of the wind being effected also by the rotation of the earth. What then constitutes the practical problem of rounding Cape Horn under sail in the teeth of the westerly gales? The wind is not a particularly great hazard as, to a sailing-ship, it is motive power, thousands of horse power to drive her through the water. It is the violence of the terrific squalls, thundering out from dense masses of cloud, invisible in the darkness, or through an atmosphere charged with driving hail, rain, or sleet, or snow, for days, even weeks, even months on end, which makes the hazard of being caught with too much sail on the ship, an ever-present danger of being dismasted, or the ship borne down upon her beam ends, particularly when loaded with grain, coal, or other cargo liable to shift in the hold.

South of Cape Horn the surface of the sea is seldom smooth even on calm days, when a series of westerly gales have died away, and before the infrequent easterly wind has blown up, long westerly swells roll forward from west to east, and within a few hours can be turned into mountainous ridges of roaring water, with dark forbidding valleys between, into which the crests break in a smother of foam and spindrift, which is whipped up by the screaming wind and blown headlong over the surface of the sea in a deluge of smoking vapour. The combination of sustained gales, with squalls of hurricane velocity, and mountainous seas of devastating power upon a ship beset in a wall of darkness, or enshrouded in a deluge of hail, rain, sleet or snow, rocketing every few seconds through an arc of perhaps sixty degrees in the inpenetratable void above her, make the hazard of Cape Horn a living reality, which for a century or more has demonstrated its invincible power by the long list of missing vessels.

It was a tribute to the skills of the designers and builders of sailing-vessels, but even more so to the courage and endurance of the seamen of the Cape Horn breed, that thousands of vessels made that dangerous passage, and continued to do so, undeterred by the fact that many fine vessels and their crews were lost, to lie buried beneath those raging waters which nowadays, long after the ending of the sailing-ship era, are seldom disturbed by the intrusion of man. Those ordeals were endured by seamen for approximately 150 years prior to the opening of the Panama Canal route from the Atlantic to the Pacific in 1914.

The many who perished were victims of Cape Horn's invincible wrath: and those who survived have become seamen of a vanishing breed. Yet their lore, and the lessons they learned, may at some time in the future become valuable, if the thoughts of men ever turn again to harnessing the mighty power of the winds which blow unused in an era of mechanical propulsion. If that should ever happen the lore of Cape Horn may be revived: for, strangely enough, the 'Invincible Cape' had in fact been conquered by Man's technical skill, when windjammers received their final death-blow by the opening of the Panama Canal. The vessels of the German 'P' Line of Hamburg, some of which were specially built and equipped for the Cape Horn route, had improvements in their technical design which enabled them to be worked to windward round the Horn without the dangers, discomforts and delays which occurred on that passage in older vessels of other nations, including Britain. It was the westward passage which was the more difficult and dangerous in vessels of traditional design and equipment. The eastward passage, when a vessel usually ran free before the wind, required a nice judgment of the amount of sail that could be carried to keep her before the wind and seas, and to avoid being pooped: but with westerly winds from any point aft she could run through Drake Strait in a few hours, without undue discomfort, or danger, unless the weather conditions were exceptionally violent.

On the westward passage, a vessel of conventional design, with a low freeboard amidships, beating to windward on long tacks, had to stem and ride over seas bearing down on her from only two or three points before the beam. In this situation her weather side reared up as an obstruction to the thousands of tons of water rushing towards her in each huge sea. When she was in the trough it was a matter of a few moments only to decide whether she would rise and ride the avalanche of water crested above her, or have her decks submerged in a flood which filled them from rail to rail, perhaps to press her down beyond the buoyancy margin of safety by the addition of hundreds of tons of water on her deck. She was then at the mercy of the seas for those few moments, with water cascading from her scuppers and wash-ports, before she freed herself to rise and meet another oncoming sea.

In those conditions, if it was necessary to shorten sail or

haul around or brace up the yards, the sailors of the watch
or of both watches, worked at risk of life and limb in swirling
water up to their waists, since practically all the running
gear was belayed to the pin rails on the main deck.

The Germans of the Flying 'P' Line had overcome this
difficulty by designing and building most of their vessels
with a long midship deck raised above the level of the
bulwarks, ranged fore and aft, except for well-decks between
the forecastle head and the forward end of the midship deck,
and likewise between the poop and the after end of the
midship deck. This construction eliminated the danger of the
vessel's being borne down by the weight of water on her
decks, which was kept to a minimum in the two well-decks. It
enabled the crew to work the vessel in comparative safety,
instead of wading thigh-deep to man the braces, buntlines,
clewlines and downalls; but, in addition, there were hand-
operated winches for the braces and halyards, so that the
yards could be braced up, hauled around, or hoisted
quickly, by the labour of the watch on deck only.

Those facilities in general, and ample manning by disciplined seamen and numerous cadets, made it possible for
shipmasters in 'P' Line vessels to make or shorten sail quickly,
without calling all hands on deck, which was only too often
the *modus operandi* in British vessels. Apparently judging by
the excellent passages of some of these German vessels round
Cape Horn at all seasons, one writer has assumed that all
other vessels, if properly handled, could have made similar
passages; but that comparison disregards the superior design
and equipment in the German vessels, and the fact that most
other vessels on the Cape Horn route were ageing if not
obsolete during the first fourteen years of the twentieth
century.

So it happened that, at the end of the sailing-ship era, the
practical problems of rounding the Horn had actually been
overcome; and the windjammers went into the discard at a
time when technical perfection in working them had been
attained after centuries of effort.

13

IQUIQUE

FOR eleven days we made little progress westward, making sail as the weather improved only to shorten down to lower topsails again as the wind increased to gale force. After a moderate gale in which the wind had hauled into the south-south-west, the wind died away to a calm and left us rolling heavily in the long oily swells, the sails slatting back and forth violently with every roll, and water pouring in through the washport doors and surging across the deck. Albatrosses and mollyhawks in great numbers flew about, skimming the tops of the great rollers, and soaring high into the air with no discernible movement in their wings, to settle on the water as white dots in silhouette against the horizon for a moment before fading from view as the swell on which they rode so easily subsided into a deep valley.

After a day of calm, a light breeze came out of the east. We set every stitch of canvas and set a course to the westward, all hands frolicking in the warm sunshine which now shone down from a cloud-flecked sky, the wind gradually increasing until we were making seven knots with the ship breasting the long westerly swells which roll forward unceasingly in these latitudes.

After two days of sailing, in which we had left behind us 350 miles of turbulent waters, gradually altering course more northward as the margin of safety from the iron-bound lee shore of Tierra del Fuego increased, the wind died away again, and for another day we lay becalmed, but happy in the knowledge that a westerly wind, which a falling barometer indicated, could no longer raise a barrier to our progress northward. As the wind came out of the north-west we headed away on the port tack, coming up to our course for Iquique while the wind hauled to the south of west with increasing velocity.

Vessels arriving in West Coast ports after rounding the Horn during the winter months often had to report both sickness and casualties among the crew, after sustaining such extensive damage to the ship and loss of spars and sails as had necessitated having to put back to Port Stanley in the Falkland Islands, or some Atlantic coast port to effect repairs.

We, therefore, had good reason to thank the wind-gods for letting us off so lightly, but, even so, it might still have been necessary to tell a very different story had the *Caithness-Shire* not been so well found, with hull, masts, spars, rigging and sails in the best possible condition, with a Master who knew his ship from A to Z and when prudence would best serve the interests of his owners. It was not destined that Mrs. Hatfield, the Captain's wife, should undergo the terrible ordeal of Captain Barker's wife in the *British Isles*, when, for seventy-two days off Cape Horn in the winter of 1905, she was confined to her cabin under the poop, with two young children, in a fetid atmosphere, with every port-hole, door and crevice to the deck, and the light of day, securely blocked against a deluge of hail, rain, snow, and sleet being driven down by the roaring wind upon a ship labouring, and rolling through an arc of fifty or sixty degrees in mountainous seas.

We had not seen again a four-masted barque which had sailed past us previously, which the Old Man said was one of the famous German Flying 'P' Line Ships of Herr Laeiss from Hamburg, most probably now in port with half her cargo discharged; as, with German thoroughness, their organisation in the West Coast ports equalled, if not excelled, that to be found in most of their Cape Horn ships.

These vessels had hardly finished mooring before lighters were alongside and the first of their cargo was going over the side. While British ships, and those of other nations, were frequently idle awaiting empty lighters from the shore, an adequate number could always be seen moored alongside a 'P' Line vessel, discharging simultaneously from all her hatches, and loading bags of nitrate immediately a hold was empty. As the contents of the last lighters of nitrate were being hoisted in, the ship's crew were heaving in the anchor cables, casting off the gaskets to loosen the sails, and breaking out the stern moorings, the vessels frequently being under way and leaving the harbour as the last bags of saltpetre were being hoisted in. These vessels were seldom in a West Coast port more than two or three weeks to discharge a full cargo, and load another, while British sailing-vessels were usually two, or even three, months discharging a cargo of coal, and loading a thousand tons of ballast. One of the reasons for the rapid turn-round of the German ships was that members of their crews seldom skinned out or allowed themselves to be shanghaied by the crimps in the West Coast ports, as they knew, when leaving their homes, that they would be back in a few months. With a full crew on board, and priority in discharging or loading cargo, such vessels as the *Patosi* and *Preussen* could make two round voyages from Germany to Chile and back, via Cape Horn, within twelve months.

Sailing northward, with a following wind on the quarter, we passed through the Howling Fifties and Roaring Forties with no more discomfort than strong winds, and, at times, rough seas, with an occasional flooding of the deck as a following sea broke over the topgallants rail as the ship rolled to windward.

The crew were in great heart, as no doubt they were able to visualise our near approach to the ship's destination, and such diversions as the largest nitrate port on the West Coast could offer, probably disregarding, even if they had heard, when the articles were gabbled over in Port Talbot, that shore leave for the crew was at the discretion of the Master, also that between one and two miles of water would still separate them from the taverns and other interests of a seaport, from where the ship would lay moored in the tiers of ships loading or discharging their cargoes. Now well beyond the bad-weather latitudes the wind gradually died away, to leave us in a belt of calms and light breezes, which delayed us for another two days, all hands taking the opportunity to wash salt-laden clothes, which draped the fore end of the ship in a mantle of diverse coloured raiment, with soiled and battered donkey's breakfasts spread over the forecastle deck among a litter of old boots, and pin-up pictures, torn from magazines, which had adorned the damp and musty bulkheads beside the bunks in the forecastles. Picking up the south-east trade wind we made slow progress northward, which gave us an opportunity to send down, and stow in the sail-locker, our No. 1 bad-weather sails and bend to the yards and set, the fine-weather suit, as we ambled along, assisted by the coastal current.

We had now been three and a half months at sea, and stores of food and fresh water were getting low, but our joint cook and steward managed to make the crew forrard a Christmas dinner, with Christmas pudding, from the canned foods remaining, and the substitutes provided in the Board of Trade scale of provisions, as such things as fresh meat, potatoes and vegetables had long since been either consumed or dumped overboard after deterioration owing to the absence of refrigeration, or other means of keeping them wholesome for long periods. We, in the afterguard, were more fortunate, as the Captain's wife made excellent puddings for the officers, and apprentices, from the private stores the Master had provided for his wife's comfort on the voyage.

With about seven hundred miles between us and our destination we sailed and drifted northwards as we closed in towards the land, the crew working in hilarious mood as the bower anchors were hoisted out and secured in the tumblers, gangway taken from the hold and rigged ready for securing overside, and all made ready for entering port.

As the sun rose into a cloudless blue sky over the towering peaks of the Andes Mountains, framing the port of Iquique in a golden dawn on January 8th, 1910, the *Caithness-Shire* drifted into the bay under full sail in a light breeze which ghosted the ship along, the crew standing by halliards and running gear to get the canvas off her as we approached the anchorage. On the forecastle head the Mate stood, with an iron bar in his hand, ready to turn the tumbler and release the anchor, while below, the carpenter waited at the windlass ready to release the brake and let the anchor cable run out. At last came the order 'Let go'. With a roar and a rattle of chain cable the bower anchor plunged to the bottom, the last of the sails were clewed up, and the ship rode quietly at anchor in the bay of Iquique, 123 days out from Port Talbot in Wales.

At 8 a.m. the discharging of coal began, six seamen and three apprentices climbing into the hold to form three gangs, the apprentices holding the mouths of the bags open while the men shovelled coal into them until they were full. Another apprentice, with a skein of twine around his middle, sewed up the mouths of the bags as they were filled, while each gang in turn made up a sling of five bags, which were hoisted up by the donkey engine, landed on the scales and weighed, before being lowered into the lighter. As the coal was discharged, and the men got lower into the hold, where such breeze as might be blowing on deck did not penetrate, the heat in the hold became stifling, a brazen sun burning down on them from a cloudless sky, while underfoot the coal, already heated from the airless confinement of 123 days, gave off clouds of choking dust as six shovels stirred up the mass off gas-impregnated material in which they laboured, stripped to the waist, with eyes and gaping red mouth, outlined against a blackened face and torso, on which rivulets of sweat carved a tracery of web-like pattern in the dust and grime.

Our charter party stipulated a rate of discharge of 100 tons per weather working day, this being the usual clause for sailing-ships discharging coal in West Coast ports, and 250 tons per day for steamers. The business of a shipmaster in the West Coast ports was fraught with many pitfalls for the unwary, or the uninitiated, but as most of the shipping business was transacted in the ship-chandler's premises,

there was always a number of Masters congregated there
each morning, discussing their problems over a glass of Pisco
or other beverage, and the advice available from such a
tribunal was usually sufficient to counter any move by the
charters or agents to misinterpret any clause in the charter
party.

Surf days and feasts days were the principal snags facing
a Master in relation to discharging or loading a cargo on the
West Coast.

14

TRIALS OF A SHIPMASTER

THE Bay of Iquique, like many others on the West Coast of South America, was wide open to the Pacific Ocean, with a coastal current running across the mouth of the bay from south to north, over a sea-bed frequently disturbed by volcanic tremors, in a geographical situation where the south-coast trade wind blows throughout the year. This is not always a true wind from the south-east, but may come at times from any point in the south-east quadrant. In the bay there is always a swell setting in from the ocean, varying from slight undulations to a moderate, or even a heavy swell, making it impracticable for lighters to lay quietly alongside a vessel without being seriously damaged, or even sunk, by the heavy bumping and grinding of two vessels moored together in the swell.

The difficulty for the shipmaster arose from the absolute authority to declare a 'surf day' being vested in the port authority, and as 'surf days' did not count as lay days, frequent declarations could prolong the ship's stay in port indefinitely.

To discharge 3,000 tons of coal at an average rate of 100 tons per day, placed upon the charterers the obligation of supplying the ship with sufficient lighters and bags per day to effect that purpose. With a large number of ships in the port, sometimes as many as thirty or forty, with some working to guaranteed steamer despatch, the lighterage problem became a difficult one for the charterers.

Shortages of lighters frequently occurred owing to difficulties in discharging the lighters at the jetty, where, from a number of ships, they would accumulate faster than they could be emptied. The obvious solution was to invoke the 'surf day' clause to build up a supply of empty lighters, with the result that the stipulated thirty days on paper became thirty-one, or even forty-one, or more, without compensation to the shipowner for the delay to his ship, and extra expense for wages and victualling the crew. Demurrage was another thorn in a shipmaster's side. This was a sum of money payable by the shipowner to the charterers for every day over the stipulated number of lay days which the vessel took to discharge her cargo, owing to shortage of crew, breakdown of ship's equipment, or other cause for which the ship was responsible.

Obtaining ballast was another opportunity which could operate adversely to the shipowner's interest. Most sailing ships required some hundreds of tons of cargo, or ballast, in their holds to even stand upright in port, and before the last few hundred tons of cargo were discharged it was necessary to take in ballast. It is on record that the loss of several sailing ships, which disappeared without trace, whilst on a voyage in ballast to a loading port, was attributed to an insufficient quantity of ballast in their holds. Some ports on the west coast had a reputation among shipmasters for giving short weight in supplying ballast to ships. In consequence some masters were willing to sacrifice despatch by weighing one in every five or ten baskets which were hoisted on board from the lighters, but even with this precaution it was not always possible to be assured of correct weight, when the ballast, particularly sand, had been thoroughly saturated with water before it arrived alongside. When dried out later by evaporation in the high temperature of a ship's hold in the tropics this could represent a loss in ballasting weight sufficient to effect the stability of the ship.

The strategy and cunning, however, were not the sole prerogative of smart operators ashore, as the shipmaster also had some trumps up his sleeve.

When discharging a coal cargo under a clause in the

charter party which called for delivery by certified weighed weight in bags, the charterers, or ship agents, supplied a set of scales, and a Chileno tally clerk, to record the weight of each sling of five sacks hoisted from the hold and lowered on to the scales, before going overside into the lighter. Throughout each long day, in tropical heat, under a blazing sun, smothered every few minutes in coal-dust, and bathed in sweat, the tally clerk's duty was to stand on the stage and weigh every sling of coal which was landed on the scales. The mates, who supervised the discharge, and tallied also on the ship's behalf, relieved each other at frequent intervals, and even a most conscientious servant of the charterers' agents could hardly be expected to refuse an invitation to accompany the Mate to his cabin for a well-earned rest and refreshments. In the Mate's or Second Mate's cabin the tally clerk eyed the bottles of Pisco with great relish, as the officer plied him with liberal doses of fire-water while he regaled him with stories of adventure in far-distant lands, until his fast-closing eyes heralded the approach of that siesta, so dear to the heart of toil-worn Latin gentry at mid-day, but which, on such an auspicious occasion as now offering, could be extended indefinitely without loss of prestige in the eyes of his employer. Hour after hour the officer on the stage worked alone with diligence and care, tallying the slings of cargo and their weight, as they came on the scales, but whether from lassitude in the heat of the day or the sweat pouring down his face obscuring the graduations on the scale, it became frequently necessary to lean heavily over the bags of coal to read off the weight registered by the scale, and, at times, when his attention was diverted for a few moments by the necessity of attending to other matters, he could not be sure whether the sling now on the scales had been weighed or not, so gave the ship the benefit of the doubt, and weighed the sling a second time.

Having slept off the effect of the Pisco he had consumed the tally clerk returned to the stage and copied into his book the details of discharge so effectively recorded during the past two hours. When the last ton of coal had been discharged by weights recorded on the charterers' scales, and certified by their own trusty servant, no doubt could exist but that the surplus of fifty or more tons of coal still in the hold was due to an error in the pit weights recorded at the loading-port. As Welsh coal was worth £4 10s. per ton on the West Coast, the £225 or more received in payment for coal delivered to a purchaser at the next port of call, did much to off-set, or even defray, the extra expense occasioned by 'surf days', or demurrage, at the port of discharge.

It was amazing how often urgently needed stores were out of stock and would need to be obtained from a distant town at the ship's expense, but a raid on the tradesman's store would have disclosed abundant supplies awaiting acceptance, when an additional margin of profit accruing from an imaginary freight-rate could be loaded to the account. If at times it was difficult for a sailing-ship Master to protect his owner's interests against the stratagems adopted in foreign ports, to extract the last penny possible from a ship's disbursements, it was equally difficult at times to perform his duties, both at sea and in port, without incurring the owner's displeasure by infringing any of the standing orders laid down in their book of instructions to their Masters.

The following extracts are taken from a printed book of instructions to their Masters issued by the British Shipowner's Company, owners of the ship *British Isles*, and many others, in 1875, which was still in use in 1899 when the above-named ship was sold to Messrs. Thomas Shute & Son. These illustrate the difficulties with which a Master was faced in his endeavours to meet the exacting conditions of his employment, and receive the approbation of his owners by returning a margin of profit at the end of a voyage. Among many others the following paragraphs are of particular interest as illustrating how the onus of responsibility must ultimately fall upon the Master.

'Before sailing you will supply yourself with a good chronometer and the latest Admiralty charts, corrected to date, also *Horsburg's Book of Sailing Directions for the Ports of the*

World, with copies of the Government regulations for the prevention of collisions as well as the latest edition of the Mercantile Shipping Acts, and a copy of *Lee's Laws of Shipping & Insurance* for reference in case of need. You cannot be too careful in the navigation of your ship, and should bear in mind that we only insure our ships to about half their value.

'When homeward bound, if you take the assistance of a tug, you should not require a channel pilot, in fact we do not believe in these men at all, for the only casualties we have ever had in the channel happened with pilots on board our ships.

'When bound to Dundee, should you think a channel pilot really necessary, you had better not engage one until you are in the Downs, and before taking him try and satisfy yourself that he is a man of experience who knows the North Sea channels well, but we shall not consider that the fact of you having a pilot on board frees you from any responsibility to us.

'In the event of your falling in with a distressed or derelict vessel, unless under especially favourable and easy circumstances in fine weather, do no more than save life. We have found from experience that in the present state of the laws as to insurance and salvage, any award we may get for saving property is not nearly sufficient to compensate for the risk run, and the process of obtaining the award is, moreover, most dilatory and tedious. Moreover, should your ship unfortunately be lost whilst undertaking a salvage service, even supposing we were able to recover from the underwriters the amount insured with them, we should at any rate lose the amount which we ourselves insure on each of our ships.

'Your ship being well-found for the voyage you are expected to make, you will please take notice that any purchases of canvas, rope, ship-chandlery, etc., made abroad will be charged to your own private account, unless you can give sufficient proof on your return that the purchase of any such articles was indispensable, on the other hand, without special instructions, you must never sell anything abroad.

'At Calcutta towage is a very heavy charge, and you must do your best to keep it as low as possible. A gratuity to your pilot, judiciously given, often saves a good deal in towage. You may sometimes fall in with a return steamer which has just towed a ship outwards, and if so, you should be able to make a bargain for a cheap tow up the river. Going-up river in the south-west monsoon you should endeavour to do without steam hire, but in any case, you should do with a very much shorter tow than usual in the other monsoon.

'When homeward bound, if, on your arrival in the channel, the wind should be fair, do not incur unnecessary expense in steam hire, but do without it as long as possible, unless by taking a tug you should save being neaped.

'When bound to Liverpool you may sometimes be able to do without a tug altogether, but at any rate a tow from Holyhead at the furtherest, should, as a rule, be amply sufficient; £40 to £50 should suffice for inward towage, if you cannot manage for less, but, in any case, always make a bargain, including the docking of the ship, and endeavour to get the use of the steamer's hawser thrown in. When bound to London the outside expense you should incur for towage should not be more than about £50, and, with a fair wind, much less.

'The strictest economy must be observed in your disbursements, and we may tell you that this, together with your passages, are the chief grounds on which we form an opinion as to whether the Masters in our employ are active and pushing, and attentive to our interests, or not.

'For all your disbursements, except incidental expenses, you must send us vouchers, any items for which you cannot show vouchers or explain satisfactorily, will be charged to your own private account, you will be allowed up to £5 for incidental expenses, whilst in each port. This allowance must cover all your expenses on shore except in the case of Bombay or Calcutta, where special allowances are made you for buggy or dinghy hire. These sums are not per month, but for the whole time you are in port, and we look upon them as maximum amounts, and expect that unless you are a long time in port, you will not require to spend so much. When several of our ships are in port together, you should be able to save money by joining with other of our Captains in hiring a buggy.'

As the days passed by and the men and boys working below got deeper into the airless hold, the rate of discharge declined, as men came up from the hold, complaining of the heat and dust, and sat on deck recouping their lost energy. This was no hard-case ship, and with the Master ashore with his wife, or visiting friends in another ship, the Mate, who at all times was averse to bullying, and sympathetic to the men's continual complaints, did nothing to improve a situation which was fast deteriorating into a sit-down strike.

Another difficulty affecting the discharge of cargo, by the crew, was the clause in their articles of agreement which read, 'No liberty granted abroad otherwise than at the Master's option', and in view of the possibility, or even probability, of desertion, no shore leave was granted. After four months at sea without a taste of liquor, or any of the diversions from the daily grind available to those who enjoyed the privacy of a home and family, or the prattle of women in various guises who might be eager to share the spoils which could be garnered by flattery and brazen display of such shapely contours as they might possess, the roving disposition of men who spent their lives isolated in the confines of the steel walls of a prison surrounded by an impregnable mote, rebelled against this stricture on their liberty in diverse ways. After slaving in the dust and heat of the hold, climbing on deck physically and mentally exhausted each evening to gaze longingly at the lights of the town some two miles distant, for three of the men the last straw to break the camel's back had been reached, and they invoked the malingerer's trump by remaining in their bunks complaining of pains here and there.

A Chileno doctor, summoned to the ship, after a very casual examination, confined to questions and evasive answers, ordered the men into hospital, where it was said facilities were available for proper treatment.

Hospitals on the West Coast in those days were places to be avoided. Hygiene as known today was non-existent, as were fly-wire screens over the open windows and doors. The patients lay sweating in the humid heat of the day, fighting off the swarms of flies which milled about them, to feast where it was possible on festering sores, or stinking bandages exposed by the restless squirmings of human derelicts picked up in the streets after brawls in which knives were the favoured weapons of aggression.

Hospital treatment for sailors was an expensive item where no alternative existed to meeting the exorbitant charges levied for treatment, which was apt to prolong their stay and contribute to the maintenance of an institution of doubtful efficiency. On inquiries being made as to when the men would be fit for duty the Master was informed that the men were not progressing favourably, and would be under treatment for an indefinite time.

Every visit to the men in hospital was now met with demands to be paid off, and further assurances by the doctor that they would not be fit for duty for an indefinite time convinced the Master that he had no choice if he was to minimise the rising expenditure of delivering his cargo, but to accede to the men's demands and pay them off. On January 15th the three men in hospital were paid off, the average amount of money each received for four months, and some odd days' work, being £4 10s. 1d.

Sometime later we heard that those three men had been shanghaied and, put on board an outgoing ship soon after they were paid off, after their wages had been confiscated by the boarding-house master, with their advance wages, notes of three pounds each, when signing articles on the outward-bound ship, to pay for the meagre outfit of bed and blankets with which they had been supplied.

A month later both the cook-cum-steward and his assistant complained of illness, and after some days in the hospital were paid off. A new cook-steward, a Dane, was signed on, after the ship had been without a domestic staff for a period of fifteen days, but, between us, one of the boys and myself had managed to dish up some hash and stew, which, if not appetising, was something with which to line the bellies of hard-driven men. One look at the ship and the conditions generally was enough for the Dane, and he promptly deserted, leaving us with a French assistant steward who had been signed on, but after a week he also was paid off via the hospital. By this time, some five weeks after our arrival in port, the four years' indenture period of four of our apprentices expired, and they too left the ship.

Since the assistant steward left on March 5th, we had been without either cook or steward, and it was not until sixteen days later that a German was engaged as assistant steward at £3 10s. per month who carried on with the help of an apprentice until a cook was procured just before we left Iquique. Of the original deckhands, comprising eight seamen and nine apprentices, we now had only three seamen and five apprentices to shovel about 2,000 tons of coal, man the boat each day, and scrape the barnacles and marine growth from the ship's plating, as the immersed plates rose out of the water as the cargo was discharged.

It not being considered proper for the apprentices to work in the hold with the Chileno drifters who had been employed in place of the seamen who had left, sufficient shore labour was now employed to complete the discharge of the coal cargo and take in 900 tons of ballast. The three original seamen, and the boys when available, were put overside in the boat, and on stages, to scrape off barnacles and marine growth, or chip and scale the rusty top side plates ready for painting, their number being augmented when four good seamen who had recently been discharged from other vessels were signed on.

These four men subsequently remained in the ship for the next ten months, a verbal condition of their engagement being that they be given shore leave.

15

CALLAO FOR ORDERS

AFTER we had been discharging for over two months a large part of the main hold had been cleared and we were ready to commence taking in the 900 tons of ballast we required, as orders had been received for the ship to proceed to Callao in Peru to load a cargo of guano at, as yet, an un-named island off the coast of Peru, for the port of Wilmington in the State of North Carolina, U.S.A.

Our portable donkey engine had been giving a lot of trouble, due to steam being procured by using salt water in the boiler, and at times would hardly lift five hundredweight of bagged coal out of the hold.

In the arid desert region of the West Coast ports fresh water was very scarce, as there was practically no rainfall throughout the year, and such supplies as could be obtained at exorbitant prices were stored and used exclusively for domestic purposes.

The water was usually boiled before usage, to minimise the risk of disease from flies, mosquitoes, and other vermin which infested a dry and sunbaked land, where cleanliness was not among the virtues of the more lowly native population in handling the supplies of fresh water to ships in the bay. The remedy was to use fresh water in the boiler until the salt had been dissolved, but, as this was too expensive, the remedy adopted was to hang weights on the safety valve so that it could be operate until practically all the water in the boiler had been turned to steam by a roaring fire in the furnace below. When the water in the gauge glass had disappeared for perhaps a quarter- or half-hour, the carpenter, who worked the donkey unit, got scared as the pressure kept rising, and finally jabbed at the safety valve with a rake until it opened and blew the contents of the boiler twenty feet into the air, smothering the rigging, which shone like silver when the steam evaporated and left the rigging coated with salt.

It is amazing that no one was killed or injured in this dangerous use of a boiler, but week after week the same procedure was adopted until after, two and a half months' work, the coal cargo had been discharged, and ballast taken in for the voyage to Peru. Life on board was now more congenial, as, with the ship washed down to reasonably clean, it was possible to enjoy the routine work of preparing the ship for sea.

As the days went by, new men were brought on board until we had eight men signed on as seamen, and our original two Able Seamen, which, with five apprentices, made a total deck crew of fifteen persons, and a total ship's complement of twenty-two, two less than our original number, but a fine-weather trip up the coast to Callao was before us, and perhaps we would get more men at the next port to complete our complement.

The Master was ashore each day perusing the many documents and accounts placed before him for signature, while no doubt making a mental calculation of the credit, or debit, with which his owners would be faced when the sale of the surplus coal in the ship had been thrown into the balance at Callao.

At daybreak on April 7th, 1910, three months less one day since we anchored in Iquique, we began to heave up the anchors and break moorings, the Masters of two ships in port coming on board to say farewell to the Old Man on the poop, as they offered him advice on how to handle his ship, while drinking his whisky. Three sturdy apprentices from each of their boats assisted our crew to make sail, which was a customary procedure in all West Coast ports, when ships were sailing, unless the Master had raised the ire of other Masters congregated in the ship-chandlers by abrogating to himself the role of an elder statesman in all matters concerning shipmasters' business.

As we cleared Iquique Bay in a light breeze the two visiting Masters took their leave. Climbing down the pilot ladder they were soon on their way back to their ships, with the boys in each gig straining their backs in a race, which was usually a feature of the ship-visiting by Masters in port to ships arriving or departing in daylight hours. As soon as they were away we made all sail and stood away to the north-west.

The run of about 500 miles from Iquique to Callao was not uneventful. With very light winds, calms, fogs, and a coastal current, we drifted rather than sailed north-westward, keeping within sight of the land when possible, which appeared on the horizon as a bluish smudge, varying in density, as the rays from a blazing sun penetrated the shimmering haze about us, and threw into relief the lighter patches of sun-scorched earth which clothed the broken ridges on the mountainside.

In the cool of the evening dog watches some crew members sat idly about on the main hatch, smoking and yarning. Others washed or mended clothes while subconsciously listening to the strains of a mouth organ with which the carpenter shattered the quiet of a tropical evening. As daylight came in on the sixth day after leaving Iquique we were steering a course northward with the light off-shore breeze abeam on our starboard side, and all sail set, the ship making about one knot in a slight oil swell. But a change in our fortunes soon became apparent, as the cold wind, blowing from off the mountains, absorbed by direct evaporation from the warmer sea water, the lower layers of cold air becoming heated by contact with the water, caused a low-lying sea fog as they rose and were again chilled by the upper air.

These early-morning fogs are usually confined to an area near the surface of the sea, and from the upper yard on the fore mast it was possible to see over the low-lying fog, so a lookout was posted on the upper top-gallant yard as we continued towards our destination. Suddenly the lookout man hailed the deck with a cry, 'Masts of a steamer in sight', and I was sent aloft by the Master to watch the vessel's approach and report if our courses converged so that action could be taken to avoid collision.

From the fore upper topgallant yard the scene was eerie. Beneath me banks of fog swirled about, blotting out the deck and everything below the lower topgallant yards. From out of the pall of vapour came the sound of a blast from our puny fog horn every minute, indicating we were on the starboard tack, in the hope that the feeble squeak would be heard by the approaching vessel. Dead ahead, perhaps five or six miles distant, the upper part of two masts protruded out of the fog, and one glance was sufficient to assure me that the steamer was bound south on a course which might not take her clear of us. Reporting this to the deck I was ordered to remain aloft and report any alteration of the steamer's course. Overhead the sky was clear and bright, but no vestige of water could be seen through the pattern of drifting fog in which our main and mizzen topmasts appeared to be floating.

Yelling to the deck that the steamer would not clear us on her present course, the Master joined me on the yard, from where he could see what was happening and shout, down orders to the Mate who had been stationed by the wheel. By the rule of the road the steamer had to give way to a sailing-ship, but it was clear that our presence was, as yet, unknown to the steamer, as she had no crows-nest on the mast for a lookout man, who was probably stationed on the forecastle head, where we would be invisible to him, as also to the officers on the bridge.

We could now hear the steamer's whistle, and the throb of her engine, which indicated she was steaming at full speed, with her two masts still in line, dead ahead of us, and getting closer. There was now no time to be lost if a collision was to be avoided, but what action to take was a problem only the Master could solve, but whatever decision he made could, in certain circumstances, be evaluated by a court of inquiry as wrong.

To back the main yards, and heave to, was only to make us a sitting duck, and unmanageable if manœuvre became necessary or possible. To alter course to starboard was also impossible, as the yards were already near the backstays, and at the most we would only come up another point closer to the wind, and what little way we were making would then be lost.

To run off to port, before the wind, was the only manœuvre possible, and that only by contravening article 21 of the rule of the road, and invoking its footnote for cases of emergency when action by both vessels becomes necessary to avoid collision. Was our presence known to the steamer? That was the vital question to be answered, and upon it all else depended. On deck the covers had been stripped off the lifeboats and all made ready to swing them over the side quickly, one watch was standing by the fore braces and the other at the main braces, with lifebelts handy on the hatchways, ready for instant action when the crisis came upon us, the men peering into the fog as they listened to the steamer's whistle blasts getting louder and louder, stunned to anxious silence in an atmosphere tense with foreboding.

Waiting no longer the Old Man yelled, 'Hard up the helm, mister. Square the yards and keep her away before the wind,' and to me, 'On deck, Mister, and ring the bloody bell on the foc's'le head, and keep it going. He can't hear that pip-squeak fog-horn, but he might hear the bell!'

By now the two vessels were probably little more than half a mile apart, and still she bore down on us at a speed which would cover the intervening distance in four or five minutes. On the foc's'le head I slammed the clapper of the bell back and forth and produced a volume of sound which ought to be heard for miles around, but what would be the steamer's reaction when he heard it?

A continuous ringing of a bell from a ship in the open sea, in hundreds of feet of water, could not be construed as the fog signal of a vessel at anchor, neither did it indicate whether it was from a steamer or a sailing-ship, or in which direction it was heading, but what it did indicate to those on the bridge of the steamer was unmistakably an emergency, coming, as it must have seemed, from almost under their bows.

We had not long to wait for the answer, as, within a minute of first ringing the bell, we heard one short blast from the steamer's whistle, followed a few seconds later by a pause in the pounding of her engine, before it reached a new crescendo as, with her rudder hard over and engines reversed, the steamer sheered away to starboard in a direction which would take her across our bows. As the short blast of the steamer's whistle sounded, the Old Man, still aloft on the fore topgallant yard, yelled, 'Haul away the starboard braces. Bring her up on the port tack!' As we swung away to port the dim ouline of a steamer became visible in the fog with his side almost parallel with ours, but now both ships were swinging away from each other, and a minute later the receding stern of the steamer, and the tips of her propeller blades as they churned the water into a creaming wake, were swallowed up in the fog. As soon as the steamer's whistle became faintly audible in the distance we again wore ship, secured the lifeboats and gear, and proceeded on our original course towards Callao.

On the evening of our ninth day at sea we hove to for the night, as by calculations we were about thirty miles from our destination, and on this coast, where calms and fogs are prevalent, to approach too closely the port you are bound for during the hours of darkness without a steady favourable wind may result in your being carried past by the prevailing northward current, if the wind dies away in the early morning and leaves you becalmed, or comes away off the land.

Many ships have drifted past their ports on the West Coast, and have sailed 800 or 1,000 miles beating back against the prevailing southerly winds, after sailing out into the Pacific Ocean far enough to get clear of the coastal current.

On April 17th, ten days after leaving Iquique, we sighted

the island of San Lorenzo, at the entrance to Callao Bay. With the yards braced up on the starboard tack, we sailed into the bay, and, rounding up to the wind, anchored in the lee of a promontory named La Punta. After anchoring, our agent, Mr. Joseph Drew, came on board in a great pother, and wanted to know where we had been: 'Ten days to sail 500 miles; two miles an hour. Why, Captain,' he said, 'I could walk the distance in less time than you have taken; I expected you five days ago and have had my lighters standing idle all that time to give you a quick despatch.'

From Mr. Drew I learned that our orders had been changed and we were now to load a full cargo at Santa Island, instead of the Chincha Islands where we had previously been ordered to load.

There were a number of ships in the port, some at anchor in the bay and others in the dock, as Callao had a large import and export trade in general merchandise, but was also the clearing port for cargoes of guano, loaded at various islands off the Peruvian coast.

Callao in 1910 was a thriving port, with a steam tug to assist ships in and out of dock, where the facilities for hand-ling cargo were far more efficient than in the open anchor-ages of the southern ports, where everything had to be con-veyed between the ships and the shore in lighters, but like all the West Coast ports, in bays wide open to the expanse of the Pacific Ocean, the swell affected the loading and dis-charging of cargo, even in the dock, where ships at the wharf ranged and rolled while straining at their moorings, which had to be attended continually.

16

CALLAO

CALLAO, Peru's principal seaport is only a few miles distant from Lima, the capital, situated on a flat plain between the Andes Mountains, and the Pacific Ocean. In 1746 an earthquake destroyed Callao, but the city rose again from its ashes, and was under Spanish rule until 1826. In Lima, which for centuries was the seat of Spanish Government and power, may be found many relics of the Inca occupation in museums, and others dating back for centuries before the Incas. Among the many beautiful churches in the city that of Santo Domingo is a famous landmark which dates back to 1549, its twin towers being a prominent landmark.

The Plaza Bolivar, once known as the Plaza of the Inquisition, is famous for a building in which infidels were tried, but no evidence now remains of the pain and suffering inflicted within these walls, which, fortunately, have not the power of speech.

Ashore, in Callao, after sunset, it was wise to watch your step anywhere in the dock area, as men of all nationalities, creeds, and customs, roamed about in search of diversion in the saloons and dance halls, where wine, women, and song was often a prelude to a free-for-all brawl, in which knife-throwing with deadly accuracy was among the finer arts countenanced by the assembled populace.

Since last I was in this port in 1906 the business of boarding-house masters had declined, probably owing to the publicity which the nefarious trade in human merchandise had received in the public press, and the pressure of public opinion on controlling authorities. More important, however, was the change taking place by the gradual adoption of a seafaring career by men, whose inveterate habits had been fashioned by the discipline of a more stable environment and the advantage of better education.

It was now more the exception than the rule to find men in the forecastles who could neither read nor write, and whose signature in the articles of agreement was a cross. Their subjugation by the artifices of hired thugs rarely now occasioned the replacement of the majority of the forecastle crew, but was confined to those birds of passage whose horizon was limited to the next port of call. The new men we had shipped in Iquique had settled down, and although attempts had been made to induce them to desert, they remained steadfast, and apparently content with the knowledge that the *Caithness-Shire* was no hard-case ship with a blue-nose Master and bucko Mate.

Having met Mr. Drew on several occasions while in Callao in 1906 I was able to converse with him on the most friendly terms, and as a result spent some pleasant evenings at his home. Sunday being a holiday, I went ashore and spent the day sightseeing in Lima and visited the cathedral, a magnificent structure, which I believe dates from the Spanish conquest of South America, wherein the embalmed body of Pizzaro the Conqueror lies in state.

To me the most impressive building in the city was the beautiful church of Iglesia La Mercea, with a massive façade and central arched doorway between projecting walls rising in three tiers, supported by turned pillars with inset statues and intricate carving decorating the entire front of the structure.

Back on board, after an exciting day ashore, I found the Captain had made arrangements to sail on the morrow, if possible.

Our crew had now been augmented by a bosun, signed on at a wage of £4 per month, a seaman at £3 per month, and a cook at £4 10s. per month. The surplus coal had been discharged and the hold at both ends thoroughly swept down and prepared for a few hundred tons of guano, which would have to be loaded at Santa Island before our ballast in the main hold could be discharged overside. One of the Pacific Steam Navigation Company's steamers had arrived, and the scene, both on board her and around her, was animated as these vessels were stocked with every conceivable commodity, and assumed something of the nature of a market. Small vessels, called balandras, were transhipping cargo, and buying all sorts of produce, equipment, and edible stores for villages along the coast, while buyers from the shore in small boats called fleteros and challoopas vied with each other to gain a favourable position alongside the steamer, from which to receive the goods purchased on board for cash.

In the midst of this animated scene, under the glare of arc lamps illuminating the sides of the steamer, as she rode at anchor in the darkness of early evening, the Old Man, and myself, in two of the ship's boats, ranged alongside, after spirited encounters with boatmen, and finally got on board and loaded the boats with stores of all kinds for our impending voyage.

These included large stocks of English tobacco, also cigarettes, men's wearing apparel, for the Master's slop chest, to be sold to all and sundry at a suitable profit.

With all our purchases made we cast off and pulled away into the darkness towards the tapering masts and spars of the *Caithness-Shire*, which lay dark and silent on the still waters of the bay, awaiting in all readiness the dawn of another sailing day.

17

TOWARDS SANTA ISLAND

GETTING under way from an open roadstead in a sailing ship, without the assistance of a tug, always involved much activity and hard work for all hands, even the tradesmen, carpenters, sailmakers, and sometimes the cook, whose duties were normally confined to their respective trades, being called out to assist in the pully-hauly on deck which accompanied the manœuvre. At the crack of dawn on April 21st, 1910, the Master called the Mate and myself up from the saloon, where we were having early morning coffee and instructed us in the manœuvre he intended to execute.

'Get all hands on deck at once, Mr. Laird,' he said to the Mate. 'Man the capstan, and heave the cable short. There is a light breeze off the land, and very little swell so she should come round easily if we get sail on her smartly.'

Yelling 'All hands on deck,' the Mate and I walked forrard and hustled the men on deck to the forecastle head where the capstan bars were shipped, and to the rhythm of the shanty 'Stamp and Go' the men toiled round and round, as the cable came slowly in over the wildcat of the windlass below, and was flaked in the chain locker by a man stationed there with a chain hook. With the 15-fathom shackle of the cable in sight in the clear water of the bay all hands were sent to breakfast for half an hour while the Old Man settled down to some final business with Mr. Drew, our agent, who had come on board with detailed instructions from the government contractor, who was to load the ship, as to where we were to anchor at Santa Island. After seeing Mr. Drew off at the gangway, the Old Man mounted the poop ladder and galvanised everyone into action, as orders came thick and fast.

'Starboard watch, man the capstan. Port watch, starboard forebraces. Two boys aloft and loose the fore upper and lower topsails. Two boys the main, lively now, lads. How's your cable growing, Mr. Mate?'

'Cable up and down, sir.'

'All right, heave away. Let me know when your aweigh,' and to me 'Sheet home the fore lower topsail, mister.'

Things were now reaching the climax.

'Anchors aweigh, sir,' comes the cry from the Mate.

'Hard up the helm, m'son,' roars the Old Man. 'Set the fore topmast staysail and inner jib. Stand by the port fore braces.'

The ship's head was now paying off before the wind, with the foreyards aback, and the head sails set.

After a pause came the orders, 'Square the foreyards. Upper topsail halliards to the capstans, steady as you go, m'son,' to the man at the wheel.

With the ship under control, moving slowly before the wind with the yards square, the tension eases. On the forecastle head the Mate cats the anchor, while the Second Mate roars out orders, as sail after sail is set to the light off-shore breeze, and the ship gathers way until, under a cloud of billowing white canvas, she clears the bay, and shapes a course northward in the open sea.

Our course and distance to Santa Island was North, True, 183 miles which, with a strong fair wind, we should have sailed in twenty-four hours, but, with the ship's bottom foul from immersion for nearly a year, and light winds as our only motive power, it seemed probable this short coastal voyage would be a repetition of our ambling gait over the 500 miles from Iquique to Callao.

In the dining saloon we were all agreed that we now had a good crowd of seamen in the foc's'les. Working the ship out of Callao Bay under sail had been the crucial test, and their instinctive reaction and response to a spate of orders in a crowded half-hour had put the hall-mark of efficient seamen upon them.

With only a short run to our loading port it was necessary to have the hold ready to receive cargo on our arrival, and the watches on deck were kept in the hold, to work the levelled ballast back as far as possible to make clear floor space for the guano, for loading would probably start as soon as the Master was able to notify the charterers that the ship was ready to receive cargo. These considerations meant nothing to the crew, who preferred seamanship jobs about the decks, or aloft, in the warm tropical sunshine, but to the Master, whose competence was judged in terms of distributed profits to shareholders, they were of paramount importance. An April 24th, three days after leaving Callao, we sighted Santa Island, some eight miles distant off the starboard bow, and with a light south-east breeze on our starboard quarter, closed in towards our destination.

Santa is actually a group of two steep rocky islands, separated at the northern end by a narrow channel, only twenty yards wide, the southern, or largest, island, being about one and a quarter miles long and one-third of a mile across at its widest point, with a range of hills rising to 445 and 475 feet, laying nearly north north-west and south south-east through the centre of the island, which lies about two miles distant from the mainland.

There is no lighthouse, or any aids to navigation. Our orders were to anchor on the eastern side of the southern island and the government contractor, who was to load us, had erected a flag pole from which a red flag was to be flown to enable the island to be identified from seaward, as, against the range of mountains rising from 1,200 to 2,000 feet, less than one mile inshore on the mainland, Santa Island appeared as part of the coastal range.

With light winds, calms, and fogs as the prevailing weather conditions, it was difficult to identify and approach the island as it was too hazardous to coast along close inshore, with the possibility of the wind dying away and leaving the

F

ship becalmed, or enveloped in fog close in on a rock-bound coast, and from a distance off-shore, as we have seen, the island was indistinguishable from the dominating land masses behind. There was, however, one aid to navigation which Providence had seen fit to establish for the guidance of worried mariners, the millions of birds which appeared as a dark cloud over the island, isolating it from the sombre and forbidding background, as they wheeled and scurried high above a definite rocky eminence, in a vast and continuous armada of pulsating wings and screeching throats, as a ghostly apparition, with towering pyramids of canvas, gleaming in the dazzling sunshine, glided silently towards their hallowed orbit, to invade and destroy their solitudes.

Making about three knots, we steered for the passage, two miles wide, between Santa Island and the mainland, sailing along only one mile distant from the high precipitous cliffs which ranged down sheer into sixty feet of water, studded for three miles from Point Chimbote to Bahiade Caisco with isolated rocks protruding from the sea, close in to the cliffs, and the Cerro de Chimbote, a mountain of 1,950 feet only a half-mile inland, dominating a wild and inspiring range of six mountain peaks, compressed within a distance of only two miles.

With Point Santa, a promontory on the mainland, dead ahead, we passed the southern point of Santa Island, ghosting along with the sails alternately hanging from the yards, and bellying out to the light gusts which traversed the valleys and gullies of the land barrier, rising as an inpenetrable wall to the intrusion of the trade wind into the sheltered anchorage of unruffled water.

With the t'gans'ls stowed, we drifted in under four tops'ls, inner jib and spanker, with all hands standing by for the last orders which would bring the ship to anchor.

At the fore braces, awaiting the order to brace up the yards as we rounded to, the conversation and exclamations of the men were illuminating: 'Jumping snakes, Ike, look at that', as a cloud of birds took off, screeching and bawling from a nearby cliff, frightened by the sound of the upper topsail

yards coming down with a run, and the hoarse cries of the
men hauling on the downfalls and buntlines, 'Stand from
under there, me bullies', as a rain of bird-droppings came
down from the squarking armada passing overhead.

With the helm hard down, and the yards braced up, we
rounded up to the wind, shattering the stillness with an
almighty roar and rattle as the anchor plunged to the
bottom, and sixty fathoms of heavy chain cable clanked and
clattered out through the hawse pipe.

The response by the local inhabitants was instantaneous
and amazing. From the length and breadth of the island there
arose a thunderous volume of ear-splitting cries and screeches
as a vast cloud of birds soared into the sky, churning the air
with a drumming beat of thousands of wings to circle wildly
above and about the ship in protest at the violation of their
sanctuary.

Around the base of the cliffs a rising crescendo of barks and
grunts focussed the attention, as hundreds of seals and sea-
lions slithered off the flat rocks at the water's edge, and
churned the water into seething foam as they swam aim-
lessly around the ship. Apparently satisfied, and lulled into
tranquillity by the cessation of alarming noise, they laboriously climbed out of the water and resumed a sleeping
posture on the sun-warmed rocks so recently vacated.

It was about 4 p.m. when at last the sails were stowed,
ropes coiled up, and the ship settled down after the turmoil
of the past hour, so the crew were sent below to idle about
until the cook was ready with the dry hash, which was the
tea menu for the day.

We now had time to look about us and take stock of the
surroundings, which Mr. Drew in Callao had assured me
would probably be our anchorage for several months and
the scene and probabilities did not appear inspiring. On the
island desolation prevailed, not a blade of grass, tree or sign
of vegetation was to be seen, only patches of red-brown
ammonia-laden deposits of guano, apparently forty or
fifty feet deep in places, interlaced with layers of sand, blown
by the wind from the mainland over centuries of time. Six

miles to the south-eastward of us, around the high bluff of Point Chimbote, lay the small town of Chimbote, with a hospital, churches and some of the conveniences of civilisation.

The waters in which we lay were teeming with fish, and, with wild-fowl and tropical fruit nearby as a reward for sailing or pulling three miles to the shore. The prospects of a change of diet from bully beef and salt horse were most encouraging.

As the dark mantle of night closed in about us the stillness was oppressive. Not a light was to be seen beyond the ship, not a breath of air stirred the clammy atmosphere, the dark water lay still and silent over the teeming life which roamed its depths, while ashore the cormorants, gulls, terns, and guanos lay undisturbed, except for an occasional plaintive cry from one whose privacy was being invaded.

18

SANTA ISLAND

CHIMBOTE, a small seaport about four and a half miles to the south of our anchorage off Santa Island, is situated in a rich coal and iron ore area, about four miles inland from the high coastal range of mountains on the northern shore of Bahia Ferral Bay, reached by passing through Passji Del Norte, a channel separating Point Chimbote from Blanca Island. The land around Bahia Ferral Bay is a bare sandy plain, with some slight vegetation at the northern end, adjacent to the town of Chimbote.

From Chimbote the railway runs north to Tambo Real, a large sugar plantation area, and thence to Huaras.

The mountain scenery is really beautiful in this region, and nearby are to be found the stone ruins of the Chavin civilisation, said to have been between third and the seventh centuries. The people are small in stature and rather unapproachable, but friendly to strangers who can converse with them in their own language.

With my previous long sojourn in the West Coast ports of South America while serving in the *British Isles*, I had acquired a working knowledge of the language, and was therefore able to have some disjointed conversation with those I met as I wandered at large ashore during some week-ends, usually on a hired horse, or mule, visiting Tambo Real, only four miles from the village of Santa, or to the village of Coisco, in the Bahia de Coisco Bay directly opposite our anchorage. Only three miles from Santa Village, where we collected mail and provisions, there were some stone ruins of Inca houses. These we explored many times, digging here and there in the hope of uncovering some relics of a bygone age in the form of pottery, jewellery, or other trinkets, but instead uncovered several scorpions.

Our programme, as unfolded by the contractor who was to load us, was not very encouraging. We learned that labourers were to shovel the guano into bags over an area as close as possible to where the ship lay at anchor, and stack them on the cliff-top, from where they would be run down a chute to the boats below, manned by Lancheros, which would ply between ship and shore.

When the adjacent deposit had been worked out, the ship was to kedge along to one, or more, convenient areas until the loading was complete.

For a week we did nothing but make preparations, rigging a stage from the main hatch to the topgallant rail, to enable the ballast to be dumped overside in baskets, hoisted out of the hold by the donkey engine. Similar preparations were made at the fore and after hatches for loading a stiffening quantity of guano, by hoisting single bags, with a dolly winch, on the stage between the ship's side rail and the hatchway, and tipping the contents of the bags into the hold, until there was sufficient weight of guano in the ship to enable all the ballast we had brought from Iquique to be dumped overside.

Thereafter we were to load guano into the main hatch in sling loads of bags, hoisted in by the donkey engine.

The weather each day was perfect, with the sun a fiery ball shining out of a cloudless blue sky, the placid waters of the anchorage a deep transparent blue, in which shoals of fish scurried to and fro, while hundreds of birds dived into the shoals and flew away with silvery fish in their beaks.

Starting at 6 a.m. each morning, except Sundays, the work went on till 6 p.m. with an hour each for breakfast and dinner, the shore labourers digging out the guano, and filling the sacks, which were carried to the dumping ground on the edge of the cliff, where a large sieve was erected through which the guano was passed to exclude foreign matter, and was then re-bagged and stacked until sufficient was available to keep the lighters going. Usually this took two or three days, the men ashore working in the blazing sun, with streams of water running from their eyes, and bodies caked with sweat and ammonial dust which burned into their skin, swinging their shovels around their heads when inquisitive birds flew around them with flapping wings and screeching cries.

As nearby deposits became exhausted and more distant areas were worked, donkeys were used to carry the bags to the loading point. On board the ship conditions were little better than they were ashore. Clouds of ammonial dust rose out of the hold, and were carried by the breeze into the saloon, cabins, and crew's quarters in the foc's'le, where beds, blankets, and wearing apparel were impregnated, and unless great care was taken even the food and water were perfumed with ammonia. It was not every day that cargo, even when stacked, could be brought off, as a swell sometimes rolled into the anchorage and would break against the rocks. This made it dangerous for lighters to approach, consequently every advantage was taken of these conditions by the charterer's agents to claim surf days, when no cargo was available for shipment, and many arguments eventuated as to why lighters could not be loaded on days when conditions appeared to the Master to be reasonable for such purpose.

After work ceased for the day the hatches were put on and the decks washed down, to make the ship more habitable. The contractor, and sometimes a chemist, who took samples for analysis, would come on board for tea and stay through the evening yarning as we lounged on the poop on improvised canvas stretchers under the awning, the incessant squarks and cries of the birds stilled, and, save for the murmur of human voices from the huts and tents ashore, not a sound broke the stillness of the night.

Of mosquitoes, flies, and insects there were none, the rock surface of the island offered nothing to the denizens of more fertile pastures, and we slept, or went about our daily tasks, undisturbed by the pests which pursue civilisation. It was always a pleasure to yarn with Señor Carlos, our contractor, about life on the coast and I learned a lot about the country and his work and experiences among the islands.

At the Chincha Islands, about ninety miles south of Callao, millions of tons of guano had been shipped to different parts of the world during the later years of the nineteenth century. Some of these deposits were 100 feet deep, and could be shovelled directly into a chute down the cliff-face into boats, which were loaded in a few minutes.

In his memoirs Captain David Cowans says that in 1850 his ship the *Collector* was loaded with about 1,000 tons of guano in from six to seven hours, down a chute directly into the hatchway as the ship lay moored alongside the cliff. Those immense deposits are gone now, together with the large fleet of sailing-ships which plied in that trade and the Chinese coolies and Peruvian convicts who toiled and sweated in the vast accumulations of bird-droppings.

What now remains is rigidly controlled by the Peruvian Government. Further south, on the headlands of the Chilean coast, there are many similar deposits which attracted ships during the boom period of the guano trade, but some were dangerous anchorages for sailing-ships owing to earthquakes and subterranean upheavals.

Mr. F. W. Wallace, in his book *In the Wake of the Wind Ships,* Hodder and Stoughton, 1927, gives the following vivid account of the catastrophe which occurred in the roadstead of Pabellon de Pica, a guano port, on May 9th, 1877. 'It was a quiet evening until about 11 p.m. when the ships began to swing around their anchors. There being no wind, this unusual disturbance brought the crew out, and, the rotary movement continuing with considerable force, before long the deep laden ships began to break adrift from their anchorages and career among the shipping. From a quiet peaceful spot the anchorage became a maelstrom of terror and tumult. There was no raging sea, naught but rotary currents of immense force, there was no wind and the stars twinkled clear from an unclouded sky. Yet the currents, twisting the ships from their anchors, sent them crashing into another throughout the night. Some foundered, others crashed on to the rocks, many were dismasted and drifted about with their topsides stove in and sides scarred by drifting wreckage. Launches were swamped and smashed on the beach, and the sea rose and submerged the town of Pabellon de Pica, sweeping hundreds into eternity.'

At our anchorage we were not disturbed by any unusual phenomenon and the ship lay quietly riding to the wind, and, occasionally, in the dead calms, laying broadside on to the swell which rolled in from the Pacific Ocean. Being only 540 miles from the Equator we had expected the weather to be unbearably hot but in the hottest part of the day, the forenoon, the temperature seldom rose above ninety degrees, and at night the average was about sixty degrees. These conditions are said to be due to the cool Peruvian current which flows northward along the coast.

In the ship's hold conditions were very different, the sun beating down on the steel sides of the ship raised the temperature to, at times, on calm days, 120 degrees, and in this inferno men had to work, shovelling the guano up under the deck while buried to their knees in the stinking mass of ammonial matter, choking in the fog of fine dust which filled the hold, and bathed in a lather of sweat and grime.

Once a week I took the gig, manned by four boys, to the village of Santa for provisions and mail, and to take the Captain and his wife ashore, or call for him when he had remained ashore. These trips were a pleasant change from the conditions on board. Usually we set out early in the morning, and rowed the three and a half miles to the village, and for most of the day roamed about, but found little of interest in the small settlement and among people who we could not intelligently converse with, although, by their gestures, they wanted to be friendly.

In the late afternoon, to avoid beating up under sail against the trade wind, when returning to the ship, we usually rowed along parallel to the sandy beach by the lagoons until opposite the ship, when we were able to hoist the sail and run down to the anchorage with a fair wind.

Our dreams of wildfowl on the ship's menu did not eventuate although we landed several times on the beach by the lagoons and stalked the birds with a rifle, but beyond a few near misses the results were negative, except to provide an amazing spectacle as hundreds of birds took to the air *en masse*.

On the other side of the island there were several caves, which we explored by climbing down the cliff-face to those above sea level, and in the boat to those which the action of the sea, over thousands of years, had hewn out of the rock face. Some of these caves were very large, and being open to the sea might well have been used by pirates in the days when Spanish galleons sailed from Callao laden with treasure, but our exhaustive search revealed nothing but rock, against which the Pacific swell broke in a booming and reverberating cannonade.

These excursions were a small break in the monotony of life on board, as week followed week, and month followed month, in a dreary routine of work, eat, and sleep, which frayed the nerves. Every tune played on a mouth-organ in the still, cool, air of the evening, by the men sprawled about the decks, jarred on the senses. You had heard them a hundred times before. Everything about you seemed changeless, men became morose and drifted into the seclusion of silence, weary and waiting, waiting only for the day when we would again feel the thrust and surge of the ship as she listed to the pressure of the clean salt-laden wind, and moved again in her predestined element.

During the first week of September we were loading the last hundred tons of our cargo, and preparing the ship for sea. There was much to be done in overhauling gear aloft which had lain under a coating of ammonial dust in a hot sun for months, to make sure it was not rotted, bending the foresail and mainsail, which had been sent down to enable the yards to be used for handling cargo, stowing away awnings, dismantling cargo gear and stages at the hatchways, and cleaning up the mess in lockers and accommodation which day to day efforts of the steward, cook and peggies had failed to completely eradicate.

19

A MAD DOG TAKES CHARGE

During the forenoon on September 9th, 1910, four months and fifteen days after our arrival at Santa Island, we hove short the anchor cable, loosed the sails, and let them hang in their gear in the warm sunshine, while awaiting the freshening of the trade wind which would carry us away from this desolate region towards the civilisation which had for so long been denied us.

The crew were in a gay mood, and needed no urging to the many tasks which departure from our anchorage entailed.

By 2 p.m. a fresh breeze was blowing from the south-east and all hands were sent to stations for getting under way. The ship was riding to the south-east wind, and with the fore yards aback, would cast her head away from the island into the open water of Bahia de Corsco Bay, ready to turn northward and round the island into the open sea.

With the cable hove in short, and the helm hard up, the fore lower topsail was sheeted home, and the ship's head sheered away to port, the men on the forecastle head heaving around the capstan to the rhythm of the shanty 'Rolling Home', until the welcome cry of 'Anchors aweigh!' brought forth the usual spate of orders from the Master on the poop.

By this time the ship's head had paid off until the wind was abeam, so the fore yards were hauled around to fill the lower topsail, the jibs were run up, and the main lower topsail sheeted home on the yards, which had already been squared in. With the wind on the starboard quarter the ship forged ahead past the northerly extremity of the island, as sail after sail was set, and we felt again the surge and heave of the ocean swell.

Under full sail we stood away, close-hauled on the port tack, to the south-westward, on our long voyage around Cape Horn to Wilmington in North Carolina, but unlike a steamer, we could not traverse a direct route, against winds and ocean currents, but had to sail away westward into the Pacific Ocean to get clear of the coastal current, setting northward along the coast of Chile and Peru.

As darkness set in we lost sight of the coastline, as mist enshrouded the high mountain range of the Andes, sixty miles inland, and the low-lying islands and hills in the foreground were merged into the deepening shadow of the land masses. With the watches picked, the sea routine again prevailed but there was much to be done, and for at least the next three months there would never be an idle moment for the watch on deck, as a survey of the ship disclosed the havoc which a mantle of ammonial dust could cause. Day after day, as we sailed south-westward in a steady trade wind, the clang of chipping hammers shattered the daylight hours, as white paintwork was scaled or chipped off, and the steel primed and made ready for the finishing coats of paint which would be applied after Cape Horn had been rounded, and the fine-weather latitudes of the Atlantic Ocean reached.

Losing the south-east trade wind in Lat. 25°S. we entered the wide belt of the variable winds and calms of Capricorn, which, at this season, extended for nearly a thousand miles, working the ship along by the unremitting toil of pully-hauly, as the yards were trimmed to catch every breath of air.

One afternoon as we lay becalmed, rolling gently in an undulating ocean swell, in my watch on deck, the wheel had just been relieved at four bells, 2 p.m., and with the exception of the man aloft on the main upper topsail yard, fitting a new lift which had been made, and one of the apprentices seizing on battens in the mizzen shrouds, the rest of the watch were spread at intervals along the bulwarks, scaling and priming.

It was a very hot day, with the sun blazing down relentlessly from a clear blue sky, softening the pitch in the deck planks, which squelched under the tread of the men's boots as they moved restlessly in cramped positions by the bulwarks as they wielded slices and scrapers on the hot steel plates, or wandered away forrard under the foc's'le head for a surreptitious smoke, while renewing the edge of their scrapers on the grindstone.

Suddenly the air was rent by savage growls as Crokie, the huge bull-mastiff, which had been stretched out on the poop deck, in the shade of the saloon skylight, panting and slavering at the mouth, leapt to his feet, and, bounding down the ladder, tore along the main deck with foam-flecked gaping jaws and blazing eyes, scattering paint pots, brushes and brooms in a mad rush forrard, where he crouched under the foc's'le head emitting savage yelps and growls.

As he tore past, the men working on the main deck stood petrified for a moment before raising a piercing cry of 'Mad dog, mad dog,' as they jumped for the rigging, and climbed up beyond the reach of the animal as it retraced its steps along the main deck, and headed for the open door into the poop accommodation.

At the first cry of 'Mad dog', I ran from where I was standing, near the man at the wheel, to the rail at the forward end of the poop deck, the men in the rigging yelling to me, 'Crokie's gone mad, mister. He's forrard under the foc's'le head. There he is, he's coming aft again. Christ, look at the bastard! Look out there, Joe, he'll tear you to pieces.'

From the watch below a man stepped out of the foc's'le to see what the commotion was about, but one look at the savage dog, crouching ready to spring at him, was enough to make Joe leap back into the foc's'le and slam the door shut, before a huge body crashed against it.

Diving down the poop ladder I jumped into the alleyway and slammed shut the door which led on to the main deck, rousing the Old Man and the Mate with a yell into their cabins of 'Crokie's gone mad,' as I raced up the companionway to the poop and barricaded the top of the ladder from the main deck, so the dog could not get on to the poop and attack the man at the wheel, who with blanched face, and trembling hands on the spokes, eyed the mizzen rigging, his only hope of salvation, if the beast should suddenly appear.

With the centre of the poop deck isolated by the chart-house and cabin skylight structures, any approach to the wheel must come from one side of the deck leaving the other free for a hasty dash to safety in the nearby mizzen rigging.

Within minutes of the first warning cry, all doors on the main deck had been slammed shut, and at every port-hole tense faces peered out trying to see what was happening, and every few minutes their vigil was rewarded by a momentary glimpse of a huge and ferocious animal bounding past in its continuous traverse of the deserted deck, of which it was now the undisputed master.

Coming up to the poop deck from his cabin, the Old Man surveyed the dismal scene in silence for a few moments, looking aloft at the sails, idly backing and filling on the squared-in yards, as light draughts of air breathed into them from the starboard quarter. Earlier in the afternoon a squall of wind and rain, from our star'bd side, had sent the hands running to the braces to haul the yards around, and we forged ahead perhaps two or three miles before again being becalmed, with the heat even more oppressive than before.

On the horizon a dark cloud had been rising for the past half-hour, and it was evident another squall from that quarter would soon be upon us. Something had to be done, and done quickly, with a squall bearing down on us from the starboard bow, on a ship with deserted decks, and the helm useless, as she lay dead in the water, unable to bear away before the oncoming squall, or stand by braces and t'gal'nt halliards to trim the yards, or take in sail, if the wind in the squall should prove to be of great velocity. Running below, the Old Man reappeared, a moment later, with a rifle, and a revolver which he handed to me.

'Watch your chance, mister, and make a dash for the top of the apprentices' deck-house. I am going down on to the

main deck, and when the dog rushes me I will empty the
gun into him as he passes the foc's'le, but if I miss, or don't
stop him, empty your gun into him, while I run up the poop
ladder, but don't fire until he is close enough so you cannot
miss.'

In the rigging the men chatted excitedly among themselves, snatches of their conversation and remarks reaching
us on the poop.

'I wouldn't get down on that deck for quids, Bos,' a man
named Fraser suggested to the Bosun.

'Don't you believe it, Jack, you may bloody well have to,
or all hell will break loose around here if that squall takes us
aback.'

Sure enough, on the horizon a white line of broken water,
thrown into relief by the dense black cloud poised above it,
was moving directly towards us, and unless the yards could
be hauled around on to the backstays, we must inevitably be
caught aback, and with all sail set, this would probably
mean some sails being blown away, or even being dismasted
if the squall was very heavy. There was not a moment to be
lost if disaster was to be avoided.

For the last few minutes the dog had been under the foc's'le
head, emitting savage growls. It was now necessary to
entice him out, and only a human target would suffice.
Yelling to a man in the fore rigging to jump down on deck
for a moment and attract the dog's attention, the Old Man
stood calmly awaiting developments, while casting apprehensive glances towards the advancing squall.

Jumping to the deck, a man named Davis whistled to the
dog, which immediately whirled about, and rushed towards
him, as he leaped on to the pin rail, and up the rigging, the
momentum of the dog's rush carrying him along the deck
to where he could see the Old Man.

Crouching for a moment, growling ferociously, with foam-
flecked jaws, the huge brute suddenly lunged forward and
rushed straight for the Old Man, who, standing like a rock
in its path, pumped shot after shot into the brute's head and
breast until it collapsed on the deck, not ten feet from

where he stood, with three shots also in its body which I had managed to get home from my safe perch on the deck-house.

'Lee fore brace, hard up the helm, stand by t'gal'nt halliards,' roared the Old Man, as he ran for the poop ladder, leaving the great carcase lying in a pool of blood, where it had dropped.

'Lower away t'gal'nt halliards, lively there, lads,' as the first blast of the squall drove into the top-hamper, and stretched the drooping canvas into rigid concaves of driving power, which heeled the ship over as she turned away before the blast, faithfully answering the helm, which once again controlled her destiny.

In 38°S. Lat. and 85°W. Long., we picked up the first of the westerly winds, and set a course to the eastward of south for our run down to Cape Horn, where we could expect to encounter the last of the winter gales in mid-October.

All preparations were now made for bad weather, with heavy deal planks lashed down over the main hatch, life-lines stretched along each side of the main deck, extra lashings on the anchors on the forecastle head, and lifeboats on the after skids and forward deck-house, relieving tackles rove off to the steering gear, and preventer lashings, to the spare spars on the main deck.

As we got deeper into the Roaring Forties the westerly wind backed into the north-north-west and the barometer began to fall.

With all sail set we tore along with the yards nearly square, and the wind a point on the starboard quarter, making ten knots in a moderate following sea. These, the first few hours of a rising gale, are, as nearly as possible, the ideal sailing conditions with a fair wind. The moderate sea impedes the progress of the vessel very little as it is driven onward by the force of a strong wind steering a straight and steady course.

Hour after hour we stormed along, keeping well to the westward, while making as much southing as possible before the wind hauled into the south-west, and we had to brace the yards up and bring the wind abeam to maintain our course.

As the afternoon waned into evening, the blur of a distorted sun sank behind the dense masses of cloud banked high and menacing round the western horizon, their upper formation an ever-changing pattern of dark and light patches, as they rose slowly into the heavens, against the reflected light of the afterglow, as they faded out in the darkening sky. The following sea began to rise, the white caps of the waves no longer a quiet profusion extending as far as the eye could reach, but a seried expanse of tumbling water moulded into cresting hills, with creamy foam breaking from the smother as the roaring wind caressed and imposed its will on the surface of the sea which surrounded us.

In the six to eight dog-watch the Master came out from the chart-house on the poop, where he had been working out the ship's position

Standing beside me, as I stood at the weather rail, he said, 'Get everything ready, mister, to haul up and stow the mainsail at eight bells with all hands, then haul the staysails down with the watch.'

As the apprentice on the poop struck eight bells the Mate came on deck and roared out, 'All hands haul the mainsail up, man the clew garnets and buntlines. You take the starboard sheet, mister, and I will look after the port. Ease away together when I give the word.'

It was now blowing hard and the huge sail was bellied out as stiff as a board, with both wire sheets from the clews through the leads in the bulwarks to the main-deck capstans humming with vibration under the tremendous strain. As we slacked away the sheets the men hauled the sail up to the chant of 'Haul, we heigh, we ho, haul, with a will heigh-ay,' until it lay snug in the buntlines, close up under the yard.

'Up and stow,' roared the Mate. 'Go aloft with them, mister, and see it is well secured in the gaskets.'

Fortunately the canvas was still dry, and in less than half an hour we had the sail secured in a harbour stow. With the wheel and lookout relieved, and the watch sent below,

I turned into my bunk for the three hours' well-earned repose.

At a quarter to midnight an apprentice of the watch on deck opened my cabin door and sang out, 'One bell, sir,' while at the same time crossing over to light the oil lamp, fixed to the bulkhead.

'What is the weather like, Wilson?' I asked.

'Blowing hard from the north-west, mister,' he answered. 'The Mate says we are in for a snorter.'

Going on deck to relieve the Mate, I found the Old Man himself was on the poop, standing near the wheel, watching the steering. The upper t'gan'sls had been taken in, and the ship was tearing along as the Old Man tried to get every mile out of her before the rising sea cut her down.

About 1 a.m. in the darkness astern we saw a welter of foam, and a moment later a terrific squall slammed into the pyramids of canvas, bearing the ship down until the sea flooded in over the lee rail. Jumping to the wheel, the Old Man seized the spokes on the lee side, and helped the man at the weather side to keep the ship steady, as she was yawing badly in the heavy sea, under the press of sail she was carrying.

All through an anxious night the Old Man drove her down into the Howling Fifties. Squall after squall screamed out of the black void about us, where sea and sky seemed merged by a veil of rain and sleet, which thundered down and tore at the labouring ship. With the coming of dawn there was a lull in the velocity of the wind, and advantage was taken of this to furl the lower t'gan'sls. The ship, which previously had been vibrating under the strain of being driven deep into the seas, now rode easier as the lower topsail sheets were eased off, and the upper topsail yards eased down, to give more lifting power to the sails, but she still yawed badly, and it was necessary to have a second man continually at the wheel.

20

AROUND CAPE HORN

THE dawn is an inspiring sight from the deck of a ship traversing the storm-swept seas of the Southern Ocean, and the dawn which was now breaking about us was no exception

As the hidden sun rises higher into the heavens, the faint red glow on the horizon spreads in a deepening hue over the eastern sky, until it is bathed in a blood-red mantle. Shafts of evil-looking green, yellow and grey tinge the upper layers of the cloud masses, as the pattern of their contours continually change before the onslaught of the screaming wind, which tears them asunder. The dense black cloud to windward breaks in a withering squall, which pours forth a deluge of hail and sleet, to wipe from our sight all else but the seething cauldron of sea immediately about us.

'Hard up the helm, m'son,' shouts the Old Man, as the wind shifts suddenly in a squall, and blows from abeam. 'Lee fore brace, lively now, mister, let the yards run forrard a point. I am bearing away now to south-east.'

Fortunately the speed of the ship through the water saved her from being taken aback, as she answered her helm, and paid off, while we slacked away the weather braces and let the pressure of the wind carry the yards forrard. Squall now followed squall in rapid succession, the Cape Horn snorter had the ship in its savage grip, tearing at her with a wind of hurricane velocity, which howled and screamed as it vomited a deluge of water over her, torn from the foaming crests of the towering greybeards to cover the raging sea in a smoking vapour.

Hour after hour, and day after day, we tore along, sighting several ships during daylight hours, hove to under lower topsails, one moment reeling high, as a mountainous sea passed under them, pouring water in cascades from their flooded decks through gaping washports, to vanish from sight the next, leaving only the white sails, with bare masts and yards above them, protruding from the sea at a crazy angle. As we ran before the gale huge seas rose up and towered high above the stern, as it sank into a trough, threatening at any moment to break over the ship in a devastating avalanche which could destroy the wheel and everything in its path.

Again and again, after a sickening moment of suspense, in which the men at the wheel cast frightened glances over their shoulders, the stern would rise as a great comber broke and roared over for the kill, carrying the ship forward, as the sea parted and flooded in over both rails to fill the deck in a raging torrent which surged to a boiling cauldron in the waist as the greybeard expended its fury and the bows sank into the depths behind the receding wall of water.

Unceasing vigiliance was necessary in steering the ship to avoid broaching to, that is, the ship becoming out of control when the stern is lifted high by a following sea, and the rudder left half out of the water.

Many ships have foundered, or been dismasted, by broaching to, and its possibility was an ever-present anxiety to those whose duty it was to sail ships through these tempestuous waters. Being pooped was another peril of the sea which resulted in the loss, or disablement, of many ships in the Southern Ocean. With the stern deep in the trough before a sea forty or fifty feet high, roaring out of the darkness towards the fleeing ship, the man, or men, steering, and the Master and Mates on the poop, stood in danger of being swept into eternity, or maimed, by the mountain of water, if it broke over the stern, and the records show the appalling damage such seas have done to ships running before these ferocious gales.

Yet again the prevalence of icebergs on the route around

Cape Horn was a hazard which claimed many victims in the days of sail.

Many ships have been embayed in fields of bergs and foundered, owing to being becalmed under a mass of ice, rising hundreds of feet out of the water, or sailing head on into a berg enshrouded in the mist and fog prevalent at some seasons in these waters.

Standing on the poop, as the officer of the watch, in sole control while the Master is below, running before a gale, is an experience never to be forgotten, particularly during the hours of darkness. All around you the roar of the wind, and crash of breaking seas beats upon your ears, the dim light in the compass binnacle at your side shines through a blur of snow or sleet, which an apprentice, on watch with you, wipes away. You feel, rather than see, the helmsman, a muffled figure with water streaming from his oilskins, laboriously heaving at the spokes of the wheel to counter the yaw of the ship, as the hammer-blows of the sea turn her from her course.

Gazing aloft every few minutes you see the outline of bulging canvas, stretched almost beyond endurance, and frozen into rigidity by the roaring wind, laden with needles of ice, coming from the frozen regions of Antarctica. Only an occasional hurried glance to windward is possible in the face of the deluge of sleet, snow, and spindrift driven towards you by the great wind, but you see nothing, as the range of visibility in any direction is perhaps only a few hundred yards.

In these crowded waters many ships may lie in your path, hove to, or head reaching in the gale, as they struggle westward. Their side-lights, in stump lighthouses, like your own, each side of the foc's'le head, immersed every few minutes in the smother of foam and spray, as the ship rolls, or dives steeply in the mountainous sea, useless to you as a warning of their presence, as the straining hull beneath you hurtles on into the darkness. Hour after hour you stand on the weather side, legs braced wide apart as you balance against the motion of the ship, clinging to the rail, or a stanchion, when a particularly heavy roll threatens to throw you across the sleet-covered deck, while freezing water runs into your sea-boots, and the howling wind whips your oilskin coat up about your waist.

Perhaps there comes a lull in the velocity and frequency of the squalls, and for the first time in an hour or more you see an horizon, and a break in the clouds to windward. Hurriedly you look at the barometer, which is very low, and has now begun to rise, and you realise in a flash what this could portend as you recall the words, 'The first small rise, after low may indicate a stronger blow.'

With mixed feelings you send the apprentice down to report the change to the Old Man, whose appearance on the poop will relieve you, for the moment, of further responsibility for the ship's safety, but may well send you wading through the icy water on the main deck to make, or take in sail, and spend an hour or more, perhaps of your watch, below, in an icy blizzard on the reeling yards aloft.

Not least of the worries which beset the Master of a sailing ship, running before a heavy and prolonged gale in the Southern Ocean, is when to heave to. With the ship reeling off 200 to 300 miles a day, towards her destination, the decision to heave to and abandon these favourable conditions is a most difficult one. Every instinct is urging him to carry on, and every hour the mighty greybeards are breaking closer, with that occasional sea of mighty proportions thundering its warning, as it towers threateningly above the stern.

Many ships have suffered the consequences of carrying on too long, with the loss of many lives, others have foundered or limped into the nearest port under jury rig, to cost many thousands of pounds in refitting, or be written off as a total loss. In five and a half days, after passing the latitude of 50°S. in the Pacific Ocean, we were in the Howling Fifties of the Atlantic Ocean.

The ship was well-found, and our No. 1 topsails and foresail had proved to be equal to the severe testing to which they had been subjected, in the heavy gales and terrific squalls they had withstood. Apart from furled sails blowing loose in the gaskets, which had to be made fast, and tangled ropes being hauled in and secured, our rounding of the Horn had occasioned little bodily risk to the crew, who, in their watch on deck, were usually kept busy under the foc's'le head where they were able to enjoy such warmth as their activities provided.

What tragic stories lie hidden on the sea-bed beneath these icy waters in the many ships which have foundered, and entombed their crews, in the furious gales, or even in calms when an avalanche of ice, smashing down on the decks, follows the resounding crash of a collision with an iceberg.

21

TOWARDS WILMINGTON

THE westerly wind drove us northward, through the Roaring Forties and into the variable winds and calms of Capricorn, extending before us for nearly a thousand miles at this season.

One day the Old Man called all hands aft. When they were mustered he came to the break of the poop and said that we were running short of provisions, and from that day the rations would have to be cut, as two casks of salt beef and one of pork had broken adrift in the bad weather and lost all the brine when they were stove. The meat, being now unfit for use, had been dumped.

In addition, the dry stores were getting low, and it was his intention to signal the first vessel we sighted, to, if possible, obtain some provisions. This was most unwelcome news, as, being a sailing-ship, we had to follow a track where the most favourable winds could be found, a track where steamers, who could steer direct from point to point, were seldom sighted, and it seemed most improbable another sailing-ship, if sighted, could spare anything from the meagre stocks usually to be found in such ships. Fortunately there was still a good stock of biscuits, pantiles as hard as flint in the lazarette tanks, and a more liberal issue of these was now made daily, with bully beef and other preserved meats of which we still had a small stock.

Picking up the south-east trade wind, in 22°S. Lat., we ran northward with a strong fair wind, making seven and sometimes eight knots, which was the best speed we could now make after fifteen months out of dry dock, and nearly eight months at anchor in ports, accumulating masses of barnacles and marine growth on the ship's submerged body.

Day followed day with every eye of those on deck scanning the horizon every now and then for signs of a ship, but the sea stretched away in a vast circle about us, devoid of any trailing smoke, or a white speck rising into the form of a sail. Passing the dreaded Cape San Roque, but well to the eastward, and, later, the island of Fernando Noronha, we carried the trade wind across the Equator, and into 5°N. Lat., where we entered the Doldrums.

Here we were held up for several days, in the calms and light breezes which prevailed, the watches below lining the rails to catch fish, which were a welcome change to the diet we had existed on during the past few weeks. During a calm day, as the sails hung limp from the yards, we hoisted the gig over the side, and the Old Man and myself, with four apprentices, rowed around the ship and were amazed at the carpet of weed which trailed out from the ship's side, and floated for a moment on the surface of the water as the ship rolled gently in the swell.

For a while we rowed about in search of turtles, but did not see any, so lay astern of the ship on a long line and started fishing, but could not understand why only the heads of some fish came up on the hooks until the Mate looked over the stern, to see how we were getting on, and suddenly yelled, 'Keep your hands out of the water, there is a shark under the boat.'

Shipping the oars, we cast off the bow line and pulled back alongside the ship with a bucket of fine fish, the Old Man prodding at the shark with a boat-hook as it swam away.

Picking up the north-east trade wind, we stood away to the north-west to make the coast of North Carolina in the vicinity of Cape Fear. After a few more days without sighting a vessel the food problem was getting acute, with the crew getting restless and complaining, so the Master decided to bear away towards the islands of the West Indies in the hope of intercepting a vessel.

One morning smoke was sighted on the horizon and much excitement prevailed, even the watch below turning out to line the rail, as they chatted among themselves in anticipation of some fresh provisions to eat, perhaps potatoes, cabbages, or other green vegetables, which they had not tasted for months, and such food was urgently required if the risk of scurvy was to be avoided.

Gradually the smoke, which trailed like a screen on the horizon disappeared, without the vessel appearing, and in disappointment all hands resumed the normal routine. Late in the afternoon another pillar of smoke indicated the presence of a vessel, but she was passing a long way off, and we never sighted her. The situation was now assuming a more serious aspect, although it was difficult to see what more could be done to avert sickness among the crew.

Two more days were passed in anxious expectation before a cloud of smoke, evidently just below the horizon, showed the presence of a steamer, which was soon in sight, steering a course which would carry her past us about four miles distant. This looked more hopeful. Not a moment was lost in hauling out the ship's numbers, name, and the international code flag signal meaning 'Short of provisions, starving', and hoisting them up on the mizzen mast, all hands watching every move of the steamer as she sailed majestically on.

As the answering pennant, meaning 'Your signal understood,' rose on the signal halliards above her bridge, the vessel, a large passenger liner, swept around in a semi-circle and headed straight for us.

To make our flags visible to the steamer we had hauled up to the wind, and now the long-awaited moment had arrived the men needed no urging as the Captain bellowed out a spate of orders to the Mate, standing ready with all hands on the main deck.

'Haul the clews, corners, of the mainsail up, Mr. Laird, haul the staysails down, and the main yards aback.'

'Hard down the helm, m'son,' to the man at the wheel,

thereby laying the ship to, in irons, while I, and a number of men in my watch, cleared away, and swung out, the port lifeboat and lowered it to the bulwark rail, while four apprentices made themselves reasonably presentable to man the boat for going alongside a passenger ship.

By this time the steamer had stopped, about a quarter of a mile from us, blowing off steam from the exhaust pipe on her funnel, which, even from that distance away, made an awful din in the relatively calm weather prevailing.

Many years later, while serving as an officer in a passenger ship, I was able, from a personal experience, to mentally re-enact the course of events which probably took place on the steamer, after we were first sighted from her bridge, by the officer of the watch—a sailing ship, well off the usual track of such vessels, flying a hoist of signal flags.

When the *Caithness-Shire* was sighted, from a distance of perhaps ten miles, it would be improbable that our signal flags could be read. The officer of the watch, reporting the situation to his Captain, would be told to acknowledge the signal when interpreted. In the meantime, under a full head of steam, the engines would be pounding out the maximum revolutions required for the speed the vessel was maintaining.

On the bridge the officer of the watch would, from time to time, endeavour to read the flag signal of the sailing-ship, without any undue anxiety, until he was finally able to read the flags, and ascertain their meaning from the international signal book. In the moments which followed, the whole peaceful routine on board would be changed to a dramatic interlude, as word reached the passengers that the vessel, now only a few miles away, was in distress, and all sports and other activities would be abandoned, as they crowded the rails of the passenger decks to watch, the expected drama unfolding before their eyes, chattering among themselves excitedly and conjuring up all sorts of fantastic situations.

Called to the bridge, the Captain would take over. Orders would now flow thick and fast, as the steamer's course was altered towards the vessel in distress, the engine-room telegraph on the bridge put to stand-by, thereby causing a mild flurry of activity in the engine room below, as the engineers tried to reduce the great pressure of steam in the boilers, in anticipation of having to stop the engines.

Called to the poop I received a letter my Captain had written and was ordered to deliver it to the Master of the steamer. This gave the name of our barque, and that of her owners, with a request for provisions, and that we be reported 'All well' to authorities ashore.

With four apprentices at the oars we pulled away towards the steamer, bucking a moderate ocean swell which, when viewed from the deck of the ship, seemed to be of slight proportions, but from about two feet above sea level, was big enough to make pulling the heavy boat a back-breaking job for the apprentices, who laboured on without complaining.

To them, as to all those watching our progress from the *Caithness-Shire*, this errand of mercy meant some good wholesome food for the next few days, and the most comforting aroma of tobacco, which was sorely needed to satisfy the longing and calm the frayed nerves of men denied for so long the comforts of civilisation.

Approaching the steamer, we saw that her rails were tightly packed with men, women and children, all agog with excitement, as they watched us pull alongside, and make fast from the bow and stern to ropes thrown down from the deck above.

With hundreds of eyes watching we sent our Captain's letter up in a bucket, which was lowered from the well deck, and then cast off the ropes and pulled clear, to avoid damage to the boat by bumping against the steel plates of the ship, as we rose and fell in the ocean swell, while alongside the steamer.

From where we lay to, perhaps fifty or sixty feet away, we had a front stall's view of the crowded decks above, from where a torrent of questions were shouted back and forth from the passengers, and those of us in the lifeboat, until some young ladies forced their way through the crowd at the ship's rail, and held up boxes of chocolate, cigarettes, and other sweets, while making gestures to us to come alongside to receive them. This, of course, was like showing a red rag to a bull, so, without more ado, we pulled alongside and were showered with gifts by many people who responded to the gesture initiated by the young ladies.

In the distance, our barque lay hove to, rolling easily, her sides streaked with rust from the rail to the water's edge, and a green field of grass rising and falling in the water alongside. From above us, batteries of binoculars explored every detail of her fabric, and cameras here and there recorded her silhouette, and took photos of her lifeboat's crew, as they gazed with envy and malice at the male escorts of charming young ladies.

We were not allowed on board, as it might have complicated health and other regulations for the steamer at her next port, but we were quite content, and enjoying the experience of again being reunited with our own kind, but were rudely awakened to realities again when ordered to haul the boat forrard to receive the stores, which were now ready for lowering into the boat. In about twenty minutes our boat was loaded down with provisions, including fresh meat, flour, vegetables, potatoes, jam, tea, sugar, coffee, medicines, and the inevitable salt beef and pork in barrels, before we finally pulled away. Cries of 'Good luck' and '*Bon voyage*' came from the onlookers, as the steamer turned on to her course, and dipped her Ensign in salute to our barque as she passed by.

Back on board we hauled up the lifeboat, and with the yards checked in for a breeze from the starboard beam, sailed slowly northward on the last leg of about 1,600 miles, the Old Man puffing away at a nice big cigar, while awaiting a tea menu of ham, salad and cheese, to round off a day of excitement and fruitful endeavour.

Fifteen days later we sighted the coast of North Carolina and closed in toward Cape Fear, at the entrance to the Fear River, on which the port of Wilmington is situated.

During the night of December 15th we sighted the Fear River light on Bauld Head, and beat in against an off-shore wind.

This is a dangerous approach for a sailing-ship during the hours of darkness, in a strong wind or thick weather, but fortunately it was a fine night, with good visibility, a moderate to rough sea, and strong wind, with no steamers about to complicate our freedom of approach. Our crew, who were now at the peak of seamanship efficiency, worked with a will, as we tacked and beat up throughout the night, and, just before daylight, hauled the mainyards aback and hove the ship to, signalling for a pilot.

As daylight came in we sighted the pilot vessel, a sailing schooner, about four miles to leeward of us. It was amazing, when she saw our signal, to see her go about, and claw into the strong wind which was now blowing, as she beat up against it to where we lay, watching in admiration her beautiful lines and perfectly rounded bilge, as she heeled over steeply under full sail.

The men who sailed that vessel most surely knew their business, and worthily upheld the great traditions of their countries' magnificent wood clippers, in which they had probably learned their trade.

With the pilot on board, we filled away under all sail, and beat in towards the entrance of the Fear River, between Bauld Head and Oak Island, coming to anchor off Southport about three miles inside the river entrance, during the forenoon of December 16th, 1910, ninety-eight days out from Santa Island, after a voyage of about 10,000 miles.

22

WILMINGTON

SAFELY anchored we awaited the arrival of our agent from Wilmington with letters from home, and orders for the disposal of our cargo, a part of which, our pilot had informed us, would have to be discharged into lighters at Southport to lighten the ship sufficiently to enable her to be towed to Wilmington.

In those days the Fear River was too shallow for a deep loaded ship, such as the *Caithness-Shire*, to navigate safely the twenty-five miles which still lay between us and our destination.

The near proximity of an American city, teeming with life, and offering such opportunities for amusement, and the diverse pleasures so dear to the hearts of seamen in a foreign port, had apparently infused new life into our crew, as they worked like beavers to get all the gear rigged for discharging cargo, and by 6 p.m. when they were sent below, the ship was ready, and awaiting the lighters, which we learned were ordered to arrive at 8 a.m. the next day.

For three days we discharged the cargo into lighters, the shore labour cursing as they grovelled in the mess below, when every shovel which was driven into the caked and settled mass of guano raised a cloud of ammonial matter, which was inhaled through nose and mouth as they coughed and spat their way deeper into the hold. With the ship lightened sufficiently we hove up the anchor, and with a pilot on board, and a tug ahead, commenced the long tow of twenty-five miles upriver to Wilmington.

Late in the afternoon of December 19th we were berthed in a slip or basin, between warehouses which bordered on the harbour at the northern end of the town. Under the direction of the foreman, a form of gantry, known as a wooden A-frame, was ranged alongside and the topping, bridge of this structure lowered across the ship above the main hatchway.

At 8 a.m. next day the work of discharging the cargo commenced, the guano being shovelled into iron tubs by men in the hold, which were hoisted up to the bridge by a steam winch, and traversed back to a hopper on the wharf, into which the cargo was dumped. From the hopper the guano was run into tram cars on overhead tracks, which were pushed by dockmen along to chutes by the railway tracks, and fed into box cars for conveyance to various destinations.

The large iron tubs, brim full, were hoisted up vertically out of the hold, spilling over some of their contents, as they were jerked from the line of their vertical progression out of the hold, to a horizontal traverse below the bridge, smothering the decks with a thick layer of dust, which mingled with the falling rain of matter ashore. As the tubs were tipped into the hoppers and box cars, the dust was carried back by the wind into every nook and cranny of the ship from stem to stern.

Throughout the day, the din and clatter of iron tubs, and shouting men, went on, as the cargo was discharged under the direction of the foreman, who manœuvred the iron tubs into position in the hold with his unvarying order to the winch driver of 'Up a hur' or 'Down a hur', the cries of the men below, floundering in the stinking mass of bird-droppings, being anything but polite, when, instead of a hur, hair, the tubs were jerked up or down a couple of feet.

At 6 a.m., when the hands were turned to, six men were found to be missing, but as their gear was still in the foc's'les it seemed probable that they were sleeping off the effects of a first night ashore, in the local gaol, or a boarding-house master's unsavoury premises. With the near proximity of large seaports like Newport News and Philadelphia, the demand for seamen was constant, and the men had a wide choice in determining where they would like to go.

There were also many opportunities ashore for steady able men in large industrial areas, where employers were not yet subject to the stringent union rules of employment in vogue today. Good seamen, flexible in mind, with a flair for adjusting themselves to any environment and situation where improvisation was an asset, were in frequent demand.

While the cargo was being discharged, the Mate and I had no opportunity to go ashore, as, to keep the ship from being hogged, we had to see that the distribution of weight in the holds was kept within the margin of safety. In consequence of this some arguments arose, with the stevedore, who deplored the waste of time involved in moving the gangs in the hold, and the bridge across the hatchway, with all the shore appliances, to work cargo out of another hatch, when the rate of discharge in tons per hour had reached a satisfactory figure.

At first the Mate was on duty all day, and myself during the night, as eternal vigilance was necessary to keep off thieves, in sea parlance 'wharf rats', who would come on board when an opportunity occurred and steal anything which would sell ashore, for a dollar or two; their cheek was amazing.

One night, while in the cabin having a cup of coffee, I heard a slight noise on the poop deck overhead and knowing there was no reason for any of the crew to be there, crept up the companion-way to investigate. As I stepped out of the chart-house door I was just in time to see the figure of a man leap from the poop rail on to the wharf, with a bundle under his arm, and calmly walk away. Running for the gangway, to give chase, I found the man who had been engaged as night watchman running aft from the galley, where he had been making a cup of tea and had seen the man jump to the wharf.

Ordering him to keep by the gangway in case the thief had a mate still on board, I started to go down the gangway, but was stopped by the watchman, who said, 'Don't be a fool,

G

mister, let him go. Those rats don't work alone; he's got pals somewhere on the lookout, they would kill you if you got in their way.' Hot-headed, and with the thought of a dressing down from the Master in the morning, I rejected the good advice given me and ran down the gangway and along the wharf in pursuit. Hearing me pounding along behind him, the thief started to run, and the chase went on through several streets until I lost sight of my quarry, after he rounded a corner. Nearing the corner I heard running feet behind me. Looking round, I found a policeman chasing me, so stopped to explain the situation to him. Pounding up to where I stood panting, with his night-stick swinging menacingly, the officer grabbed me by the arm before I could open my mouth, swung me round, and pushed me against a wall, where he frisked me in a search for arms, and told me to shut up when I tried to explain that I was chasing a thief.

Unfortunately for me, I had grabbled my Smith & Wessen revolver from my cabin before I went on to the poop, and had it, loaded, in my pocket, which, added to my unkempt appearance, satisfied the officer that I was a criminal. With a firm grip, on my arm he arrested me, and marched me off to the nearest police station.

In most sailing-ships engaged in the Cape Horn trade, to the West Coast of South America, the apprentices were the only members of the afterguard who wore a uniform cap and badge on board, and a brass-buttoned monkey jacket when going ashore; the Master and Mates wearing any old clothes on board, particularly when such dirty cargo as coal or guano was being discharged or loaded.

In conformity with this practice on board *Caithness-Shire* I was clad in a pair of blue dungarees trousers, blue guernsey, battered felt hat, and, worst of all, a pair of sand-shoes, which had become a habit, owing to our practice at sea in fine weather, of wearing them when on watch at night, to avoid waking those below with the heavy clump of boots over their heads. With dirt and grime on my clothes and hands from the handling of guano, and grease-covered gear on board, I realised I was a disreputable figure as I marched along the street, and, having been found in possession of a loaded gun, the situation would need a lot of explaining.

Arrived at the police station, I was pushed up in front of a long desk, behind which sat the officer in charge. Reporting to his superior officer, the policeman said, 'I caught this bum running away from some job he had pulled, and found this on him,' putting my gun down carefully on the desk, well beyond my reach.

'Wat's your name, buddy?' said the officer,

'William Jones.'

'Where you live?'

'On the barque *Caithness-Shire.*'

'Oh yeah! You just sleep there, and bum a feed, eh?'

'Oh, no, I am Second Officer of the ship.'

'You look like a prize bum to me.'

'I can't help that. The ship is filthy with guano.'

'Wat's your Captain's name? Do you know that?'

'Yes, Captain Hatfield.'

'Orright, we'll see.'

'Look, officer, this isn't funny, I am the officer on duty on the ship; if you don't believe me, send the officer down to the ship with me.'

'Oh yeah, nice and easy like; carrying a loaded gun you were. I'm holding you till I find out where you've been.'

Fortunately for me, a more senior officer arrived. After a lot more questioning my request to be sent in custody to the ship for indentification was agreed to, and in the early hours of dawn I was marched down to the ship by the burly policeman, feeling very uncomfortable under the inquiring gaze of the few people who passed by in the street.

Arriving on board, the Old Man was hauled out of his bed to identify me. After hearing my story we made a search on the poop, and discovered the signal halliards on the mizzen mast had been unrove and stolen. The watchman who had tried to warn me came aft and verified my story of seeing a man jump from the poop and giving chase, so I was exonerated from blame. Over a cup of coffee later in the saloon, with the officer of the law, I was advised to leave the arrest of waterfront criminals to the police, if I wished to live longer.

On reflection I had to admit that the policeman's appreciation of what he saw must have left him with the impression that I was up to no good, and most certainly I was a sorry figure to impress anyone with the assertion that I was an officer, acting in performance of his duty.

The work of discharging the cargo went on smoothly from day to day. We now had a new, and very reliable, night watchman, armed with a gun, so it was considered unnecessary for an officer to be on night duty, and after the day's work ceased I was now free to go ashore.

Like many other sailors I found being ashore in a strange port for the first time a most uninteresting experience, which usually resulted in a parade up and down the main streets.

As I walked along, a dead-beat full to the bung with rot-gut liquor, said in a guttural voice, 'Happy Christmas, brother.' Not flattering perhaps, but his heart was probably of gold, even though his brains were addled, so I acknowledged his greeting, and passed him by, to mingle with the throng which milled about the pavement, too busy and distracted to be gay on this festive evening.

Back on board, laying in my six by two and a half foot bunk, in the stillness of the night, far away from my relatives and friends, cast away among a brotherhood of seamen, with them, but not of them, as my rating held me apart and aloof, because it is said 'Familiarity breeds contempt'. I find myself alone or in company daily with two men only, with whom I can converse, if they happen to be in a convivial mood, but one being my Master, and the other my senior, I have to be wary in my approach, and cautious always in conversation.

'Why do I do it?' I ask myself. 'What is it that makes me persist in accepting all the hazards, discomfort and isolation from people, from the crowds I have seen tonight, the gaiety of life among the multitude, for weeks, months, years, yes, even for the whole period of my active life, to roam around the world, always looking for something, but never seeming to find it?'

Perhaps that is the dominating force that drives me on. Maybe it is the glorious canopy of the celestial concave in a tropic night or the vista of a tropic sunrise, or the blue lagoon beyond the waving palms and sparkling white sands of a tropic isle, clothed in a shimmering mantle of green foliage.

Or is it the sea, a challenge, the animal instinct in me aroused, something to conquer in its fury, the deluge of sleet, snow and hail, the vicious sky as it looms dark and foreboding with masses of cloud scudding by? But, no, it is called Ambition, the quest to reach the pinnacle, where money alone can lift me out of this squalor into the light of a world where men pass on their lawful occasions in peace and happiness, unhindered by the urge to drown their sorrows and loneliness in waterfront taverns, among the harpies and wild women who batten on those who circumstances cast among them.

With such thoughts I ponder the future; I can be free for the asking, paid off and left in a foreign land to work out my own destiny, to perhaps become a hobo, like the fellow who greeted me in the street, but, fortunately, the wearied mind presently resolves my problems in a profound sleep, and I awake again to the clang and clatter of stevedores, delving into a mass of bird-droppings below.

On December 24th all work ceased for the Christmas and New Year holiday period, and we spent a hectic day, after cargo work ceased, washing decks and cleaning the ship generally, to make it habitable for the crew, which, with the return of the absentees, was again complete.

Throughout the Christmas and New Year holiday period very little cargo was worked, and the crew spent most of the time ashore, returning on board for their meals, when it suited them, but seldom doing a full day's work, drifting away in ones and twos during the day, and openly resenting any restraint, when the effects of liquor were upon them.

It was a difficult situation, and one in which the bucko mates of legend might have excelled, but alongside a wharf with drifters from the shore coming and going with the men, and rot-gut liquor flowing freely, to try and enforce an order, would probably result in being abused, and perhaps injured in a free for all, among a crowd of brawling men in hostile mood.

With the holidays over, cargo work was resumed, and we tried to establish some semblance of law and order in the work of the ship, from day to day. Apparently some of the men had tasted the joys of living without restraint, and now adopted the time-honoured practice of passive resistance, and useless endeavour, to get the Master to pay them off.

Eventually four seamen and the cook deserted. A few days later three more seamen went to hospital sick and were paid off.

By January 14th another seaman and the assistant steward had gone the same way, both being paid off, also one of the apprentices, who had been injured on board, was sent home to England, making a total of eleven crew members short, eight of whom were seamen, out of a total of twelve seamen on board when we arrived in Wilmington.

For twelve days, from January 5th to the 16th, we had no cook on board, and such scratch meals as were served up were cooked by the assistant steward, a German, who on January 14th would no longer carry on and was paid off.

Conditions on board were now intolerable, with no decent meals, and only four seamen and four apprentices to scale and paint the hull, which was rusty from the bulwarks to the waterline after the long voyage from Santa Island, and tons upon tons of barnacles and weed adhering to the ship side-plating which had now risen out of the water several feet, as the cargo had been discharged. Working from 6 a.m. to 6 p.m. it was frequently necessary to call the hands up from overside to do necessary work on deck, for taking in stores for the impending voyage and, attending to the wants of the stevedore discharging the cargo.

The Master was harassed almost beyond endurance, but as his wife had left the ship the day after we arrived, to return to England, he was able to give his undivided attention to the many problems with which he had to contend, in discharging the cargo and taking in 900 tons of ballast.

Orders had now been received instructing the ship to proceed in ballast to Port Arthur, in Texas, to load a full cargo of case oil for Australia. Sailing day had been fixed for January 25th, or thirty-six days after our arrival in the port, and there was much to be done in preparing the ship for sea. It was now imperative to replace the crew members if we were to be ready to sail on time, and the usual avenues of recruiting now got busy in finding the eight seamen we required.

On January 16th the Old Man engaged a Dutchman from Rotterdam as cook and steward, at a wage of eight pounds per month, ten shillings more than the Chief Mate, and three pounds more than I received, making him second to the Master as the most highly paid man in the ship, also a cabin boy at three pounds per month. On January 18th four seamen were unexpectedly obtained and signed on in the presence of the British Consul, two of whom were British, and two Americans.

By this time all cargo had been discharged and the loading of sand ballast completed. Although we were still two seamen short of our complement, a tug was made fast, and we commenced the long tow downriver to Southport, where we anchored well off shore just before darkness set in. There were no sails aloft on the yards, and the ship was in a terrible mess about the decks, with sand and guano everywhere, as the cleaning of the hull overside had been given priority over all else, as it affected the ship's sailing quality when at sea.

We were now able to exercise some authority, and drove the men from 6 a.m. to 6 p.m. each day bending sail, levelling off the sand in the hold, and washing decks.

On January 21st another seaman was put on board, and three days later a second one, both Fins, who signed the articles on board the ship. The crew was now considered complete with ten seamen and four apprentices, making a total of twenty-one persons on board, instead of the twenty-seven with which we had started the voyage from Port Talbot in September 1909.

This meant there would be five seamen and two boys in each watch, which, with one at the wheel, and one on lookout, would leave three seamen and two boys available to make or take in sail, or haul the yards around, in a large vessel of 1,641 tons gross, which, being a bald-headed vessel, was heavily sparred aloft.

We were not unduly worried, however, as it was a short voyage through tropical seas to Port Arthur, and if we were lucky all would be well, but there still remained the possibility of encountering one of the West Indian cyclones, as we neared the region in which they were prevalent.

After a lapse of half a century I look back in amazement at the conditions which prevailed in the manning and operating of many British sailing ships in the decades at the turn of the century, when ten seamen could be considered sufficient to man a vessel in which thirty would have been inadequate in the heyday of the sail era.

What hope had we, with three seamen and two boys in each watch, even if they were always fit for duty, to press on and make a passage? The success or failure of a voyage between ports depended solely upon the crew's ability to handle the ship under all conditions of weather, but there was a definite limit to what an inadequate crew could do.

Of the six new seamen who had joined, two were from steamers, and the remaining four from sailing-ships, making a total of eight seamen on board familiar with the working of a ship under sail.

23

THE WRECK

At daybreak on January 25th, 1911, after laying at Southport for seven days, we hove up the anchor, and, with a tug ahead, proceeded to sea. About five miles out, with the four topsails, jibs, and staysails set, we cast off the tug and made all sail in a light breeze, close-hauled on the port tack, on a voyage to Port Arthur in Texas.

The course the Master had decided to take was to the eastward of the Bahama Islands, in preference to the inner passage between the Islands, or through the Straits of Florida, before rounding up to pass the island of Cuba, and across the Gulf of Mexico to Port Arthur, which was situated in the north-west corner of the Gulf, between New Orleans and Galveston.

With light winds and moderate seas we made slow progress towards the Bahama Islands, the crew settling down well with the prospect of a fine-weather passage before them. The days passed pleasantly, as in the warm sunshine the hands worked about the decks, washing and cleaning, as we endeavoured to get rid of the last traces of guano which still fouled the bulwarks and deckhouses.

At 10 p.m. on February 3rd the light on San Salvador Island was sighted, from the topgallant yard, bearing S.23°W, the weather at the time being fine and clear, with a light breeze from the eastward. The ship was close-hauled, on the port tack, sailing by the wind, and making from two to three knots through the water under all plain sail.

By midnight the light on San Salvador Island was in

sight from the deck. On the course the ship was making, between south half west and south-south-east by compass, we expected to pass well clear of the reef, which extends seaward from the eastern side of the island. It had been my watch below, from midnight to 4 a.m. and at 3.45 a.m. the apprentice on watch called me, and reported that the light was in sight.

At 4 a.m. I relieved the Mate on the poop. He informed me that San Salvador Light bore four points on the starboard bow, at 3.50 a.m. and that he had reported the bearing to the Master.

With the man at the wheel, and on lookout on the forecastle head relieved, I checked the course the ship was making. The Master had by this time come up from his cabin, on to the poop, and was taking bearings of the light and checking our position on the chart. Calling the watch aft I went down on to the main deck to sweat up the weather fore braces, which had stretched sufficiently to allow the foreyard to grind against the forward shroud of the rigging. Returning to the poop, the Master informed me that his bearings placed the light fourteen miles distant, and that we should have it abeam, six to eight miles distant, between 6 and 7 a.m. I was to call him if there was any change in the weather, or when the light came abeam.

From time to time I looked at the binnacle, and noted that although the wind was variable, within two points, the ship was making a mean course of about south by east. The Walker taffrail log, which we were now using, was practically useless to check the speed we were making through the water, as past experience had shown that it was erratic, and unreliable, unless the ship was making more than three knots through the water.

The bliss log we usually used, which was reliable at all speeds, had been lost a few days previously, when fouled by a shark, or some floating object, thrown overboard from a passing vessel.

We had no hand log line and reel on board, so there was no way to check the speed of the ship, and the distance off the land, other than by bearings of the light, which, when abeam, would give us our distance from it, providing we knew accurately the distance we had covered over the ground while altering the bearing of the light, through an angle of forty-five degrees.

At 4.50 a.m. the light came abeam. With the ship still making the same course, I reported this to the Master in accordance with his instructions, and in doing so informed him that by the log distance run, over the four-point bearing, we were three and a half miles distant from the light. Returning to the poop to continue my watch, I did not feel uneasy about our distance off the light, as, by the chart we were using, we were in deep water, beyond the outer extremity of the reef. I did, however, feel uneasy about the variable wind, as I knew that, at a speed of two or three knots, the ship might not come about if the wind hauled more southerly, and we had to tack ship.

With only about one mile of clear water to leeward, to be forced to wear ship, and run off before the wind towards the reef, would be courting disaster. In the meantime we continued on our course. Although we had a good and very reliable man at the wheel, who had been in the ship since we left Port Talbot, I warned him not to let the ship run off the wind, and watched his steering carefully.

After coming on deck the Master first looked in the binnacle to check the course and then at the weather leech of the main upper topgallant sail, to make sure the ship was sailing as close as possible to the wind. It was the darkest hour before the dawn. Away to starboard the faint outline of the land was visible, and on the starboard quarter the illuminating beam from the lighthouse flashed its warning at intervals over the darkened sea.

At 5.15 a.m. there was a heavy bump as the ship struck a submerged object, a trembling vibration passing through the ship, but she continued sailing, and remained under control, with all sails drawing freely. The heavy bump brought all hands out on deck on the run. They were immediately ordered to stations to tack ship.

With the helm hard down, the ship's head came up slowly to the wind, but she missed stays, owing to having insufficient way through the water, and lay for a few moments, without any steerage way, before falling off again before the wind as the sails again filled. The helm was now put hard up, and an attempt made to wear ship, with the mainyards squared in, but, although the ship's head turned shorewards through several points, she was too close in, and her turning circle in the light breeze prevailing too great, for her to come about, and clear the reef.

After some moments there came a succession of bumps and grinding crashes as she encountered isolated boulders, or rocks, before finally coming to rest, firmly wedged among the reefs, twenty minutes after first touching ground at 5.15 a.m.

The ship had gone aground under full sail. She now began to bump heavily as the ocean swell lifted her momentarily, and the pressure of the wind in the sails edged her deeper into the reef, as all hands worked like beavers to clew up the sails, before going aloft, to make them fast in the gaskets. This was a dangerous job, as each time the ship lifted on a swell and crashed down again on the rocks, the masts and yards rebounded violently with the heavy shocks. The braces, which secured the yards, stretched to the rigidity of harp-strings as the ship was thrown over momentarily to an angle of thirty or forty degrees, then snapped under the strain and left the yards on which we lay struggling to furl the sails, whipping back and forth in violent jerks which threatened to throw us headlong to the deck below.

In the first light of dawn the scene about us was amazing. From aloft, as we worked feverishly on the yards, the outline of the island rose clear and stark, beyond a stretch of green water. A mass of boulders and coral heads beneath the surface lay in profusion around the ship on all sides, as far as the eye could see in the clear water, with masses of kelp and weed floating idly on the surface. Away to seaward the eastern horizon sparkled in the growing light, with the white caps of wavelets dancing gaily across the intervening sea to the urge of a freshening breeze, which foretold more wind in the offing.

Over the reef the long oily Atlantic swells rolled in, sucking the water back, and exposing huge coral boulders for a moment, before surging forward in cascades of foam and broken water, to expend their fury in a white mist of smoking vapour, which swirled about over the writhing shallows.

All around us the sea rose in pyramids as the onward rush of the rolling swells broke in confusion against the wall of steel, which lay as a barrier in its path, sending sprays into the air to deluge the ship in a torrent of water. As she was lifted by the upsurge of the advancing swell, it bore her over in a sickening lurch, which set in motion a vast and thundering clang and clatter, as the whole towering mass of top-hamper came alive, in a resounding chorus of grinding steel and tortured wire.

Aloft the situation had become so dangerous that we were ordered down on deck. Preparations were at once made to lay out anchors in an attempt to haul the ship off the reef. It was now broad daylight, and through binoculars we could see a small crowd of natives on the beach, about two miles distant, chattering and gesticulating as they gazed in wonder at the apparition cast up on their shore. From the poop, the Master, Mate, and myself searched the water for signs of the passage through which the ship had reached her present position on the reef, but from where we stood the mass of coral boulders in the depths around us seemed unbroken by any passage of clear water sufficient for our passing.

Calling all hands aft we prepared to swing out the lifeboat on the lee side. After some difficulty we got it into the water, with the gunwale and some planks stove in. Being in ballast trim, with a high side out of the water, and the ship being rolled over and pounded on the rocks every few minutes, while lowering it in the davits it was grinding against the ship's side one moment, and the next would be swinging ten feet away as the ship rolled over, to fall back with a crash against the steel plates in spite of the frantic efforts of four men to fend her off with boat-hooks.

Once afloat, we hauled the boat round under the stern, and after the Old Man had scrambled down into it, we pulled away to make a survey of the reef, and find a channel through which to haul the ship out into deep water. By this time the wind had freshened considerably, and a nasty sea was running over the reef.

All about us large boulders of rock were visible in the depths, ten, twelve, twenty and more feet below the surface with hillocks of coral rock here and there nearer the surface with the heads shorn off, as with a scythe, by the ship's hull as she ploughed her way through the shallow water. Further to seaward the boulders of rock were more scattered, and only faintly visible in the depths, so we were able to make a fairly good assessment of the task involved in hauling the ship off the reef.

By mid-morning there was a strong wind blowing. We were being deluged with spray, as the men at the oars laboured to pull the heavy lifeboat against the rough sea, so the survey had to be abandoned, and we pulled back to the ship, wet and hungry after not having had a meal since the previous evening. While we had been away two kedge anchors and heavy hawsers had been got ready on the poop. The Mate now took charge of the boat. With four fresh men as a crew he prepared to lay out the anchors to windward, for hauling the ship off.

We lowered one of the kedge anchors down to the boat, where it was hung below the stern on a slip rope, and the attached hawser coiled down in the boat, ready to be paid out. Heading into the rough sea the boat was almost unmanageable at times, and made slow progress, with the men toiling and sweating at the oars, the anchor hanging below the stern frequently fouling the reef and bringing the boat up all standing.

More than once the boat nearly capsized, as she took a heavy list when men hung over the side to free the anchor, and the coiled hawser, piled high in the boat, slid over to the lee side. In the meantime we on board had been paying out over the stern a second hawser, as the boat pulled away, which had been secured to the one taken away in the boat.

After an hour's hard work about twenty fathoms had been towed out by the boat, which could now make little headway with the heavy drag astern, so the rope in the boat was now paid out, until its length was exhausted, and the anchor let go in a suitable position, about 700 feet from the ship.

On board we hove the hawser as taut as possible, with a main-deck capstan in double gear, while a second hawser and stream anchor were prepared for laying out from the opposite quarter. It was now my turn to take the boat away, and after three hours of solid work I was able to get the second anchor laid out in a suitable position, just before darkness set in.

All afternoon the wind had been blowing strongly from the eastward, even to a moderate gale force. A heavy sea was running over the reef, and the position on board was now most dangerous, as the ship pounded and heaved on the rocks, listing over thirty and forty degrees as she was swept, from stem to stern, by a deluge of water from the seas breaking against the hull.

Several of the heavy steel yards kept whipping back and forth, with each roll of the ship, carrying away ropes, wires, and pennants, with heavy blocks and shackles, which crashed down on to the deck at intervals, while loose ropes and gaskets streamed out to leeward in the wind, from torn and threshing sails aloft.

In the poop, under the mizzen mast, on which there were no yards, there was less danger than forrard, so in the sail-locker, right aft, the crew now settled down for a well-earned rest. At about 11 p.m. the carpenter reported that water was entering the hold. As it seemed possible the ship might at any moment start to break up, the Master decided to abandon the ship for the night.

With all hands we worked feverishly to get the second lifeboat, which was on the weather side of the ship, into the water. This was a difficult job. The weather davits were useless for the purpose, and tackles had to be rigged to lift the boat over the standard compass, to the lee side, where the davits could be hooked on, and the boat lowered into the water in the usual way without sustaining any damage. While this operation was in progress the cook and cabin boy had prepared a good meal for all hands, with cold canned bully beef, pickles, jam and biscuits.

With hot tea, made on the cabin stove, we all ate a hasty meal, sitting around the saloon, with our backs against the bulkheads on the sloping deck, listening to the crash of the seas and groaning of tortured steel, as the hull lurched and worked deeper into the coral reef.

At midnight we left the wreck, all hands sliding down ropes some fifteen feet into the lifeboats, which had been laying to leeward on long lines from the ship. It was about two miles to the shore, over a reef on which a heavy sea was running. In the dark it was courting disaster to try to find a passage through the reef, which our experience in making a survey, and laying out anchors in broad daylight, had shown to be both a difficult and dangerous hazard which could easily result in the boat being smashed against the rocks, and the crew left struggling in the water.

Before leaving the ship it had been decided to lay off the wreck to leeward all night, on long lines, and we settled down to get what rest we could in a boat which tossed and dived into the seas, sending heavy sprays over us every few minutes, until we were wet through and forced to bail out the water which swirled about our feet.

As the night wore on we could hear the continual noise of seas breaking over the wreck and the shrill scream of metal against metal as the swinging yards clanged against each other. We could see that the fore upper topgallant yard had broken away from the parrel and was swinging, cock-billed, on one of the lifts, which might give way at any moment and send the yard crashing down to the deck.

With the first light of dawn we pulled the boats up to the wreck and clambered on board, wet, weary, and hungry, to find that both the hawsers, laid out to the anchors astern, had carried away during the night. A hasty survey of the ship showed that water was now seeping into the hold and that it was now imperative to get assistance if the ship was to be saved.

After a hasty meal, and a change of clothes, we got the gig over the side, as it was much lighter, and less deep in the water than a lifeboat. With four apprentices at the oars, the Master and myself now set out to find a passage through the reef, to the shore. Around the ship there was eight to ten feet of water, with lesser depths over coral boulders, but towards the shore the reef lay in shallows, with coral heads, and rocks, near the surface. As we got nearer the shore the sea flattened out. We were now able to see, in the clearer patches of water, the pattern of the reef below.

By turning here and there we were able to avoid rocks near the surface, except in patches of heavy kelp where we grounded several times and had to get over the side on to the reef to haul the boat off. By 8 a.m. we had landed on a sandy beach, and were surrounded by a number of West Indian natives, both men and women, who spoke English.

One man, who seemed to be the principal one present, described himself as the peublic officer, which we understood to mean he was a public official or policeman. He informed the Master that word of the wreck had been sent, the previous day, to Cockburn Town, the main settlement, which was on the other side of the island, and that no facilities existed on the island for salvage purposes, except some native divers.

Obtaining the loan of a horse, the Old Man set out, with the peublic officer as a guide, to find his way to the settlement and get into communication with Nassau, the capital of the Bahamas, ordering me to haul the boat up on the beach, and await his return. About noon the Master returned with two native divers, so we pulled back to the ship, where the necessary gear was put into a lifeboat, which, with the Mate in charge, and the two native divers, was sent away to find the ends of the broken hawsers, and secure them together for another attempt to haul the ship off the reef.

Since returning to the ship at daybreak, the hands, except those with us in the boat, had been, in relays, working the main pumps continuously to keep the water in the hold down, and it was now our turn to engage in this backbreaking work under the blazing sun of a hot tropical day. Fortunately the wind and sea had died down during the forenoon. Although still listing over heavily, the more violent lurches of the ship had ceased as she finally ground the coral into a hard bed on which she rested more comfortably.

By about 4 p.m. the divers had succeeded in recovering the ends of the broken hawsers, which were secured together, and again hove taut on the capstans, in a second attempt to haul the ship off. With the deck under our feet at an angle of about thirty degrees we strained at the capstan bars, the sweat pouring down our faces in the blazing and humid heat, as we strove to move the ship, some men able to exert useful service, as they pushed against the capstan bars downhill on the sloping deck, while others could only contribute feeble help as they pushed uphill.

Hour after hour through the night we toiled at the capstans and pumps, with the men working in watches to enable everyone to get some rest, but the ship remained hard and fast on the reef in spite of every effort to release her. On February the 5th, the day after we struck the reef, the exhausted men, who had worked heroically through a long and arduous period without adequate sleep or nourishing food, were disheartened and complaining as they toiled at the pumps and capstans in a losing battle against the forces of nature.

Despite their efforts, the water in the hold was gaining, and without immediate assistance it seemed the ship must become a total loss.

24

THE UNWRITTEN LAW

THROUGHOUT the next day, February 6th, the weather remained calm, and there was no change in the ship's position, or the leakage of water into the hold.

The Old Man again went ashore, to report the condition of the ship, and try to get immediate assistance. While he was away we lay off on the reef in the boat where we were able to catch a few fish, for a welcome change of diet. Towards evening we returned on board, the crew being again divided into watches to keep the pumps going, and attend the hawsers throughout the night.

At 6 a.m. on February 7th a moderate breeze was blowing with an oily swell rolling over the reef, setting up a vibrating and rocking motion through the hull so the capstans were manned, and the heaviest strain possible put on the hawsers, in the hope that the rising swell would make it possible to haul the ship off, pumping being renewed with men refreshed after a good sleep.

About 8 a.m. a dense cloud of smoke belched up on the southern horizon. All eyes were immediately riveted in that direction as the Captain, and the Mate, hastily scanned the international code signal book, before hoisting signal flags of distress.

At the capstans, and pump handles, the men speculated on the chances of our flags being seen, or what help, if any, the steamer could render to a ship so far up on the reef.

Suddenly a babble of voices in excited comment arose,

as from the smoke cloud the outline of a warship appeared which rapidly resolved into that of a large cruiser.

She was apparently steaming towards us at high speed, throwing into stark relief a huge bow wave, which rolled away along her side in a glittering overfall of broken and agitated water, as the rays of the sun caught the tumbling masses of foam and spray cast up by her passing.

As always, the unwritten law of the sea had prevailed, the call had gone out, a ship was in distress, and the lives of seamen in jeopardy. As she came nearer we saw, standing out stiff and unyielding in the strong wind the rush of her hull through the water created, the Stars and Stripes of the United States of America.

We watched eagerly as the bow-wave flattened out and her massive hull crept silently through the water, with the roar of escaping steam belching from her exhaust pipes, as the engineers tamped down the great pressure of steam in her boilers.

Men swarmed about her decks as a boat was cleared away, and swung outboard, seamen in the chains chanting continuously as they hove the hand leads from each side, and plumbed the depths of water which lay beneath her keel. Coming to anchor outside the reef at 9 a.m. an eight-oared pinnace pulled away, and headed towards us.

With the crew straining at the oars, to prevent her being slewed broadside on to the cascading and broken water, she came in over the reef, until eventually she pulled alongside, and an American naval officer from the cruiser *Birmingham* climbed on board and saluted the Master.

With the Master and Mate, the naval officer made a close survey of the ship. The native divers, who had been kept on board, were sent into the hold to ascertain, if possible, the extent of the damage to the hull, and where it was situated.

They returned on deck, after about half an hour below, to report that the bottom, at each end beyond the ballast, was set up in several places, and that the bottom, under the ballast, was also set up, as all the toms had fallen down.

Since daylight, the wind had been freshening and now

blew strongly. A heavy breaking swell was rolling in, which shook the vast fabric of wire and rope aloft into a clattering medley of spine-chilling sound, which beat heavily upon the ears of the men as they laboured at the pumps under the avalanche of quivering structure, poised high and threatening above them.

In the saloon the Master discussed the situation with the naval officer, whose ship could not approach near enough to render towing assistance. The only question now to be answered seemed to be whether the Master would abandon his ship and transfer the crew to the cruiser. From time to time signals were made as the naval officer reported to his captain, and received replies.

The decision to abandon the ship was the Master's, and his alone, but while there remained the slightest chance of saving her, his duty was to use every endeavour to do so. In the present situation there still seemed to be a possibility that, with adequate pumps and other salvage gear, she might yet be pulled off the reef. Calling all hands aft the Master informed them of his decision not to abandon the ship immediately or transfer the crew to the warship. A number of the men demurred, stressing the danger of remaining on board under the shadow of the teetering masts, and the hardship of living under the conditions which the abnormal position of the ship would impose upon them. After some discussion it was agreed to transfer the crew ashore, on San Salvador Island, to live, while arrangements were made for salvaging the ship.

Lining the rail, the crew gave a rousing cheer as the warship's pinnace pulled away, on her return trip to the warship, which immediately weighed anchor, and, dipping her flag in salute as she steamed away, was soon lost to sight in a cloud of trailing smoke. Preparations were now made to land the crew on the beach for the night. Some sails and provisions were loaded into the three boats, and in the gathering dusk of the evening we pulled away for the beach, leaving the Old Man on board as evidence to anyone who might try to board the ship and take possession that she was not abandoned.

With the masts and oars from the lifeboats, and the sails we had brought ashore, we made several tents on the beach. As the dark mantle of a moonless night, calm, still, and oppressive, closed about us, we were able to lay down on beds of canvas in our, improvised shelters, to obtain a much needed rest.

While we had been actively engaged in rigging the tents we had not been interrupted, except by natives passing along the road, who stood hesitatingly for a few moments on the edge of the sand watching, before padding away on bare feet, to be lost in the darkness of the adjoining scrub. In the stillness we now heard the sound of men slap slapping as they fought off the droves of mosquitoes which invaded the tents.

Within half an hour all hands were out gathering dried seaweed and burning it by the tent flaps, in an endeavour to ward off the massed attack of these pests, which now filled the air with a continuous drumming. The cure, however, proved to be worse than the complaint, as the burning weed gave off clouds of black stinking smoke, which soon filled the tents, from which came the sounds of coughing and gasping men, as they dashed out into the night air to get relief. In the hope of getting some sleep we now vacated the tents, and built a big fire of seaweed on the open sands. Laying down in a circle around it, we still had another enemy in our midst, as we discovered, when swarms of tiny sand-flies entered our clothes, to bite, and cause an itch, while scratching and rubbing resulted in patches of inflamed flesh, which irritated almost beyond endurance.

There comes a time when resistance to fatigue is no longer possible, and in a state of near exhaustion I drifted away into a profound sleep among the circle of grotesque shapes on the naked sand, while a plague of cannibal insects feasted upon our naked bodies. How immeasurable is the gulf which separates the influence of darkness in depressing the mind's evaluation of a strange environment, and the uplifting surge of elation, as the warming light of a rising sun spreads before the seeing eye a vista of nature in unclothed beauty.

25

THE CASTAWAYS

REFRESHED from a long and deep sleep I woke as a dazzling light flooded over the white sands. Not a breath of air stirred. The calm sea stretched away to the far distant eastern horizon, unbroken by any signs of the hidden menace which lay in its depths, fringing the shore, and beyond to where the silhouette of a noble ship lay in its death throes, on the treacherous reef.

All around, the birth of a new day breathed rejuvenated life into the weary band so recently cast upon the shore, as men awoke to find themselves comforted by glorious sunshine, which evoked both laughter and banter, as they shed the remnants of civilisation which covered them, and plunged naked into the warm sea. In the scrub beyond the beach the birds twittered, and all manner of pests came alive. The croaking of frogs, buzz of mosquitoes, mingled with the whirr of bees and flies, as they swarmed about the fire where the cook and cabin boy were busily making tea, in a large hash kit, and preparing a scratch meal from the assortment of canned foods we had brought ashore.

With the meal consumed we made preparations to return to the ship, leaving two stalwart apprentices to guard the camp. Launching the three boats we pulled back to the ship through the placid water, which now offered little resistance to our passing, as we knew the conformation of the channel we had traversed, and climbed on board refreshed, fit and ready for whatever task lay before us.

A survey of the ship now revealed the magnitude of the task

which lay ahead if the wreck was to be salvaged. The hull was flooded to a depth of seventeen feet, small fish swimming around as evidence that the plating was badly holed, in an inaccessible position. The wreck was firmly wedged in the coral rock, which had been ground away in her labourings to a comfortable bed, on which she now lay, still and quiet, with a moderate list, under the weight of thousands of tons of water in her hold. Aloft the masts had miraculously withstood the terrible pounding shocks to which they had been subjected, but the wire rigging had been stretched almost to breaking point, and some topmast backstays now sagged on the lee side as the masts leaned drunkenly to the list of the ship.

In the saloon the situation was discussed. The Master decided to go ashore and take passage to Nassau in a schooner which traded among the islands, which was fortunately now at Cockburn Town, on the western side of the island, where he could get into direct communication with the owners in Glasgow, and the necessary authorities to arrange salvage operations, if the position as disclosed warranted such action, and was approved by the interested parties. After landing the Captain in the gig I returned to the ship, where a number of the seamen were busily engaged in getting the remainder of the edible canned and bottled food out of the lazerette, which was now full of water, before stowing them in the saloon.

The Mate had been instructed by the Master to make a rough survey of the reef in the vicinity where the ship had stranded. He now set about this task by checking the deviation of the compass. With horizontal bearings of prominent landmarks, vertical angles of the lighthouse, taken with a sextant from the poop, also from a lifeboat anchored in various positions on the reef, he placed the ship's position as 1·6 miles distant from the lighthouse, bearing N.55°W. This position, when plotted on both the British Admiralty chart, and American chart with which the ship had been navigated, placed her in deep water immediately outside the charted extremity of the reef.

In the meantime I had been ordered to unbend and send down all the sails from aloft, after securing the yards, which were again awry in a tangle of broken ropes and wires. The first task was to secure the yards, which pointed in various directions as they swung loosely, unsupported by the braces which controlled their movements.

The crew were in good heart. They seemed to like the unusual conditions, in which they now enjoyed more freedom from restraint, lingering, while perched high on one of the t'gal'nt yards, to survey the surrounding scene, pointing here and there as a bullock cart came into view among the scrub, or natives going about their daily tasks padded along the road, carrying heavy loads.

The officers were well aware that diplomatic handling in the present situation was necessary to avoid an upsurge of discontent among the men, who were unavoidably being denied even the meagre amenities to which they were fully entitled. In the galley the cook and cabin boy were labouring under difficulties as they prepared meals for all hands on a cooking range unseated from its bed, and without a chimney to carry away the smoke which filled the galley and contaminated the contents of stew-pots, which had to be hung over the fire from the iron grid above, owing to the range top being at an acute angle.

Fresh water was also a problem. The main tanks in the hold had been sprung by the heavy bumping on the reef, so we were reduced to using the fresh water from the lifeboat water breakers, which, very fortunately, could be re-filled from the shore daily as required. By early afternoon we had the yards and all the loose gear secured, the courses, t'gan'sls, jibs, and spanker unbent, and stowed in the sail-locker.

Calling the men aft, the Mate explained the situation, that in the present calm weather it was quite safe to remain on board, but if the wind freshened, or a heavy swell rolled in, there would be a danger of the masts falling, giving them the option of remaining on board or going ashore again for the night.

Without hesitation the men decided to go ashore. It had been agreed the Mate and I would take turn and turn about sleeping on board, to avoid complete abandonment of the ship. The Mate elected to stay on board this night, using the second gig, which we had launched and moored to leeward during the afternoon ready for him to use in getting away, if the weather deteriorated and made it necessary for him to leave.

Landing on the beach we unloaded the stores, and personal belongings, which we had brought ashore, then hauled the boats up high on the sand. After a while the public officer appeared and I had a long talk with him, sprawled out on the warm sand near my tent, which had been set a little apart.

He was a man of about fifty years of age, with a very dark brown skin, and sombre blue eyes, clad in a loose blouse of a reddish brown material, which hung loosely below his waist over dark turned-up trousers.

It appeared that he lived in the scattered settlement on our side of the island. He was a mine of information concerning the inhabitants who cultivated the land, the majority of the workers being women, some of whom had seldom seen a white man, and then only from a distance when someone in authority had passed by.

Not knowing the people's habits I was concerned about the safety of the stores we had piled on the beach, with personal effects, which included watches and clocks, which I surmised might be in short supply in the community. We had discussed the problem on board and arranged to rope off the area of beach we occupied, the men to keep four-hour watches against pilferage, also to keep a lookout for signals from the ship, if the weather deteriorated or the officer on board needed help.

With axes we cut suitable saplings out of the scrub, drove them into the sand, and roped off the area, piling the stores together before covering them with a hatch tarpaulin. In my tent I had the Old Man's two rifles, also a revolver and a lot of ammunition, together with cutlery, charts and books, the chronometer, and sextants.

So far the position ashore was much better than that of the previous night. The fresh easterly breeze, that was now blowing, kept the flies and mosquitoes away, so we ate our evening meal of cold salt beef and potatoes, which had been cooked on board during the day, with soft bread, baked under difficulties, with a liberal issue of jam and butter, in reasonable comfort as we sat around a table of hatch-boards, on full and empty provision cases.

With the coming of darkness all hands now settled down to sleep in the tents, but in the early hours of the morning the wind died away, and the mosquitoes descended in swarms to drive us into the open, where we waded chest deep in the warm sea, or dozed around the seaweed fire, until the glaring sun made further rest impossible.

It was soon apparent the night watch on the camp had failed miserably, as, near one of the tents, a basket of eggs, and another of fruit, was found. No one had seen or heard the donor of these very acceptable gifts, which later became a frequent occurrence, but under somewhat different conditions, as I fear they were encouraged by surreptitious offerings of jam and other delicacies, purloined from the stores.

With everything on board secured there was little we could do until a message was received indicating whether salvage operations were to be undertaken, or the ship finally abandoned. This being a Sunday, and a fine calm day, it was decided we would all go on board the ship, where the cook and cabin boy could prepare a hot meal on the galley stove, instead of eating cold viands on the beach, pestered by the flies and mosquitoes who seemed to prefer the white flesh of the visitors, to the dark tanned skin of the native inhabitants, who gleefully watched the spectacle of enraged men squirming and slapping, while they sat unmolested in the shade of the scrub.

There were still some bags of potatoes left. With salt pork, boiled potatoes, and canned peas, we later enjoyed the first really square meal we had been able to have, since the ship first grounded on the reef. With the meal over all hands were anxious to get ashore again, as the possibilities of gratifying diversion seemed to be hovering near the camp, which was now a magnetic attraction for the younger generation of the local female species, and by late afternoon the frivolities were resumed.

26

LIFE AMONG THE NATIVES

THE inventive genius of man can be amazing when his appetite is whetted, and so it now proved. The arena on the beach now became a dazzling display of black, brown, and white limbs, as men vied with each other to invent games which were destined to inadvertently reveal nature's beautiful contours in fleeting glimpses to those who watched and waited.

Someone suggested a game of leapfrog. After a purely male demonstration, which produced much giggling and excited appreciation among the gallery of women, bolder spirits among the contestants succeeded in introducing several of the more comely girls into the intricacies of the game. This resulted in many spills, as men and women fell together in the warm sand in jumbled heaps, with arms and legs awry in a flutter of flying skirts, which alone seemed to provide adequate protection against the ravages of a tropical sun.

In the twilight a game of hide-and-seek kept the assembled company in high spirits, but in the darkening shadows of the approaching night, one after another of the hunters disappeared into the scrub in search of his quarry, and emerged only when the propriety of family life in the settlement could no longer be evaded.

Two more days were spent in idleness as we awaited the decision which might result in a prolonged effort to refloat the ship, but unless operations were commenced very soon it would be too late, as a strong wind and heavy sea on the reef would probably send the masts crashing over the side, tearing the decks and side plating apart as the mass of steel hurtled down.

With nothing else to do I wandered about the island, which is roughly twelve and a half miles long, and five and a half miles wide, almost surrounded by reefs of coral rock, which extend for three and a half miles beyond the shore at the northern end of the island, and for about one mile on the western side, with a fairly clear passage of water in the approach to Cockburn Town, situated at about the island's mid-length.

On the eastern side, where the wreck lay, the reefs extended off-shore for nearly two miles. Through its length the centre of the island is a series of brackish water lagoons, separated by small wooden hills, varying in height from 100 to 140 feet, the lighthouse, a stone tower, being on Dixon Hill near the northern end of the island, with the Columbus monument, about two miles south of the lighthouse, in a prominent position on the shore near the northern end of Fernandez Bay.

From where we were camped on the beach it was a distance of nine miles to the main settlement at Cockburn Town by a rough road which followed the shore line around the northern end of the island, and seemed to be the only way to reach the other side of the island, as the lagoons were deep, and could only be crossed by boat, of which, at that time, none were available. While walking along the road towards the lighthouse one Sunday afternoon I was passing a cottage, which had the door wide open, and an old native man sitting on a rough bench outside.

I greeted him and received a friendly toothless grin from the old man, so approached and sat down on the bench beside him for a rest and a chat.

I judged he would be about seventy years of age, with a deeply lined face and shrunken figure, but he was very voluble, and by questioning I soon learned that he had been on the island for many years, first as a labourer, and later as a supervisor, until he became too old to work. After a while I heard a rustling inside the dwelling and a most comely native girl, about twenty years of age I thought, with bare feet, came out through the door and asked me whether I would like a cup of tea. Feeling very much in need of one, after walking more than a mile in the stifling heat of the late afternoon, I accepted her offer with gratitude, and followed her into the dwelling. The interior comprised one large room, with a baked and hardened earth floor, in two levels, partly covered with rush matting, and divided transversely by a draw curtain, which at the moment was pulled aside, revealing a double mattress and blankets on a rough wooden base, with a wash basin and water jug on a pedestal nearby.

In the outer section of the room, where I now stood, there was a well-worn couch, a wood-fire stove in a corner, an old saddleback armchair, two other chairs, and a high stool. Seating myself on the couch, I had time to study my hostess as she busied herself at the stove, boiling a very blackened kettle, to make a pot of tea. She was a graceful creature, lithe and supple as a panther as she moved about in a light print dress, which appeared to be shrunken to a degree, evidently by much thumping on the rocks, which now left it clinging tightly to her figure, which, by any standard of perfection, could only be described as beautiful in its contours.

She was dark-brown-skinned, about five feet three inches in height, with classic features, somewhat spoiled by rather thick lips, her long black hair was combed back and hung loosely about her shoulders. As she turned, with a radiant smile on her face, towards me, her lips parted to reveal a set of natural pearly white teeth.

I had been so engrossed in the conversation, and the enchanting figure poised before me, that I had forgotten the old man on the bench outside the door, but now, hearing him wheezing, I became intrigued as to where he fitted into this picture and sub-consciously glanced towards the only bed.

Apparently following my glance, and interpreting my thoughts, this beautiful girl, without hesitation or any trace of embarrassment, told me she was lonely at night and was grateful for his company.

Thanking her for her hospitality, I made my way back to the camp on the beach, and although I later looked for her among the women who frequented the camp, to in some measure return her hospitality, I never saw her again.

One seldom met any of the native males, who apparently worked at distant plantations. After sunset all activities ceased, and the dwellings lay dark and mysterious in the solitude of the night, the flicker of an oil lamp showing momentarily through a crevice in a wooden door, as an occupant arose to perform a duty. On the beach one evening the sailmaker came along to where I was sitting on the sand, near my tent, in the smoke from a kelp fire burning nearby, in a vain attempt to obtain some peace from the persistent mosquitoes which swarmed about the camp, to ask about our plans for the morrow.

Old Tom was one of the real breed of old-time sailmakers, who had sailed in both China tea clippers and Australian wool clippers, in the last quarter of the nineteenth century. He was fifty-nine years of age when he joined us in Port Talbot and now, in his sixty-first year, was feeling the effects of many sleepless nights, and the rigours of the life imposed by our present surroundings. Having nothing better to do we settled down and yarned about generalities until I was able to wheedle him into talking about some of the ships he had sailed in.

Old Tom was a dour Scot from Glasgow, not easy to converse with, and evasive in answering the many questions with which I endeavoured to learn more of the incidents of what I felt sure had been an adventurous life in the hey-day of the sailing-ship era, but his mood for conversation had passed, and presently he wandered away to get such repose as the invading pests from the swamps and tangled brush nearby might in their merciless wanderings permit.

The next day orders were received to commence dismantling the ship, as the cost of salvage operations was estimated to far exceed the value of the vessel. Sailing-ships, of which there were still several hundred under the British flag, were rapidly being eliminated from the trade routes of

the oceans by the competition of steamers, the owners of
such famous vessels as the Lock Liners and Bank Liners,
which had traded regularly with cargoes of general merchandise to Australia, and the Far East, were selling their ships,
and those that remained were fast being relegated to the
more lowly adventure of carrying coal, nitrate, and guano,
in a last despairing effort to operate such ships profitably.

In Nassau the Master had chartered a coasting schooner
to load all the salvaged equipment from the *Caithness-Shire*
and carry it to Nassau, where it was to be sold by public
auction, the crew, after demolition was complete, being,
also sent to Nassau, where they would be paid off, and sent
to their destinations as distressed seamen.

H

27

STRIPPING THE WRECK

On board we commenced the task of dismantling all the gear aloft. This meant unreaving the ropes and wires, which were then coiled up, and stoppered off for easy handling, also a mass of shackles, made up in bundles, hanks from the stays on which jibs and staysails were set, blocks (pulley) of all sizes, both wood and iron, mooring ropes and wires, and the whole mass of portable equipment in usable condition, which might have some value on the open market.

Working aloft on fine calm days in the warm sunshine was an exhilarating experience. From a cloudless blue sky the round disc of the sun blazed down on the wreck, and the many half-naked figures of the crew, with their skin burned to a coffee-coloured hue, and rags of bright clothing adding a splash of colour which harmonised with the surroundings, which, under other conditions, would have been ideal. To seaward the deep blue water of the ocean lay still and silent in a vast expanse which lay between the circle of an elusive horizon, shimmering in the haze of a mirage, and the reef fringing the shore, on which the clear green water was dappled by floating kelp and the reflected radiant light from beds of coral laying beneath the surface.

When the Old Man returned he abrogated to himself the task of dismantling the accommodation under the poop, stripping down the saloon panelling and the cabin fittings, while the carpenter worked laboriously tearing down the teak-wood chart-house, teak-wood rails and other fittings for transportation to the shore.

Day after day, when the weather permitted, the work went on, tearing the ship to pieces and piling a mass of material on the beach, in a shuttle service of lifeboats which had been stripped of all buoyancy tanks and fittings, to provide space for carrying the goods, the deep-laden boats often grounding in the shallow water close to the shore, which necessitated unloading the cargo and manhandling it ashore while wading waist deep in the water.

During one of these incidents I was unfortunate enough to walk over some coral in bare feet and gashed the sole of one foot. This was distressing, with no doctor available, and was in future months to cause me much pain, and difficulty in walking when the wound healed over a fragment of coral embedded in the flesh.

On the beach life was both miserable and gay. The friendly unspoiled women and girls who now clustered the camp were eager to do any chores, and tend the wants of men who now revelled in the unaccustomed servile pampering, and fetch and carry porterage, which was now an accepted diversion from the daily grist.

In the distance couples roamed at will, or languished in blissful isolation in the restful seclusion of a wave-lapped inlet, while those less favoured waged a losing battle against the hordes of mosquitoes and flies which descended after sunset and drove them into the water.

Day after day we plied between the ship and shore, until finally all salvageable equipment had been landed and transported around the island to Cockburn Town, to await the arrival of the schooner from Nassau. The ship was now a skeleton of steel plates and stark beams, from which projected towering steel masts, and a profusion of crossing spars pointing hideously in all directions. Shorn of restraining harness, they hovered over the avenging reef to await the ravages of rust and decay which would send them crashing down, to rot, and mingle with the despoiled hull, as it crumbled away and was erased for ever in the overgrowth of the live coral.

On February 26th, three weeks and one day since we

stranded on the reef, we made a last survey of the wreck and pulled ashore to pack up and make preparations to join the schooner on the morrow, which was now loaded and awaiting our arrival at Cockburn Town.

There was both gaiety and sadness on the beach that evening as new-found friends parted for the last time. After a final restless night, in which the insect pests redoubled their efforts to annoy us, we left the beach in the first light of a new day. My last view of the *Caithness-Shire* was one I have never forgotten as she reared up on the reef, a grotesque figure, clearly outlined against the golden rays of the rising sun beyond, a fitting monument to the elusive power which lay hidden in the depths beneath her.

By a strange coincidence I was, many years later, to meet a shipmaster who, while an apprentice in a steamer, was wrecked on San Salvador Island quite close to where the *Caithness-Shire* stranded, but by that date all trace of the sailing-ship had disappeared.

At about 10 a.m. on February 27th we sailed in the schooner for Nassau, 180 miles distant to the north, making ourselves as comfortable as possible on the stacks of salvaged goods, as the vessel ran westward before a strong easterly wind, making seven and eight knots through the water. She threaded her way among the many islands and cays which lay in her path.

The schooner's crew, of four men, were a veritable mine of information concerning the waters which we now traversed, as they sat among our men telling of their experiences, both ashore and afloat, while trading among the vast concourse of people of many nationalities inhabiting the islands which studded the waters bordering the Caribbean Sea.

With the mind at ease again after the strenuous exertions of the past few weeks, one's thoughts became focussed on the idyllic surroundings which encompassed us in waters where pirates had roamed at large, and committed many crimes against humanity, which were common in their trade.

What horrible tales may lie hidden for ever in that beautiful tropic isle we are now passing. The glittering white sands, under those leaning palms, may have borne the footprints of pirates as they hauled their boat up out of the water, after skilfully riding the outer breakers into the smooth and sparkling blue waters which lap the shore, but today, as we pass by on our lawful occasion, we have nothing to fear, as the sea about us lies tranquil under the arch of the firmament above us, from which a blazing sun beats down and lulls the senses into repose.

Passing the southern extremity of Cat Island, just before dark, we entered Exuma Sound, and hauled up to the north-westward with the wind on the starboard quarter.

In the early dawn we turned westward, through a passage between Cistern Cay and Hawksbill Cay, and shaped a direct course for New Providence Island, on which the city of Nassau is situated.

With about fifty miles to go, the breeze held steady on the starboard quarter, and by early afternoon on February 28th, we were sailing up the channel which lay between Hog Island and New Providence Island, to make fast at the wharf about 3 p.m. after a fine passage from San Salvador Island at an average speed of a little over six knots.

28

NASSAU

History records that Nassau was once infested by pirates, who roamed the adjacent seas and raided the eastern coast of the mainland, and the Caribbean waters bordering the islands of the West Indies, until they were destroyed early in the eighteenth century by British naval and military forces.

There are 700 islands in the Bahama Group, covering about 70,000 square miles of the surrounding seas. It would be difficult to find a more perfect and equitable climate than that enjoyed by the people of Providence Island, where the temperature in winter and summer varies only between 70 and 80°F. with glorious sunshine most of the year.

After three and a half weeks of trials and tribulations since we first stranded on the reef, we now found ourselves in a veritable paradise, which nature had fashioned for those fortunate people who could spend their lives in such ideal surroundings, and the favoured few who languished for a space in this enchanted haven, to escape the rigours of the northern winter. Comfortably settled in a nice hotel I was ashamed to be seen among the well-dressed visitors in the torn and tattered garments in which I had landed, and stole away to eat a frugal meal in a small café nearby.

Purchasing a ready-made suit the next day and other necessities, I was able to mingle with the people in the hotel and converse with many who were interested in our presence among them. The arrival of a shipwrecked crew, in the height of the tourist season, had not passed unnoticed, as we found ourselves a centre of attraction and were treated in a most hospitable manner wherever we went.

We had to answer innumerable questions, particularly in the case of ladies, who seemed to envisage the most frightful situations which a wreck must have entailed, and who chided us with excessive modesty when we could not always agree with their flights of fancy. My injured foot added to the interest being taken by those with whom we made daily contact. As a result I was invited to join sight-seeing parties, and was driven here and there in motor and horse-drawn vehicles, sometimes most comfortably seated between charming companions of the fair sex. With some very nice people from New York I went one day on a tour of the islands, visiting an ancient buccaneer's tower, from where it was said they kept a lookout for the white sails of a ship on the horizon which might be worth plundering, also to Fort Charlotte where we saw old-fashioned guns and dungeons where prisoners were kept in solitude to ponder on the pain and suffering awaiting them at the hands of their captors.

All the ship's gear we had so laboriously salvaged had been stored and catalogued in a shed on the wharf, and was to be sold by public auction. At the appointed time I attended the auction, and found a large crowd of people, some elegantly dressed in summer clothes, eyeing with curiosity the assortment of old wire, rope, chains, blocks, buckets, canvas, spunyarn, harness-casks, barrels of salt beef and pork, old sails, timber, cutlery and pots and pans on display, but there was little which could appeal as mementos to take home of a happy holiday spent on a tropic isle. The millionaires and wealthy business men, who puffed at fat cigars, while they stood around as unwilling escorts to ladies seeking excitement and diversion, were not interested in the auctioneer's persuasive tirade as he tried to dispose of the goods, and the assembly gradually dispersed, until only a few fishermen and island traders remained.

I heard later that the sum of money realised from the sale was about £200, which perhaps in some measure helped to defray the cost of chartering the coastal schooner to bring the goods 180 miles, but in no sense could be considered adequate compensation to the shipowner, or satisfaction to the crew, for weeks of difficult and dangerous work, while perched high among a quivering tangle of ropes and wires which might at any moment cascade into the sea, if the masts and yards to which they clung should be erupted from their foundations by the constant lurching of the hull on the reef.

The wharf was situated at the foot of a large open square, where horse-drawn vehicles, and cars, assembled to convey visitors to hotels and boarding-houses, with the usual touts currying favour for the houses they represented, and many native porters eager to handle baggage.

As the steamer from Miami in Florida came in, or left, it seemed to be the custom for everyone to join in a gay and lilting American song, to the accompaniment of waving kerchiefs and multi-coloured summer hats, as the large crowd which packed the wharf seethed with excitement in a continuous exchange of animated comment.

All too soon our sojourn in Nassau ended. Four days after we arrived three of the seamen who had been paid off left by steamer for Galveston, Texas, as passengers, where they hoped to obtain employment in the booming oil industry of that state, The remaining members of the crew, seventeen in all, excluding the Master, were to be sent to Newport News in the United States where some who had joined in the State of North Carolina would be discharged, and those of British nationality would be sent home to England as Distressed British Seamen.

On March the 18th we were all in readiness to join the American passenger steamer *Bornu* which was expected at the wharf at 8 a.m., but the day wore on without any sign of her arrival, until late in the afternoon, a message was received that owing to the easterly gale blowing the steamer would not enter the port, and had anchored on the southern side of the island in the shelter of south-west bay, where we were to join her.

Hurriedly obtaining some motor vehicles, we said a hasty farewell, and set out for the long drive to the opposite side of the island, and boarded the steamer from launches as darkness set in.

Many years later, in Melbourne, while writing this story, I had occasion to write to the Colonial Secretary's office in Nassau, N.P., for some details concerning the island of San Salvador, and in a most gratifying reply received an extract from a book called *Silent Sentinels* written by Commander R. Langton-Jones, R.N. Inspector, Imperial Lighthouse Service, Bahamas, in which he relates the following experience. I quote:

'The four brass muzzle-loading cannons, once the armament of the first lighthouse tender, flank the white mast and crossyard. High above floats the Blue Ensign, defaced in the fly by the Bahamas Imperial Lighthouse Service badge, consisting of a lighthouse set in a medallion. Behind the mast stands the old sundial from the Cay Sal Bank Lightstation (now closed down), whilst in front of the mast and in line with the cannon, is erected the beautiful figure-head of the late, Scottish-owned three-masted barque *Caithness-Shire*.

'It is representative of a woman clad in classic-style flowing robes, resplendent in white and gold raiment, with gilded hair. Once more she is facing the same broad Atlantic on which she had, through so many long and stormy years, gazed so fearlessly. When the sun is shining overhead and the nearby palm trees dapple her with alien shadows, she seems to frown. Perhaps, in those moments she remembers a certain murderous reef of the Bahamas, or, maybe, she misses the sound of the ship's bell, which, for seventeen years, gave time to her seamen during her travels around the Seven Seas, and has now found a resting place at the gate of the little Catholic Mission Church at Riding Rock, San Salvador. It still performs a service, namely that of calling the faithful to worship, the same as Columbus had done when he landed there over four centuries ago to give thanks to Almighty God upon discovering the New World.

'The vessel, built in Glasgow in 1894, was of one thousand five hundred and twenty-five registered tons and proceeding from Wilmington, North Carolina to Port Arthur, Texas, U.S.A. in ballast. On February 4th, 1911, she was wrecked under the very beam of San Salvador lighthouse and became a total loss. The crew abandoned her the following day and "wreckers" commenced their depredations quickly, removing everything they could lay their hands on or rip from the vessel. One of the natives turned his attention to the ship's figurehead, sawed off the head and carried it ashore. Shortly afterwards he sustained a fall aboard and died.

'Some years ago, on one of my inspection visits to San Salvador Lighthouse, I decided to go for a ride along the foreshore and visit a memorial set up to Columbus on a point of land a few miles away. Cantering along the sandy beach my stallion suddenly reared and I descried what must have been a perfect parabola over his head. Deciding that I much preferred the movement of a vessel under me to that of a horse, I looked around in an endeavour to discover the cause of his extraordinary behaviour and there, half buried in the sand, was the torso of the partly decayed figurehead still showing traces of the original blue and gold paint which had once adorned it.

' "It's an ill wind," etc. thought I, and proceeded to make some enquiries. Eventually, I purchased the figure and had it transported to Nassau, with some difficulty, owing to its great bulk and weight. To find the missing head, however, was not so easy. Ultimately, it was discovered in the possession of a member of the Nairn family who had set it up in his palmetto thatched dwelling as a kind of mascot. The head was in a very remarkable state of preservation, the beautifully-shaped nose had not even been chipped, in spite of her many adventures, since she left the master-craftsman's hands nearly fifty years previously.

'The hull of the *Caithness-Shire* defied the heavy rollers of the North Atlantic in a most remarkable manner, despite being buffeted by many gales and several hurricanes of great severity.

'It was not until twenty-six years after she went on the reefs that the old ship finally broke up, surely a great tribute to her builders and to the material of which she must have been constructed.

'In the year 1933, she was several times completely submerged by a series of tidal waves, estimated at about thirty feet high.

'This submarine, cataclysmic disturbance swept away great pieces of the foreshore. The natives still speak with dread of that terrible time when they took to the hills for safety.

'When it was over the gallant barque still remained, her foremast still standing with her fore-yard cockbilled, the same as I had seen her from Salvador Lighthouse gallery some years previously. Now, only her rusted stern can be seen at low water.'

29

HOMEWARD BOUND

AT daybreak on March 22nd we arrived at the American port of Newport News in the Delaware River, and had no opportunity to go ashore and see the sights of the town as we were to be transferred during the day to the British steamer *West Point*, which was finishing loading that evening and sailing at daybreak for Liverpool.

With our scanty belongings we were taken by a motor boat during the afternoon to the *West Point*, after saying goodbye to the many nice people we had met on the *Bornu*. The *West Point* was a cargo steamer which had some surplus accommodation, and was able to house the ten men who came on board for passage to Liverpool. These included Captain Hatfield, the Mate and Second Mate, one Able Seaman who had joined in Port Talbot in 1909 at the commencement of the voyage to the West Coast, four apprentices, carpenter and sailmaker. The remainder of the seventeen men who had left Nassau in the *Bornu*, comprising the cook, cabin boy, and six seamen, were paid off and left behind in Newport News.

I was now to experience the daily routine on board a cargo steamer, both in port and at sea, which would perhaps enable me to make a wise choice for future employment, after having sailed in both passenger, and cargo steamers, and sailing-ships.

If the clang and rattle of the stokehold of the *Bornu* had been annoying, the bedlam of sound from eight steam winches, working incessantly day and night, was disconcerting and amazing to one whose experience had been limited to dolly-winching single bags or baskets of cargo, or the working of a single donkey engine under the meagre pressure which salt water in the boiler provided. This was a slow and arduous process in comparison to that of the rip, tear, and bust operation which seemed to govern the exertions of the winch drivers, who disregarded the steam valve which controlled the machine's movements, whenever possible, and transferred the control to the reversing lever, in two movements of full speed or stop.

In the holds the gangs of longshoremen stowed the slings of general cargo, which were lowered into the hold every few minutes, as the stevedore, or hatchman, used every endeavour to maintain the rate of loading in tons per hour which would satisfy both the employers of the labour, and the shipowners, an endless struggle to bridge the gulf between the possible and the seemingly impossible demands imposed by fluctuating world markets, and the vagaries of wind and tide, which in some measure might be the final arbiters in the eternal race against time.

On March 23rd, 1911, we sailed for Liverpool on a voyage of some 3,000 miles across the North Atlantic Ocean, and there was much speculation as to the weather we might experience in this winter month, as the gales in this region could be as severe as those off Cape Horn, but were usually of much less duration. With the Captain's permission I joined the officers in taking sights of the sun and stars whenever possible, and gained much practical experience in practical navigation, which in the *Caithness-Shire*, where the chronometer, charts, and books on navigation were the personal property of the Master, was seldom possible.

In steam I found navigation to be a factor which affected the profit margin in the owner's ledgers, and was therefore of particular interest to an officer's employers. My first introduction to this factor was at the dining-saloon table when I discovered that the engineers had a habit of watching the ship's wake, to see if it was straight or otherwise, and commenting in the presence of the Captain at table when it trailed away astern in a zig-zag pattern, which usually resulted in a reprimand for someone for not watching the steering more closely.

The difference between a straight course and a zig-zag all over the ocean affected the bills for coal, water, oil, food, and wages, which bills weighed heavily on the Master, and chief engineer, whose responsibility it was to produce advantageous figures when the voyage was completed. This was perhaps a not less exacting responsibility than that of a sailing-ship Master, whose competence was in part measured by the length of passage he made from port to port, even though his ship could be held up in calms for days, even weeks during a voyage.

Life on board the steamer flowed smoothly and easily from day to day in the fine weather which prevailed, the Cherub log on the taffrail aft reeling off ten knots as the ship rolled easily in her onward surge before a moderate following wind and sea, with the decks dry, and the steady throb of the engine the only apparent effort necessary to transport many thousands of tons of cargo across the ocean.

In the dining saloon conversation ranged over current affairs, the deck officers at ease in their sphere of isolation from all responsibility for the mechanical propulsion of the vessel, which was vested solely in the hands of skilled engineers whose mathematical calculations of fuel consumption versus speed, were occasionally set at naught by the intervention of nature's majestic power, when the roar of the gale, and the crashing of mighty seas, again called for that knowledge of seamanship which alone might evade the devastating consequences when the efficiency of a mechanical contrivance was subjugated by the wrath of the elements.

One morning, when we were within about 500 miles of the Irish coast, a full-rigged ship was sighted, evidently making for Queenstown or Falmouth for orders.

A fresh south-westerly wind was blowing, with a moderate following sea, and we were making ten and eleven knots by the taffrail log. With all sail set she made a beautiful picture as she came on, running free with the wind on the quarter, rolling easily as the sea lifted her grey painted hull, and the pyramids of snowy white canvas pressed her down again into the sea, which fell away from her raking stem as it arched up in a smother of foam to send sprays of iridescent colour flashing along her side as the sunlight traced a pattern of light and shade on the dancing water erupting about her.

As she rolled to leeward, the symmetry of her spars was vividly outlined against the sky as they leaned far over in a graceful curve, the bulging sails quivering with life as they unleashed a mighty thrust which bore her on relentlessly in defiance of the surging water which clawed at her rust-streaked hull as it passed by.

There was no trailing smoke cloud to pollute the clean salty air, no clanging of metal and throbbing engine, only the sweet aroma of stockholm tar which clung tenaciously about the spider web of interlaced rigging which held in subjection the tapering masts, spars, and clothing of snowy canvas.

On board our steamer there was not a man indifferent to the artisty portrayed by this enchanting picture.

As she came abeam, and drew ahead, men whose calling committed them to spend their days at sea in the stifling heat of the steamer's stokehold momentarily left their allotted stations, to climb on deck and gaze in admiration at this splendid ship as it surged past at fourteen knots.

On April 4th the *West Point* arrived in Liverpool after an uneventful voyage across the Atlantic Ocean and I said goodbye to old and new shipmates, which the fates decreed I was never to meet again, and, taking train to London, was soon home again to enjoy a well-earned rest.

Today the dwindling few who remain from the crews of the tall ships of a bygone era which battled their way around Cape Horn, and withstood the perils besetting them in the Seven Seas as they proudly carried the flag of trade to far distant countries, have still at heart a yearning for the adventurous life of danger and hardship which alone could triumph when the courage and skill of their breed were pitted against the fearful odds which beset them.

No more will we see those hardened shellbacks fisting a frozen sail in a blizzard, their hands gnarled and misshapen from the eternal battle to master the elements, which strove to tear from their grasp the life-giving fabric which alone could clothe them in a mantle of safety, and suffer them to reach a haven of rest where the rigours of a voyage would be forgotten in the brawling orgies of a waterfront tavern.

The tumults of wind-whipped wastes of icy water now rage in solitude about the dreaded Cape Horn, but its place in history is assured as a lasting memorial to the gallant ships and prime seamen of a glorious era which lie buried in the depths which surround its rocky shore. This lonely rock is their epitaph.

APPENDIX: EXTRACTS FROM THE OFFICIAL ENQUIRY INTO THE LOSS OF CAITHNESS-SHIRE

The Merchant Shipping Act, 1894

In the matter of a Formal Investigation held at County Buildings, Glasgow, on the 12th, 13th and 14th, all days of July, 1911, before Wm. GEORGE SCOTT-MONCRIEFF, Esquire, Advocate, Sheriff-Substitute of Lanarkshire, assisted by Captain ALEXANDER WOOD and Captain WILLIAM L. MAIN, nautical assessors, into the circumstances attending the loss of the British sailing ship *Caithness-Shire* of Glasgow, through stranding on the east side of Watling Island, Bahamas, on or about 4th February last.

REPORT OF COURT

The Court having carefully inquired into the circumstances attending the above-mentioned shipping casualty, finds for the reason stated in the annex hereto, that the cause of the stranding and loss of the *Caithness-Shire* was due to the master over-estimating the distance of the vessel from San Salvador Light at 4 a.m. on the 4th February last, through which the vessel was allowed to get into proximity with the foul ground to the east of San Salvador Island, where she struck a rock or reef said to have been uncharted. While the Court does not find that the stranding and loss was caused by the wrongful act or default of the master, it considers that he is to blame for not having remained on deck after 4 a.m. on the day in question under the circumstances in which the vessel was passing San Salvador Island. No fault attaches to the second officer.

Dated this 14th day of July, 1911.

W. G. SCOTT-MONCRIEFF,

Judge.

We concur in the above Report.

A. WOOD,
Wm. L. MAIN, } Assessors.

Annex to the Report

This was an Inquiry into the circumstances attending the stranding and loss of the British sailing vessel *Caithness-Shire* and was held at the County Buildings, 117, Brunswick Street, Glasgow, on Wednesday, the 12th, Thursday, the 13th and Friday, the 14th, all days of July, 1911. Mr. James Morton, writer, Glasgow, represented the solicitor for the Board of Trade (Sir R. Ellis Cunliffe) and Mr. David Wright Smith, writer, Glasgow, appeared for the master (Alexander Hatfield). The second officer (Wm. H. S. Jones), who was a party to the Inquiry, appeared in person, but was not professionally represented.

The *Caithness-Shire*, Official Number 104546, was a British sailing ship built of steel at Port Glasgow in 1894 by Messrs. Russell & Company, and was registered at Glasgow. She was owned by Mr. William Law and others, Mr. William Law of 123, Hope Street, Glasgow, being designated in transcript of register as managing owner—advice under his hand received 30th July, 1894. The vessel had three masts, was barque rigged, and of the following dimensions:– Length, 247·3 feet, breadth 37·6 feet, and depth in hold from tonnage deck to ceiling at midships 22·6 feet. Her gross tonnage was 1641·50 tons, and after deducting 116·08 tons for crew space etc., her registered tonnage was 1525·42 tons. She was constructed with a collision bulk-head forward, and carried four boats—two of which were life-boats. She was provided with five life-buoys and thirty life-belts. She had three compasses, a standard placed on top of the apprentices' house situated between the main and mizen masts, and one on each side of and in front of the wheel. She was supplied with a Bliss' taffrail log and a Walker's cherub taffrail log; the former was lost previous to the stranding. It was stated that the latter failed to register the distance correctly unless the speed of the vessel was greater than three knots. There was no hand log on board. She was provided with hand and deep sea leads and lines. The master, who had to provide his own charts, obtained an American chart for the Straits of Florida and Approaches, published at Washington, D.C., August, 1908, by the Coast and Geodetic Survey, accompanied by a Book of Sailing Directions. He stated that no Admiralty charts were obtainable for that part of the world in Wilmington.

The *Caithness-Shire* sailed for the West Coast of South America in September, 1909, under command of Mr. Alexander Hatfield, who holds an extra master's certificate, numbered 037390, and who had been chief officer on the vessel on former voyages. Mr. Laird, the chief officer, was in possession of a first mate's certificate, but Mr. Jones, the second officer, was uncertificated, although he appeared from the manner in which he gave his evidence to be a highly intelligent and well-qualified seaman. The master and these two officers remained on the vessel till she was lost.

From the West Coast of South America the vessel arrived at Wilmington, North Carolina, which port she left on the 25th of January, 1911, ballasted with 911 tons of sand, bound for Port Arthur, Texas. The crew consisted of 21 hands all told. The vessel's draught on sailing was about 12 feet forward and 12 feet 6 inches aft. Nothing worthy of remark occurred during the passage till 10 p.m. on the 3rd February, when the light on San Salvador Island was sighted from the top-gallant yard. As the light appeared directly under a bright star, the bearing of this star by the compass determined the bearing of the light to be about S.23°W. The weather at this time was fine and clear, with a light breeze from the eastward. The vessel was close hauled on the port tack, and according to the master's statement was making from $2\frac{1}{2}$ to three knots through the water. The wind being somewhat variable, the vessel was making a compass course between S./W. and S.S.E., and was under all plain sail. At midnight the light on San Salvador Island was in sight from the deck when the master left the deck, giving the chief officer instructions to call him if there was any change, or when the light was abeam. At 3.50 a.m. on the 4th February the light bore four points on the starboard bow. The chief mate noted the time when this occurred in order to obtain the position by a four-point bearing when the light would be abeam. At 4 a.m. the chief officer called the master, who went on deck, and from the appearance of the light estimated that the vessel was 14 miles distant from it. He said that he thought at the same time he would pass from six to eight miles from it, and that he did not expect that it would be abeam till between six and seven o'clock. He then went off the deck. The second officer, who relieved the chief officer at 4 o'clock, called the master at 4.50 a.m. and reported to him that the light on San Salvador Island was then abeam. The master did not go on deck then, but he admitted in Court that had he been properly awake, he would have realised that the vessel was much nearer the land than he had estimated her to be at 4 o'clock. The speed of the vessel, as recorded in the log at 4 a.m. is 3.5 knots. As the vessel was only an hour in running the distance to complete the four-point bearing, her distance from the light at 4 o'clock would be under five miles. This view of the case is also supported by other witnesses, who stated that at 4 o'clock and afterwards they could see the land, which they could not well have done had it been 14 miles distant. At 5.15 a.m. the vessel was felt to strike something and pass over it, which brought the master and all hands on deck. An attempt was at once made to tack ship, but she missed stays. The helm was then put up and the after-yards squared, with the object of wearing round on the other tack. The vessel's head went off some few points when she encountered other reefs or rocks, and, 20 minutes after first touching, she ran aground and remained hard and fast, surrounded by reefs. The sails were clewed up and anchors laid out astern, but the lines attached to them were carried away.

At 9 a.m. on the 7th February the American warship *Birmingham* came to their assistance, and anchored outside the reef, but could render very little assistance owing to the reefs, among which the *Caithness-Shire* was stranded. The vessel was finally abandoned by the crew on the 3rd March, 1911, and became a total wreck.

During this Inquiry it has been seriously contended on behalf of the master that the charts for the locality are inaccurate —both the American chart he was using (No. 8 of process) and the Admiralty charts (Nos. 14 and 16 of process). The following evidence from independent sources was submitted to the Court in support of this contention:

Imperial Lighthouse Office,
Nassau, N.P., 9th May, 1911.

Sir,

As directed by your letter of the 9th ult., I have the honour to furnish the following information respecting dangers to navigation on the east coast of Watling Island.

To the southward of the line of the lighthouse bearing, approximately, west, detached coral patches exist to a distance of about three quarters of a mile to seaward of the reef. I am not able to say how far to the southward of the above line of bearing these patches exist, but it is probably not less than a mile.

To the northward of the line of the lighthouse bearing west the ground is, as far as I have observed, clear outside the reef.

I have the honour to be, Sir,

Your most obedient servant,

FRED G. LOBB, Inspector

The Assistant Secretary,
  Harbour Department,
    Board of Trade,
      London, S.W.

Imperial Lighthouse Office,
Bahamas, 17th March, 1911.

The master of the British ship, *Caithness-Shire*, stranded on the east coast of Watling Island, having appealed to me for a statement as to the nature of the bottom to seaward of the reef on that coast, in support of his own observations, I am able from personal experience, extending over the last eighteen years, to state that to the eastward of Watling Island lighthouse large boulders exist on the bank for a distance of about three quarters of a mile outside the edge of the reef. These boulders, constituting very foul ground, are not shown on the Admiralty charts. The soundings in that vicinity are few and wide apart, and apparently no close survey has been made.

FRED G. LOBB,
Retired Commander R.N.,
Board of Trade Inspector of Lighthouses,
Bahamas.

GLOSSARY OF NAUTICAL TERMS

Abaft. Behind.

Afterguard. The Master, officers, apprentices and stewards.

Aweigh. Anchor free of the ground when heaving in.

Backstays. Heavy wires from the deck supporting the masts.

Ballast. A few hundred tons of sand or rubble in the hold sufficient to make the ship stable.

Barque. Three-, four-, or five-masted vessel square-rigged on all masts except the after mast nearest the stern, which is fore-and-aft rigged.

Belaying-pins. Wood or iron pins about sixteen inches long to which ropes are belayed, or made fast.

Bending Sail. Securing the head of the sail to the jackstay, shackling on sheets, clewlines, etc.

Blacking down. Tarring the rigging.

Blocks. Made of wood or iron with a sheave (pulley) inside over which a rope or wire runs.

Boarding-house master. A man who keeps a boarding-house for sailors.

Boltropes. Wire or rope round the sail to form a strong framework.

Boot-topping. The section of the ship's side immersed by the loading of a cargo.

Bosun's chair. A flat piece of wood about 18 in x 10 in. suspended by rope legs from each corner.

Bower anchors. The anchors carried at the bows of a vessel.

Braced up. When the yards are hauled round on to the backstays for a wind before the beam.

Braces. Wires and tackles with which the yards are secured.

Brassbounder. An indentured apprentice in a sailing-ship, so called for his brass-buttoned uniform.

Break of the poop. The forward end of the poop.

Bulwanger. Wire strop around the yard arm to prevent the head ear-ring slipping down.

Buntlines. Ropes attached to the foot of the sails, which extend down to the deck through blocks for hauling the sail close up under the yard.

Cable growing. Direction of anchor cable from the ship's bows.

Capstan. A circular drum revolving on a steel column fastened to the deck with which ropes or wires are hove taut.

Capstan bars. Hardwood bars about five feet long used by seamen to revolve the capstan.

Chain-gang. A human chain formed by men hand to hand.

Clew garnet. A tackle from the clew-iron of a course to the yard for hauling up the corner of the sail.

Clew-iron. An iron spectacle frame in the lower corners of a square sail to which the sheet and clew garnet are attached.

Clew lines. Tackles from the clew-irons of smaller square sails to the yards for hauling them up.

Close-hauled. As for braced up.

Cock-billed. Upended to the required angle.

Courses. Foresail and mainsail, the lowest and largest sails on each mast.

Crimps. A boarding-house master's runner or thug.

Dog-watches. 4 p.m. to 6 p.m. and 6 p.m. to 8 p.m.

Donkey's breakfast. Straw mattress given to sailors by boarding-house master.

Drifters. Sailors who leave a ship on arrival at the first port.

Eight bells. Every four hours from noon to noon.

Fall. Wire used for hoisting cargo out of the hold.

Fife rail. Heavy teakwood rail around the main mast in which the belaying-pins for the mizzen braces are set.

Foc's'le. Seaman's name for forecastle.

Footrope. Wire rope extended horizontally below the yard on which seamen stand to furl the sail.

Forecastle head also foc's'le. A raised deck at the fore end of the ship.

Forecastles. The crew's quarters in a deckhouse abaft the fore mast.

Forrard. Seaman's way of saying forward.

Freshening the nip. Hauling in any slack caused by the stretching of a rope by bringing a fresh part of the rope into the nip where it is passed over a sheave or around a belaying-pin.

Full and by. Sailing with the yards braced up and the sails full.

Furling. To roll a sail up and make it fast to the yard with gaskets.

Futtock rigging. Iron bars from a band on the mast to the top, fitted with ratlines to form a ladder.

Gantline. A single rope rove through a block used to hoist anything aloft.

Gaskets. Lengths of small rope spliced around the jackstays for securing the rolled-up sail to the yard.

Greybeards. The name by which the huge breaking seas which prevail off Cape Horn were known to sailors.

Gyn. Large iron shell with 10 in. or 12 in. wheel inside, *see* blocks.

Half-deck. A room occupied by the apprentices.

Halyards (*halliards*). Tackles with which the yards are hoisted.

Handing. Gathering in a sail before rolling it up.

Handy Billy. Small tackle.

Harness cask. A teakwood cask in which salt beef or port is kept in brine.

Head ear-rings. An iron ring at each top corner of a square sail for hauling and keeping the head of the sail taut along the jackstay.

Head-reaching. Heading into the wind and sea under a minimum of canvas.

Heel of the mast. The lower end.

Hove to. Laying as near to the wind as the braced-up yards will allow under storm canvas.

Howling Fifties. Region of strong westerly winds and gales between 50 and 60°S. Lat.

Jackstay. A steel rod along the top of the yard to which the head of the sail is secured.

Kedge anchors. Small portable anchors used for various purposes.

Lead blocks. Pulleys arranged to lead a rope in any direction required.

Lime-juicer. Name by which British sailing-ships were known owing to lime-juice being served out to the crew to prevent scurvy.

Old Man and Old Woman. Seaman's reference to the Captain or his wife when they were not within hearing.

Parral. An iron band hinged in two sections around the mast which allows the yard to which it is attached to be hoisted up the mast.

Pin-rail. Wide rail running along inside the bulwarks in which belaying-pins are set.

Poop. The raised section of deck at the after end of the ship under which the Master's and officers' accommodation is situated.

Purchase. A heavy tackle known as a three-, four- or five-fold purchase formed with wire or rope rove through blocks in which three, four or five sheaves (wheels) are set side by side.

Ratlines. Small rope secured to the shrouds to form the steps of a ladder for climbing aloft.

Rigging screws. Powerful stretching screws with which the shrouds and stays are set up taut to support the masts.

Roaring Forties. Region of strong westerly winds and gales between 40 and 50°S. Lat.

Sails aback. The wind blowing against the forward side of the sails instead of the after side.

Sheer-legs. A tripod formed by three spars on end lashed together at the top from which a tackle is suspended for lifting heavy weights.

Sheet. Length of chain or wire shackled to the lower corners of a square sail with which the sail is set.

Sheeting home. Hauling on the sheets to set the sails.

Shellbacks. Hardened, experienced sailors (prime seamen).

Ship. A three-, four- or five-masted vessel, square-rigged on all masts.

Ship in irons. Sails on foremast full and those on main mast aback, preventing movement back or forth.

Shrouds. Heavy wires supporting the masts against lateral strain.

Spider band. An iron band round the mast with belaying-pins attached.

Stepped in. Securing the heel of the mast to the keelson.

Stiffening. A few hundred tons of cargo in the hold sufficient to make the ship stable.

Stirrups. Short lengths of wire secured to the jackstay at intervals along the yard from which the footrope is suspended.

Strop. Short length of wire with an eye at each end.

T'gan'sls. Topgallant sails, being the fourth and fifth sails up from the deck on each mast.

Top-hamper. The masts, yards and maze of wire and rope aloft.

Truss. Heavy forked bracket of iron bolted to the lower yards and hinged to the mast to enable the yard to swing through an arc while remaining projected forward from the mast.

Washport. Hinged iron doors in the bulwarks through which heavy water on deck is released.

Wear ship. The manœuvre of turning the ship around before the wind, keeping the sails full.

Weather cloth. Canvas stretched across the mizzen rigging or between stanchions on the windward side to afford shelter from the weather.

Windlass. A powerful winch under the forecastle head for weighing the anchor.

Yards aback. Wind blowing against the forward side of the sails instead of the after side.

INDEX

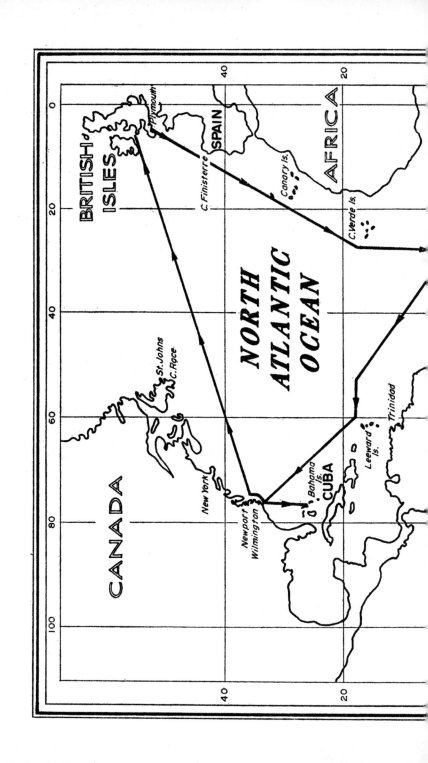